Praise for ENDANGERED SPECIES, ENDURING VALUES
An Anthology of San Francisco Area Writers and Artists of Color
Edited by Shizue Seigel

Truly stunning! Stories and artworks by "creatives of color" bring readers to the edges of awareness, endurance and beauty. I love every voice!!
> — Deborah Santana, author, seeker, founder and
> CEO of Do A Little non-profit

Nothing short of amazing. On the surface, ENDANGERED SPECIES, ENDURING VALUES is a thoughtful and inclusive curation resulting in a necessary anthology. Beneath that surface is a collective voice that says, "We are San Francisco. We will not be erased!"
> —Truong Tran, poet, visual artist, and educator
> San Francisco State University and Mills College

Essays, memoir, fiction, visuals and poetry paint an honest, complex and personal picture of San Francisco area artists-of-color. Interdisciplinary, intergenerational and inspiring pieces illuminate how natives and immigrants, domestic and international, can shape a city.
> —Elmaz Abinader, author, *This House, My Bones*,
> co-founder and program director, VONA

A treasure chest full of literary gems!
> —Naomi Hirahara, author of the Mas Arai mysteries and
> community-based nonfiction

The fact is, San Francisco and California are respectively white-minority city and state. You will be moved by this book chock full of seasoned writers of color and budding beginners of all ages. You may even want to pick up a pen yourself.
> —Dennis J. Bernstein, Executive Producer, *Flashpoints*,
> on Pacifica Radio (KPFA) and author of *Special Ed:*
> *Voices from a Hidden Classroom*

In the face of discrimination and gentrification, communities of color survive and even thrive by focusing on the positive. [Un]told stories intermixed with artworks reflect how much goodness is around us—even in dark times.
> —Lewis Kawahara, Adjunct Professor in Ethnic
> Studies, College of San Mateo and Lecturer in Asian
> American Studies, San Francisco State University

To Soheil:
Thank you for your support ♡ [signature]

Endangered Species
Enduring Values

An Anthology of San Francisco Area
Writers and Artists of Color

Edited by Shizue Seigel

The real San Francisco!
—Shizue Seigel

Pease Press • San Francisco

Pease Press
1717 Cabrillo Street, San Francisco, CA 94121
www.peasepress.com

First edition April 2018.
Printed in the United States of America.

Book and cover design by Shizue Seigel. www.shizueseigel.com
Front cover. Wasteland shop window on Haight Street, creator unknown.
Photo: Shizue Seigel, 2008.

Library of Congress Cataloging-in-Publication Data

Endangered Species, Enduring Values
An Anthology of San Francisco Area Writers and Artists of Color
Edited by Shizue Seigel
Library of Congress Control Number: 2018935379

ISBN: 978-0-9904173-4-7

 Supported by the San Francisco Arts Commission.

Why This Book?
Thoughts from the New Majority—San Francisco's Fifty-Eight Percent

Literature and artwork illuminate our common humanity by providing vital insights into how people think, feel, and live. Yet, creatives of color remain under-published and underrepresented even in the diverse San Francisco area. (I refer to San Francisco as an area, rather than a city, because escalating housing costs have forced many would-be residents to live beyond San Francisco's city limits, though they may work in, identify with, or engage in arts and activism in the city.)

The anthology *Endangered Species, Enduring Values* includes prose, poetry, and four-color artwork from San Francisco area writers and artists of color. They offer a compelling snapshot of the city's majority minority, who now comprise 58% of the residents in the nation's most diverse[1] and progressive[2] metropolis. For this book, over 70 people submitted prose, poetry, and art addressing these questions:

- In challenging times, how do heritage, history, or spirituality inspire you as a person of color?
- What sustains you and keeps you working for a just and inclusive society?
- What do you want the world to know about your heritage or community?

This book is far from a scientific sampling of the San Francisco area, however. Amid the urgency and confusion of Trump's first year in office, many people I asked to submit could not. They were occupied with simple survival— work, school, or volunteering on the evolving issues of the day.

Endangered Species, Enduring Values provides a taste of the city's diversity not only by race, but also by culture, class, education, national origin, generations in the United States, gender identity, and age. Over 70 creative people of color contributed more than 150 pieces of prose, poetry, and artwork. Contributors include established to emerging writers aged 17 to 80, from immigrant to indigenous. Their roots reach back to Native America, China, Africa, Japan, Mexico, Peru, Cuba, Puerto Rico, the Philippines, India, Iran, Afghanistan, and Europe. They are working poets and artists; physicians and healers; students and retirees; advocates for mental health, housing, and senior rights; union workers; shopkeepers; retirees; and community volunteers.

I went out of my way to look for "ordinary people." The unexpected result is that not all are accomplished writers, but nearly all feel an extraordinary

---

[1] Bay Area Census www.bayareacensus.ca.gov/bayarea.htm and www.bayareacensus.ca.gov/counties/SanFranciscoCounty.htm Feb. 7, 2018
[2] https://www.nytimes.com/elections/results/president, Aug. 9, 2017

commitment to their heritage, their communities, and their democracy. This literature is the polar opposite of the stereotypical writer alone in a garret. This is the writing of engaged and empowered people reflecting and recording even as they work towards a just and healthy society.

As people all over the world lose their connection to the places, histories, values, and traditions that shaped societies over millennia, many contributors have learned to draw strength from their heritage not only to survive but also to thrive—through compassion and collaboration rather than competition.

People of color have had to be bi- or multicultural from the outset. Every day we reflect upon what to keep, what to reject, what to adopt, and what to adapt. It makes for a sometimes confusing journey, but it has made us resilient and adaptable, appreciative of the best in many cultures, and prepared for the sudden upheavals of a topsy-turvy world.

As the dominant culture reaches an evolutionary dead-end and becomes increasingly dysfunctional, people of color point a way forward by offering a powerfully positive vision that builds on a history of resistance and adaptability, a powerful sense of family and community, and the traditions of our ancestors. These encourage us to keep moving forward with flexibility and compassion. Our way is the way of patience and cooperation in synchrony with the universe; it's never about rugged individuality striving to the top.

Until we are seen and understood in as much variety and nuance as European Americans, we remain stereotyped and at risk. As a Japanese American whose family was incarcerated after Pearl Harbor, I am viscerally aware of the present-day dangers. Today, African Americans, Muslims, and immigrants of color are at risk. Who knows who will be targeted next?

To steady us, many of us were fortunate to be fed by family and community ideals about duty, humility, integrity, and faith, as well as by American ideals of freedom, democracy, and equal opportunity. This cross-fertilization and mutual give-and-take is truly what makes America great.

And in the San Francisco Bay Area, we cannot forget the land itself. "Indigenous" means "that which occurs, lives, or grows naturally in a particular region or environment." Whether we were born here or elsewhere, many of us value the area's changeable and varied climes and landscapes—leading from sun and baylands to fog and surf-battered cliffs. When we stop to connect with our surroundings, the Earth and the ancestors can feed us ancient wisdoms, rising from the soles of our feet and up through the tops of our heads. We remember that there is much more to life than power and money, and we look into each other's eyes with renewed clarity.

How I Found the Writers. When I started taking creative writing workshops twenty years ago, I was usually the only person of color participating. The few who did soon dropped out, or were very quiet in class. To draw out more writers of color and to encourage non-writers to value their voices and their perspectives, I started Write Now! free monthly creative writing workshops in 2015 with the help of a San Francisco Arts Commission Individual Artist grant. Since I was especially interested in engaging ordinary people, I employed community outreach skills that I learned twenty years ago during the AIDS crisis. I passed out flyers and talked to anybody and everybody on the street, on the bus, and at community art exhibits, film festivals, street fairs, and other events.

The workshops were free and open to people at any level of experience. Many people's eyes lit up when they heard about the project, but they insisted that they were not writers. They wanted me to write their story. I wanted to empower them to take responsibility for their own narratives, so I replied, "If you can talk, you can write. I'm looking for the authentic voices of real people. Come give it a try." Three years later, the initial six Write Now! Fillmore and Write Now! Japantown workshops have grown into Write Now! San Francisco, still going strong. More than fifty people attended at least one workshop, and our first anthology, *Standing Strong! Fillmore & Japantown*, reached hundreds of people.

I was fortunate to receive submissions from well-established writers as well, and the resulting mix of sophisticated writing and fresh voices is invigorating. I'm deeply grateful to the following groups and individuals for helping create a rich diversity of voices: the African American Arts & Culture Complex, the Asian American Women's Artists Association, At the Inkwell, Bay Area Generations, Rene and Rio Yanez's *Día de los Muertos* art exhibitions at SOMArts Cultural Center, Eastwind Books of Berkeley, Eth-Noh-Tec, Gears Turning poetry series at Adobe Books, the Fillmore Jazz Festival, San Francisco Juneteenth celebrations, the Howard Zinn Book Fair, Kearny Street Workshop, La Lunada Literary Salon at Galería de la Raza, the Manilatown Heritage Foundation, the National Japanese American Historical Society, Nihonmachi Street Fair, Reverie Writers, the San Francisco African American Historical & Cultural Society, San Francisco Poet Laureate Kim Shuck, SOMArts Cultural Center, The Black Woman Is God project, the Writers Grotto, the Writing Salon, VONA/Voices of Our Nations Arts Foundation, and word of mouth through Faith Adiele, Tomo Arai, Lyndsey Ellis, Susan Ito, Sandra García Rivera, Margo Perin, Tony Robles, Denise Sullivan, Truong Tran, and others.

—Shizue Seigel, Editor

Table of Contents

4 in my own skin - seen and unseen

5 mother father/ gifts and ghosts

1

born here
borne
here

Shizue Seigel, *Border Fence,* digital photograph, 2010.

Juanda J. Stewart arrived in San Francisco from Oklahoma City at 7 years old. Back in 1945, her family had to ride in straight-back seats in the colored section. They were barred from the dining car, so they got sick from a four-day diet of unrefrigerated food. Juanda inherited a love of rhyme from her grandmother, who often recited poetry from memory.

She picks up her pen whenever a memorable person or event inspires her. After receiving a BA and an MA from San Francisco State University, she worked as an administrator at the U.S. Postal Service until retirement. She is an enthusiastic fan of the Forty-Niners, Giants and Golden State Warriors. She is also a world traveler and a very involved member of her church. Her priorities in order are God, family, and everything else.

Her book of poems, *The Rhymes of My Life,* was published by Dorrance in 2015. She attended Write Now! Fillmore writing workshops in 2015-2017, and two of her pieces were published in *Standing Strong: Fillmore and Japantown.*

Endangered Species
Juanda J. Stewart

Who says that I'm endangered?
Comes as news to me.
Can navy beans fear a takeover
By the black-eyed pea?
Can black keys fear the presence
Of the nearby ivory?

Does crude oil stand in fear
Of an eruption of olive oil?
No! Like tares and wheat, they coexist
And both grow tall.

You say that I'm endangered?
I sure don't feel that way.
I'm too busy breaking down barriers
That once stood in my way.

I intend to be around
'Til night turns not to day.
I'll never feel endangered;
No, I'm here to stay.

Human
Kim Shuck

Did you always know how to
Listen?
Wake up with the concrete under your nails and
Covered in salt there are
Pelicans all over that rock these days
All over that rock it's
Cold and the currents the
Currents there is something at the core of the
Island there is
something at the
Core of the IslandJoyjoy
Some people are a pebble and we are
Caught in the ripples how do you learn
How do you learn to be human?
I won't/ Set any words so solid that you might
Catch yourself on them not even
Restless a word you
Might have outgrown you
Might have outgrown it
Given time we can teach ourselves anything
We will learn to be real people
With songs and
Ceremonies that we will not blame on you
Even if your words have called things out of us
Out of these city moments a
Memory there are
Other sacred wings but that evening in the
Osage Hills it was a moth
Just as you said
Though you said it about something else
So much to learn about and
Taste and time will choose as often as
Dice or
Wisdom and the hiccup moan of
Harmonica or any of the birds back home or
Sad Native boys who were on their way to being men in those
Days some people are a
Pebble and we were caught in those
Ripples fallen or thrown the
Water still shivers

Radio Poet
Kim Shuck

New century in its teens my
Heroes moving on
Radio poet in the bay I remember you
Mica'd paint and the smell of
Copal the heartwood of this city can be
Split along growth rings and
Woven that prison place and even the idea of
Judgment the
Salt is taking the buildings that still stand
You are on Indian Land
Bay water I
Knew it pretty well back then
Fishing with my father for
Bullheads the
Crab nets that
Taught me early lessons in
How to set a trap with string or were those
Words?
There are things that I don't remember
Somehow the old bait shop by
Ghirardelli is muddled in my
Childhood with the occupation those
Spike riddled
Lures the back of the old
Toyota and
Muni pier the
Salt and
Mussel colonies how many
Crabs can I name?
Radio poet in the bay we are
Still here draped in those healing fogs the
Pelicans are back they are
Back and the
Salty prayer smoke will bring word
For now the salt still sings here and in the
Glitter sand

Kim Shuck is a silly protein. She holds an MFA in Fine Arts/Textiles from San Francisco State University. Shuck has written three solo books, one chapbook, is included in many anthologies published on various continents and plays with beads and string. She teaches things, reads in cafes and on street corners, she still knows how to play. In 2017 Kim was named the 7th poet laureate of San Francisco. Photo: Shizue Seigel. Opposite page: Family photo courtesy of Shizue Seigel

This Land Is Whose Land? A San Francisco Education
Shizue Seigel

In California history, the terra cognita is occupied by whites, but people of color have been here all along—and not merely as victims.

Untold stories are tattooed on our retinas and crowded into our corpuscles. Many of us were here before hipsters knew there was a here here. We are native San Franciscans, native Californians or native indigenous. Our stories take many forms, rough edges tumbling together in the surf. If not for World War II, I might not have lived on the city's western cliffs. I might be living 200 miles south in my mother's birthplace—the home she never stopped missing on the balmy Central Coast, on a coastal shelf now strewn with multimillion-dollar second homes with spectacular views of Pismo Beach.

One hundred years ago, in 1918, my grandparents leased that Central Cal land, 140 acres of it. Since they were Japanese immigrants, they were not allowed to buy it. A tangled thicket of laws barred Asians from citizenship and property rights. My jiichan and baachan prospered because a benign landlady did not kick them out after they improved her land so she could charge higher rents to the next tenant. Instead, she encouraged them to stay and kept their rents moderate. In gratitude, my grandparents named my mother after her. And they honored the old ones that had lived there first. When ploughs turned up stone knives and arrowheads, my grandparents brought a Shinto priest from San Francisco to invoke bygone spirits and ask permission to live there, in harmony with the sea and sky, cypress and chaparral, kelp and mussels, and rich fertile soil.

In the spirit of wa and arigatai, harmony and gratitude, they irrigated and innovated, collaborated and co-operated. Blending East with West, they formed

19

a co-op with their countrymen to pack and ship and sell their produce to the burgeoning Los Angeles market. By 1940, Japanese Americans were growing 40% of all the produce grown in California. But their very success made them targets. They lost the farm in 1942 when they were sent to Poston, Arizona, to a concentration camp built on an Indian reservation. The Office of Indian Affairs ignored the objections of the Colorado River Indian Tribes, who had been dislocated themselves.

My Nisei parents, native Californians and citizens by right of birth, had just turned legal adults when Pearl Harbor turned them into instant enemies. Their fathers were arrested by the FBI and disappeared into detention camps. Mom left sewing school for the searing Arizona desert. Dad missed his UC Berkeley graduation when he was locked up at the Stockton fairgrounds and then in Arkansas swampland. Thus began a 14-year exile that ended when we moved to San Francisco in 1958.

Mom and I fell in love with the western edge of the city. Perched on a windy hillside, our souls soared with the crashing surf, the sharp salt wind and swirling fog. Pelicans strung themselves across the horizon at sunset, and the chaparral sheltered blue lupine, golden poppies and California quail (not yet decimated by feral cats). In those days San Francisco was not yet a trophy town. It was solidly working and middle class, and thoroughly white-identified.

Dad surf-casted for perch at Baker Beach, but San Francisco never measured up to his sweltering hometown of Stockton. He tolerated the fog because he had his own reasons for wanting to work at the Presidio of San Francisco. Dad had proved his loyalty as counterintelligence officer during years of restless exile in Baltimore, Maryland, and Occupied Japan. Now he was assigned to the very same office where in 1942 Lt. Col. Karl Bendetsen had churned out the "Evacuation Orders" that had sent 120,000 Japanese Americans to incarceration camps. Within few more years, Dad became a lieutenant colonel himself. Twenty years after his own dad had been arrested by the FBI as a "dangerous enemy alien" (three times: as a Buddhist Church board member, as president of the sumo club and as a member of the Japanese Association), Dad had the secret satisfaction of becoming chief of military security of the eight Western States—Bendetsen's equivalent. Sadly, he couldn't share his triumph with anyone, not even with Mom and me, his own family, because his job was top secret.

Given what he did for a living, it's no surprise that Dad and I clashed constantly over history and culture, civil rights and foreign policy. I was a first-year baby boomer, born a few months after the camps closed. I watched my aging immigrant grandparents struggle back onto their feet in strawberry

No. 27: Are you willing to serve in the armed forces of the United States on combat duty, wherever ordered?

28: Will you swear unqualified allegiance to the United States of America and faithfully defend the United States from any and all attack by foreig or domestic forces, and forswear any form of allegiance to the Japanese Emperor or any other foreign government, power, or organization?

Shizue Seigel, *Classified*, mixed media, 50 x 34 in., 2010

21

sharecropping camps and skid-row hotels. I didn't believe in the Cold War, or any kind of war. I believed in Dad's mom, my other baachan, my grandma Yuka, who'd raised ten kids in a skid row hotel. She'd dealt with immigration laws, alien land laws, mass incarceration and good old-fashioned Japanese sexism. She'd lost children to pneumonia and a husband to heart disease. Through it all, she developed a deep Buddhist faith. She learned to live in the here and now, in gratitude, without my mother's timidity or my dad's bitterness. To Baachan Yuka, nobody was "better than" or "less than." From drunken panhandlers to self-righteous church ladies, we were all imperfect ningen, human beings. Her compassionate smile lit up dark corners in all our hearts.

I was the first of her grandkids to grow up middle class, contending with white classrooms where I was the only Asian American. To survive, I had to be as good, if not better than any white boy. Dad warned, "Nobody's going to hand you anything, you have to work twice as hard just to stay even." Silently, I added, "And twice as hard again because I'm a girl, Dad!"

By the time I got to San Francisco, I'd moved 8 times in 12 years. I learned to adapt by watching and listening to anybody and everybody. On the 4 Sutter bus, on the way to Japantown, friendly African Americans taught me how to talk to strangers, how to laugh out loud and not take s--t. To newcomers like me, the Fillmore was welcoming, while Japantown was closed—under assault by redevelopment and other factors I didn't understand.

At my largely white Richmond District schools, earnestly liberal teachers taught social change and multicultural awareness in the classroom. Class distinctions, I learned about at recess. I wasn't as middle class as I thought. When my classmates chattered about Ski Week, I wondered what fool would spend hundreds of dollars on equipment and drive hours on icy roads to risk breaking a leg¬—the only trips my parents took were to visit relatives. When schoolmates talked about their maids and gardeners, I realized—my aunties and uncles were maids and gardeners. My relatives were humble, but they were a lot happier than the neurotic well-to-do.

On the street I had to watch out for the working-class boys whose forebearers may have come from Germany or Ireland later than my grandparents came from Japan. These kids, possibly fending off memories of being called "kraut" and "mick," defended their turf by pulling up the corners of their eyes and jeering "Go back where you came from!" To get away from them, I hung out at the library, at the bookstore with the dreamy, possibly closeted-gay owner, and at the folk-music club with the "Another Mother for Peace" poster in the front door.

Aside from the fresh tang of fog and sea air, the Richmond's bland stucco was less interesting than the shabby jumble of Victorians in the Western Addition. I loved that rich mix of storefront churches, manju shops, and TV repair shops jammed beneath cold-water flats. But the neighborhood was being red-lined into blight. All too soon, in the 1960s and 70s, urban renewal "cleaned up the neighborhood," and Japanese and African Americans were displaced yet again. The six-lane Geary Expressway drove a wedge through the neighborhood. One hundred blocks of the Fillmore were demolished, over a thousand family businesses destroyed, and nearly 20,000 residents displaced, driving the desperate and homeless into the arms of Jim Jones and his People's Church. It was coming clear that "North" didn't necessarily mean freedom.

By college, I was sick of received wisdom from the left AND the right. Demonstrations and organizing were important, are still important, but I needed to work on myself first: dig myself out of internalized oppression and do my own research based on personal observation. Besides, Dad had done such a great job of raising me middle class, I thought I had the same right as any sheltered suburbanite from the Midwest to turn on, tune in, and drop out.

So I pissed off Dad by marrying a red-diaper baby, the son of a Communist. We wed at City Hall in 1966, moved to the Height Ashbury and threw ourselves into the counterculture. Determined to end war and injustice though a natural and loving lifestyle, we joined a loose community of young adults of all colors exploring different cultures and spiritualties, going back to the land, and traveling the world. My guru in India advised, "Do good, be good, see good. That is the way to God"—simple to remember; hard to do. But I learned to close my eyes and breathe to connect with universal energy—most of the time.

I returned to San Francisco, and plunged into the here-and-how of natural food, natural childbirth, alternative schools, and peace marches. But by the late 1970s, my hippie paradise fell apart. I became single parent struggling to support my kids on $15 a month child support. I spent the 1980s overworked and underpaid as an advertising art director, with a front-row view corporate life during the greed-is-good decade. My colleagues bought homes in the suburbs, with expensive mortgages and long commutes. They talked about their SUVs and bed-and-breakfast weekends in the wine country while living in terror of downsizing and outsourcing.

In the 1990s I found myself doing HIV prevention with women in public housing, volunteering at the needle exchange, and working to preserve the stories of Japanese American former incarcerees before they died. It was like a homecoming. Once again, I was watching and listening to anybody and everybody and encouraging them to tell their truths about how we live in this city by the bay.

Lost and Found
Kelechi Ubozoh

When you arrive in San Francisco, California a rebirth happens.
Not that you are becoming someone new, sometimes you are just becoming who
you were always meant to be.

Maybe, you're the black poet going through a never-ending goth phase like me.
Or, you could be the black artist stifled by her strict parent's ideas of success
like my mother.

Mama arrived in San Francisco thirty-seven years ahead of me. Growing up in
an all-white neighborhood in Long Island, New York was painful. For her older
siblings, being part of the only black family in the area was glorious. They were
invited to the best parties. Everyone wanted to watch them dance, touch their
thick afros, and be their friend. None of this was extended to my shy, frumpy,
lack-luster mama. She was a hidden gem that no one was looking for.

When I asked her why she traveled across the country to a place she'd never
seen outside of magazines, she sighed and wistfully gazed toward the closest
window.
"It's a place where the lost go to find themselves," she said.

My mother landed in San Francisco in 1976. Befriended by a Haitian
diplomat's daughter, Angeline, they built a home for themselves in the Harlem
of the West known today as the Fillmore. In San Francisco, she transformed.
Something woke up inside of her, that inner light was fed and the glow was
born. I imagine those two were quite a pretty package, and mom had endless
stories from all their "gentlemen callers," though thinking on it now, I'm sure
those stories were heavily censored.

At night, she painted skyscrapers or audited art classes at San Francisco State
University. Angeline took her to poetry readings and jazz clubs. Mama fell in
love with the cold, gray ocean and lifted herself out of the thick fog. During
the day, she worked for the Black Panthers teaching English at the Oakland
Community School. English would sometimes morph into art and math, and
whatever else she could recall from her privileged Oberlin education. Really,
anything she could do to help these kids with a fare, since they'd have to buy
their own ticket out of poverty.

Her time in California was brief. One day while she was working with the kids,
she got a call … and I'm not talking about the kind on the phone.

Despite her college major of English with a concentration of African American
studies, a voice told her it was time to serve black folks differently. Something

very loud was telling her to become a doctor. The voice wasn't her parents, siblings, or even the neighbors. I doubt she had ever been far enough from home and the noise that allows one to truly hear. The message was clear. She returned to the east coast, attended medical school, and eventually built a primary care practice in Atlanta, Georgia.

I am my mother's daughter. When I got lost, I started dreaming of foggy mythical kingdoms.

A call from outside my being whispered that I needed to go west. I wanted purpose and radical change. I wanted healing for black people who had experienced trauma like me. I needed to live in a space that invited innovation.

I envisioned stardust littered streets and finding my missing family. Imagined a place where no one would call me "white" for simply reading. In this city by the bay, maybe black was not a synonym for uneducated.

When you arrive in San Francisco, California a rebirth happens.
Not that you are becoming someone new, sometimes you are just becoming who you were always meant to be.

So, I traveled to California. Partially confronting fate, and hiding from the Furies.

Here I am in the land of outsiders, and no one is laughing at me. I'm not unlovable. Healing the hatred of myself that I've been taught for eons. Dancing in a crowded house party in the Mission. I'm working in mental health advocacy, preaching about trauma-informed care. Sometimes people hear me. When I tell my story of coming back from the dead, they always listen.

Mama was right, location is everything.
Acceptance is expensive, and the city is fluid.

There are times this place steals my breath.
I gasp when I see the blue-green ocean and the lights from the hills, like grounded stars.The view from the top, when you are feeling at the bottom is indescribable.

This city is in flux, and I don't know how long it will last.
Magic is funny like that.

One day, there will be a new city where lost souls go to find themselves.
Outcasts rebuild their identities. Black women embrace their complexity.

Poets chase their muses, and innovation is unending.

On that day, I will give my daughter a compass and trust that the voice and the message is louder than the things we have lost.

Kelechi Ubozoh is a Nigerian-American San Francisco Bay Area poet and mental health advocate. Originally from Brooklyn, New York, Kelechi holds a BA in journalism from Purchase College, and was the first undergraduate ever published in *The New York Times.* Kelechi has performed at many Bay Area readings like Lit Quake's Lit Crawl, Beast Crawl, Birds of Paradise, Lyrics and Dirges, Get Lit, Passages on the Lake, Voz Sin Tinta, Uptown Fridays, Liminal, and Bay Area Generations.

She is featured in The Voice Award-Winning Documentary, *The S Word,* following the lives of suicide attempt survivors in an effort to eliminate the stigma of mental health issues in the black community.

Young woman at the Nihonmachi Street Fair 2017. Shizue Seigel

Three generations of the Robles family: Tony Robles, second from left, with stepson Tiburio Gray-Garcia, dad Ray and brother Asian. Photo: Tony Robles.

Notes of an Uncle Tom
Tony Robles

"Tom, Tom … Come in Tom. Do you read me Tom?"

I still laugh at my father's reaction the moment I informed him—with unprecedented pride—that I'd been hired as a door attendant at a high-end apartment complex in the city. I had started off as a security guard at the same complex greeting the high-end residents with a high-end greeting (such as "Wonderful morning, isn't it?" … followed by an under-the-breath "you son of a bitch"), high-end nod, and of course, a high-end—albeit chickenshit—smile.

I always pictured a door attendant as wearing one of those outfits with a wide shouldered jacket and captain's hat—like the doorman on that classic TV show, "The Jeffersons." I was given a pair of tan pants—Dockers—a light shirt and wel-made, high-end leather shoes. I slipped into the outfit and began to feel high end. My end had never felt so high. Anyway, it's getting higher with every passing minute.

"Hey dad," I said. "I got a new job … a house negro job, a doorman. Aren't you proud of me? You think grandma and grandpa are proud, having braved the stormy seas to come to America like George Washington and John Wayne (not really, but it sounds like a good thing to say), in hopes of providing a

27

new life, new opportunities to their offspring and their offspring's offspring?" Dad paused. He's a native San Franciscan living in Hawaii. I heard the waves pounding the shore through the static of his Metro PCS cell phone. He finally spoke: "You ain't got no house negro job … you got an Uncle Tom job." I listened to the waves and the sound of the ocean over the phone. My dad, working years and years as a janitor in San Francisco; he's got the Hawaiian beaches now. Let him have that beach, he deserves it.

I stand by the door waiting. I look around. The building is big and spotless and I hear the calls of ravens outside. They sometimes call out to me. "Hey Uncle Tom, you think you can throw us a few breadcrumbs … at your convenience, of course." I got to the lobby kitchen area and look for breadcrumbs but all I find is expensive gourmet coffee. I see a resident walking to the door. I step on it, moving with the swiftness of a gazelle, reaching the door and opening it with much class. Sometime the residents say thank you, sometimes not.

I am 90 days into my Tom-hood. I am doing a decent job but I have some concerns. One of these concerns involves an old white man in a terry cloth robe—let's call him "T.C." (short for Terry Cloth). T.C comes down every morning to the lobby for his morning paper and coffee. He is pleasant, and his robe is befitting of the terry cloth prince that he surely is. He requested a cart from me to move a few items into his apartment. Like the good Tom that I am, I complied. He came back with the cart 30 minutes later. "Put it there," he said, producing a fist. He inched his fist close to me. "Give it up," he said. I looked at my hand. T.C. took ahold of my hand and formed a fist. He then, in a beautifully choreographed moment, bumped his fist into mine—a "Brotherhood of the Fist" of sorts—not predicated upon race, economic status, education or various other chickenshit requirements and/or sensibilities. It's tough being a Tom, for you forget how to make a fist and must rely on older white men to give you an occasional refresher course.

Sometimes I find myself dozing at the desk and at the door. I think of the neighborhood outside. Not long ago, my grandparents were prevented from moving here. It was in the 1950's. Grandpa was a black man from Louisiana; Grandma was San Francisco Irish. Nobody in this place knows this. I open the door and the ravens cry out. I step back inside and see another resident approach. They all look so important, all making so much money. What do they do to make so much money? I open the door and smile. "Have a nice day, sir." I don't earn enough to live in this place, yet I grew up in this neighborhood. Nobody in this place knows this.

A coworker stops by. His name is "J." We talk about the job. He mops the floor and changes the toilet paper consistently and with much expertise. He speaks of the former doorman, a fellow named Kissassman. Kissassman lasted a couple of months. "J" explained that Kissassman was running around every second, attending to every need. "Kissassman get me an umbrella, Kissassman make more coffee, Kissassman call me a cab, Kissassman arrange to have my dry cleaning picked up, Kissassman, Kissassman, Kissassman …" etc, etc. One day Kissassman left—kissed it all goodbye like a snake shedding some unfamiliar skin. His last words, "I'm tired of being Kissassman. I'm going to have my name changed … legally."

In the meantime, I stand by the door. I catch myself dozing off. My cell phone rings, a text message from good old dad. I read it:

"Tom, Tom … come in Tom … do you read me Tom?"

Below: The Work Projects Administration (WPA) commissioned murals by Russian immigrant Anton Refugier between 1941-1948 at the Rincon Annex Post Office. Refugier won the commission by competition, but his politically trenchant works drew criticism from the outset. The 27 murals and Streamline Moderne lobby and exterior were preserved when private interests developed the Rincon Center business/residential complex. Shizue Seigel.

The Brother Who Won't Go Away
Tony Robles

I was in line at the Civic Center post office in downtown San Francisco when the far off smell of salty air hit me. I looked around for something that resembled the ocean and saw a passel of light blue shirt clad postal clerks weighing and affixing postage to letters and parcels, each doing the job with a personalized diligence gleaned from years of repetition. How can one inhale the vast blueness of oceans and seas in a post office? I was in line, in whose juxtaposition I occupied a place behind 15 others whose postures ranged from assertive, hurried, bored, fatigued, ambivalent or misguided aplomb—each holding sway to the pendulum of impatience moving within. The post office is always crowded but I don't mind standing in line. Standing in line at the post office to send a handwritten letter is a resistance to our techwashed reality where everything is done via a click or press of a button. As the second hand on the clock ticks its tiny steps of supplication towards eternity, the salty air smell becomes stronger and soon my face is awash in a breeze coming from somewhere.

"Excuse me" a voice cut though from behind. I turned and saw him—an African-American man who I'd seen around the city since I was a kid. The man was about 5 foot 5 or 6. He was dressed the way I remembered from back then—rugged pants, boots, denim jacket, turtleneck sweater—topped with a wide-brim leather hat. "Do you know how much it costs to send a certified letter," he asked. I'd sent only two certified letters in my life and didn't remember what I'd paid. "No, I sure don't," I replied. His thick fingers held a fanned-out set of certified mail forms as if they were U.S. currency. He looked about for a list of postal rates. If they are posted they are well hidden, along with the machine for those whose only wish is to purchase a single stamp.

On the man's jacket was a patch that read: Karate. I tried to imagine what he'd look like in a Karate gi. He is short but solid. I remember driving somewhere with my uncle years ago when he spotted the man walking down the street carrying a shoulder bag. "That guy is a karate man," my uncle said. My uncle practiced Okinawan Karate and came across the man in that world. I looked at the man as we passed him. He looked as if he'd just returned from a long journey by ship. A merchant seaman, maybe? I'd see him from time to time, always with that shoulder bag and sometimes a guitar case. He'd pop up in different places in the city, always unexpectedly. Somehow I felt I knew him. "Hey there's that guy …" I'd think upon seeing him. I was just a little kid living in the Projects of North Beach, running in every direction except the right one. Once while running, I came upon the man again. This time he was among a crowd of tourists. "Do you speak German?" he asked someone in the crowd. "I do too." He smiled and strummed his guitar and said something that sounded like:

Spreck-a-dee doych
Spreck-a-dee doych
Stop 'n' drop…thank you!

And the tourists showed teeth that spread as far and wide as the bridges that connect one place or person to another, smiling and dropping coins and dollars in that guitar case. I was just a kid watching. "Hey, it's that guy …"I thought again, offering only a smile exposing the bashfulness of a boy in the presence of a guitar case that was a wide mouth that knew about laughter and hunger in any language.

The man stood jotting information on the certified mail receipts. I'd never spoken to him yet I felt I knew him. He was someone from the landscape of my childhood, the feel of which is on the bottoms of my feet—in the sand and pebbles and shards of glass that have collected in my shoes. I looked at the man's face. It seemed he hadn't aged at all. He didn't have his shoulder bag or guitar case. He glanced at his cell phone that was tucked into his denim jacket pocket. Standing in that line, I wanted to ask him his name, where he was from, what he did for a living. The only thing I could say was, "I remember you when I was a kid."

Displayed on the circumference of his leather hat rests a multinational array of pins proudly bearing the flags of many nations as well as the emblem of the state of California. Had he been to all those places? I remembered him talking to those German tourists long ago. I mentioned this to him. He explained that he spoke 15 different languages, including Asian, African and Polynesian tongues. I wanted to know more. Where did he live? Was he married? Where was his guitar? The line was moving and now I was at the head. The postal worker at the counter called out, "Next in line!" I turned to the man and said, "It was really nice seeing you again, sir. By the way, my name is Tony." The man just smiled and nodded. I went to the counter to take care of my transaction.

I wanted to hug the man. I was so glad to see him. The feeling I had was ineffable. Seeing him gave me the feeling that the city was still mine, still strumming with memories which move slowly though the crowds, the traffic— memories still alive, memories that still breathe. I wanted to thank him for still being here.

I walked out of the post office and the smell of salty air hit me again, reminding me of where I was and of that brother who didn't—who won't—go away. Neither will I.

Tough Flip
Tony Robles

The Pilipino guy
is the baddest looking
guy on the block

Has a scar running
over the bridge
of his nose

His name is
tattooed on his
neck in cursive

"Percival"

Works as a transport
specialist at the
Pilipino restaurant on
the corner

Transporting boxes of
lumpia wrappers, produce,
rice noodles, meat, meat
by-products and toilet paper
from point A to point B

On a
hand truck

Placing it all

Ober dare
Ober dare
Ober dare

When asked how things
are going, he
answers

So far… no good

Says he's been hanging in
there … has been hanging
in for more than twenty years.

I graduated from
Hanging In There
University, he adds

Hang-U
for short

He's one
of their many
success stories.

Published in *Cool Don't Live Here No More*, Ithuriel's Spear, 2015.

Tony Robles was born and raised in San Francisco of Filipino and African American heritage. His books *Cool Don't Live Here No More—A Letter to San Francisco* (2015) and *Fingerprints of a Hunger Strike* (2017) were published by Ithuriel's Spear Press. He is the author of 2 children's books, *Lakas and the Manilatown Fish* and *Lakas and the Makibaka Hotel*, published by Children's Book Press. In 2017, he was awarded a San Francisco Art Commission Individual Artist Commission and short-listed for poet laureate of San Francisco. He carries on the legacy of his late uncles, Al Robles, activist poet and scholar, and Russell Robles, co-founder of SOMArts Cultural Center, by serving as board president of the Manilatown Heritage Foundation and by working for housing and senior rights.

How Baseball Saved My Life
Jesus Francisco Sierra

My family and I arrived in San Francisco in 1969, a couple of years after the Summer of Love, seven years removed from the San Francisco Giants' last World Series appearance. A trail of incense and marijuana still wafted through the City. I was about to turn twelve, and it is that scent that I most remember, because it was new and it stank of drastic, indecipherable change. The cold and the streets crowded with people I neither knew nor understood cast out such distances between where I was, and where I came from, that I thought I'd never again remember home.

Only a week before, I had been in Havana, in the sun, embraced by the warmth of family. They had overwhelmed me with love more than normal, in anticipation that perhaps it would be the last time they'd ever see me. I remember their tears each time they hugged me. I was in the known.

The Cuban Revolution was evolving and making every effort to eradicate western culture. Cuba was a place where long hair and American music were not permitted. A place where wearing bell-bottoms was an offense worthy of jail time, regardless of age. I'd hear adults argue about how their freedom was being systematically stolen from them. I'd hear them talk about leaving to the United States, where they could be free. But I never understood any of that. To me, there was only one thing: baseball, and my team was Industriales, Havana's team.

I found that in this strange place even the Spanish I heard some people speak was not my own. My uncle, whom I'd never met before, was nice but still a stranger, as were my cousins. Everything that was home, that meant home, was gone and seemed irretrievable. I supposed this was what freedom was like, but I didn't like it. Instead, I felt alone, trapped, and less free than I'd ever been.

For months I wallowed in self-pity and melancholy, missing the only friends I knew up to then, the family we left behind, the blue skies, the warm sun, the pounding rains, the slap of the domino pieces over the constant chatter of the players, the red clay stuck to the bottom of my shoes, drinking water from the hose, the sweat, the laughter and the music. We all did, my sister, my brother and me. It was worse for my mother, Mima. She wanted to carry that burden for all of us, but her task was already daunting. She was a widow when we left Cuba. A lone woman with three kids making her way to a place she'd never been to make a new life.

We lived in a small two-bedroom basement apartment in my uncle's house. We were cramped, but thankful for all that we had. At least that's what

Mima kept saying. I felt different; the walls seemed to be getting closer to me each day. My brother and I shared a bunk bed. I slept on the top bunk. Some nights I'd lie down, stare at the ceiling pressing down on me, and cry myself to sleep. The more time passed, the more isolated and lost I felt.

* *

One day my uncle came downstairs and asked me if I liked baseball. I said I did. He asked me if I knew Willie Mays, Willie McCovey or Juan Marichal. I didn't know who they were. He went on to tell me all about how Mays was the world's best center fielder, McCovey a great slugging first baseman, and that Marichal's delivery was a thing of beauty that made him a great pitcher. And that all of them were Giants. He made sure to tell me that from then on, the Giants would be my team, and the Dodgers my hated rivals. I listened, but felt no passion for any of it. I didn't know the players or the team.

To me Pedro Chavez was the world's best first baseman, Tony Gonzalez the best ever shortstop and no one could ever hit Manuel Hurtado, my star pitcher. He had no idea who these guys were. He dismissed them. We argued and in the midst of that argument, I remembered home. But the memories were not external, or even in my mind's eye, like a faded photograph; these memories came from someplace deeper, someplace that suddenly made my skin once again sense the caress of the breeze back home.

As I began to pick up a little bit of English, I would hide away at the school's library, to read the San Francisco Chronicle's Sports page. Back then it was called the "Green Sheet" because they printed it in a light green color and made it easy to find. Growing up in Cuba where politics came at you from all angles, the one thing I came to enjoy most about this newfound freedom was that I didn't have to deal with it any longer. I could care less what was going on in the rest of the world. I went right to the box scores. Those were things I understood. You see in Cuba, you learn about such things as the infield-fly rule, balks, balls and strikes, well before you learn to read. In Havana, my friends and I would talk about how many hits Chavez got the night before or how many strike-outs Hurtado had, and then we'd argue about why Chavez took a fastball down the middle on a 3–2 count with two outs and men on base, or why Hurtado served up a slow curve in the sixth that resulted in a game tying home run for the opposing team.

I remember reading about the Miracle Mets when they won the World Series in 1969. I began to recognize names: Earl Weaver, Tom Seaver, Boog Powell, Brooks Robinson. Following baseball pulled me away from my struggles to adapt; still, the names were unfamiliar and strange sounding.

* *

That first Christmas, my uncle gave me a baseball glove. It was used, but it was the best gift I'd ever received. The glove was broken in, but not the way it should've been. I went on to dip the glove in water, put a ball in it and wrap a string around it. He watched me do that with a strange look on his face. I told him not to worry, that I knew what I was doing. Once the glove dried I slipped it under my mattress. I could feel the bump under my legs each night as I slept. It was like I was incubating the thing, waiting for it to hatch. After a week, I pulled it out from under the mattress and it was perfect, the pocket broken in just right. When I slid my fingers into the glove, I again sensed something that wasn't a memory but more akin to seeing land after drifting for months in the open ocean.

Our house backed into the Sears parking lot, which was often empty in the summer nights after they closed. It was still light out and occasionally I'd see some kids running around playing baseball with a tennis ball. I drifted out there one afternoon, glove in hand and asked them if I could play. There were enough kids so that one guy batted and the others fielded. We took turns hitting and fielding. To them, it was just a game. But I was playing for my country, imagining myself as a member of the Cuban National team, playing against these Americanos. We would trade gloves each time one took the field while the other one batted. When it was over, I went to get my glove from the kid I'd lent it to. He was a bit taller than me. Instead of handing it back, he punched me in the eye and ran, glove still in hand. It was as though he'd taken home right out of my grasp. I chased the kid for three blocks until I caught up to him and smacked him in the back of the head. He fell and I snatched the glove from his hand. I was about to punch him again when he covered his head with his arms. I stopped short of hitting him and yelled the worst curse words and flurry of threats that I could muster. This was my glove. I'd been yanked from my home once and it would not happen again. He looked at me, not with fear, but with a furrowed brow. You see, all that yelling was in Spanish. I ran out of breath and out of words. Finally, I just screamed "Okay?" He nodded, and I walked home proud.

*   *

Later that summer, my uncle came down on a Saturday to tell my brother and I that we were going to a baseball game on Sunday, a double-header no less. It wasn't to see Industriales, but I was nevertheless excited to see a real ballgame for the first time in my life. On Sunday my uncle, his two sons, my brother, and I drove to Candlestick Park on the South end of San Francisco. Years later that park would be derided as a "dump" of a stadium, but to me, on that day, it was a jewel. As I strolled in and through the tunnel, the green outfield

Cuba, 2015

Shizue Seigel

Ben Pease

and the manicured infield, with bright white bases perfectly aligned, unfolded before me like a colorful peacock tail. I stopped and thought of my childhood friends in Cuba—if they could only see this. Willie Mays patrolled center field for the Giants and I found out that Tito Fuentes, their second baseman, was Cuban. I became a Giants fan that day. Industriales were still a part of me, but it would be years before I'd be able to follow them again. And this place was now beginning to remind me of home. This language of baseball, I understood. It transcended borders. When I heard the first crack of the bat, it felt as though a new part of me, a new limb, reached out and touched the Havana I'd left behind.

*   *

My mother died in October of 2014. That year, she watched just about every Giant's game on TV. She loved Buster Posey, their catcher, because of his boyish looks and clutch hitting. She called me each day, sometimes at work, when they played back East and I wasn't able to watch or listen, to give me updates of the score. She was our stalwart, our star, and our hero. Her death came in her sleep, as she'd hoped. My brother, my sister, and I were devastated. It was difficult to imagine life without her. Once again, I found myself forced to leave behind a time of my life that I'd never see again.

We held a service for my mother to celebrate her life. Family and friends gathered at my brother's house after the service. By early afternoon, everyone had left. I, along with my brother, his partner, my sister, my kids, and nephews were left with the emptiness. On that same day, the Giants, in an impossible season, reached the seventh game of the World Series against the Kansas City Royals. We turned on the TV to watch the game, but also to remember my mother. We watched Madison Bumgarner stroll out of the bullpen in the fifth inning, in a do-or-die game. Salvador Perez popped up in the ninth and Pablo Sandoval caught the final out, falling back to the ground and raising his arms in victory. We hugged and cried. We all wished she'd been able to see them win. Then we all agreed she probably helped them win. Whether she did or not we'll never know.

Once again, baseball had given me the feeling of yet another limb reaching across time, across memories, across loss, to steady me and remind me that there are still a few more innings to play.

Published online at *Lunch Ticket*, Jan, 19, 2018. http:// lunchticket.org/baseball-saved-life/

Jesus Francisco Sierra received his MFA in Creative Writing from Antioch University Los Angeles in December 2017. He is currently doing an additional Post MFA semester working towards the completion of a collection of short stories. He emigrated from Cuba in 1969 and grew up in San Francisco's Mission District. His inspiration and most supportive audience are his adult daughter and son. He is fascinated by how transitions, both sought and imposed, have the power to either awaken or suppress the spirit. His work has previously been published in the *Marathon Literary Review* and *The Acentos Review*.

Avalos Shoe Repair on 26th Street in the Mission District has been in business for forty-two years. Shizue Seigel

San Pancho
Karina Muñiz-Pagán

"We found an irregularity in the cell culture. There's a fifty-fifty chance the fetus may have Trisomy 13. Most die within a few days, or at best, make it to two years old. And at your age, Mona, pregnancy is already a risk. You two are going to have to decide in the next couple of days, given how far along you are, but I recommend an abortion," Dr. Golbus said to my parents at San Francisco Children's Hospital back in 1976.

My mom has told me this story multiple times. How his words, barren and cold, matched the sterility of the room, and stung my parents into silence. Irregularity, dead within a few days, abortion; these weren't words my mom expected at her checkup. She never even expected to get pregnant. My dad had been married once before and he had always assumed, based on his first wife's rendering of what happened, he was to blame.

"I couldn't take his words, couldn't stand to be in the room any longer, much less think of questions to ask the doctor," my mom told me. Instead, my parents grieved the news underneath the shaded pines and redwoods of Golden Gate Park, and then went close by to St. Anne's on Judah Street, lit a candle and prayed. My mom, a supporter of a woman's right to have control over her own body, said of that day, "I could just feel your presence inside me. You wanted to be born."

Forty-years later, I visited St. Anne's for the first time, tracing my roots in San Francisco to make sense of my own journey before I moved away, for possibly the last time, from the beloved city that gave me life. I wanted to start from day one in understanding how my life has been shaped by the city, made me who I am, and how despite the changes, it will always be home in my memories, identity and heritage, and the guiding lens with which I see the world.

The church was empty that day. To my right was a pastel mosaic of St. Anthony, and I thought of my paternal grandmother, Candelaria, and the stories of her lighting candles for St. Anthony for members of the family. Is this why I am so obsessed with a grandmother who passed before I was born? The one who fled Chihuahua at the end of the Mexican Revolution, who was known for making batches of sugar cookies for her grandchildren, and who was pulled out of primary school to work as a domestic worker on the El Paso/Juarez border. Was I somewhere in the ethers that day with her, as my parents knelt before this very spot and lit a candle in prayer?

Maybe I carry the stories she never got to tell with me. As well as the hopes she had for her children and grandchildren to live a good life in this new land disconnected from México; the country I continue to run to and the one she was forced to flee from.

Growing up in South San Francisco, racial identity for me was often associated with place. As a mixed kid of Mexican-Swedish descent living in a mostly Filipino neighborhood, I wasn't sure what I was exactly. As I got older and started to learn about Xicana/o history; the student walkouts, the Xicano moratorium, and places like Garfield High School where Jaime Escalante taught, I secretly thought to be a legit Xicana I had to be from East LA. And as a white-passing half-breed I need not apply.

Or it meant living on the U.S./México border like my family, where Spanish flowed as easily as English. Being from those places, identity wasn't questioned; language, place, and appearance made it all clear.

I couldn't claim the Mission District either, another place you could pass the Xicana/o litmus test. And even though we spent most of our free time in the Excelsior, adjacent to the Mission, I often saw 24th Street, peering out of a window on the 14 Mission bus en route to Russia Avenu with my maternal grandmother, on the outside looking in.

Recently, I passed by my grandmother's house to visit friends who still live in the Excelsior. I saw a big gaping hole that led to the backyard. The insides of the home were being gutted. I spent hours there when I was a kid. The rooms that had become nothing but dirt and pummeled plywood, were where my grandfather assembled his 1940s Lionel train set for his five children while delivering laundry for a living. It's where my grandmother kept her rock collection inside an old Dole Food Company cardboard box, and occasionally hung her plastic bags to dry for re-use. It's also where I stole *Playgirl* magazines from my uncle's secret stash; knowing how much trouble I'd get in if I ever got caught. It appeared as if my grandma's leaky roof was finally going to get fixed, and a fresh exterior paint would cover any evidence of the people who used to live there.

As a kid I got my first geography lessons from the Excelsior. With typical street names like Vienna, Persia, Madrid and Naples, I found myself imagining what these real places were like, and who lived there. But San Francisco was its own mecca of cultures and peoples. On the bus running errands with my grandmother, I would hear Tagalog, Chinese, and the familiar cadence of words in Spanish that would flow in and out of the rooms when visiting my dad's compadres and their kids. They lived in the Excelsior too.

My favorite pastime at their house was when my cousins Gabriel and Richard would put me on a blanket and drag me through the house as fast as they could. I was on my own little rasquacho rollercoaster, squealing and laughing. I don't recall getting a chichón on my forehead or a split lip from it. I remember being too young, according to my parents, to watch *Purple Rain* with my cousins when it first came out, but managed to sneak in a scene or two, standing by the doorframe of their room with my head slowly peeking in while they pretended not to notice.

I couldn't see exactly how much San Francisco had shaped me as a child and teen until I left for college and landed in a small Christian liberal arts school in Chicago where most of my classmates were from the Midwest. I naturally gravitated towards the international students from India, South Africa, Ecuador and Palestine, who I seemed to have more in common with than students from lily-white small towns fitting the description of what "American" looked like to the outside world. Or I hung out with the few Black students from Chicago who commuted to school. We'd talk about East Coast vs. West Coast Hip Hop and I learned about a new artist named Common Sense who was putting Chicago on the map. I'd share all my Bay Area Hip Hop music with my friends, like Souls of Mischief and Del the Funky Homosapien, even RBL Posse who wrote a song about the high quality weed smoked in San Francisco. It didn't bode well for a school where we were required to go to chapel twice a week.

I had wanted to leave home, a girl trying to be grown too fast, wanting to experience the big city life, and also in search of spirituality. I took the city I was born in, with so much to offer as well, for granted. So I returned one summer from college eager to intern at a local organization. I discovered Global Exchange online, sitting in our school's computer lab, getting used to how this new popular phenomenon called the internet worked. I had learned about the Zapatista movement in my Mexican history class in Chicago, and from hanging out with my friend Tomás from Queretaro, whose parents were still active in leftist politics in México, despite living in Chicago. The Program Director from the México program interviewed me over the phone, and I was "hired" to work for free that summer, supporting the Zapatistas from this side of the border.

Global Exchange, located on the corner of 16th and Mission, gave me my first vantage point into social justice in the Bay Area. When I arrived my first day, I saw numerous Zapatista dolls and a poster on the wall of subcomandante Marcos with the words Justicia and Libertad. A few months prior to my internship, Mexican paramilitary massacred indigenous women and children inside a church as a brutal tactic to annihilate any resistance against the government in the Chiapas region. It barely made the news in the US. A call from local groups for human rights observers to arrive, bear witness and disseminate what was happening, was in full force. But the Mexican government was deporting international observers fast. That summer, between protests, media pitches and U.S. Congress sign-on letters, I worked with the team to keep the observers there and bring visibility to Chiapas and indigenous rights.

My understanding of San Francisco activism had been peripheral at best. Now, with my first protest under my belt and successful legislative advocacy, I found myself part of it, even if I was young and not clear about what targets and direct action meant.

I was getting to know the city on my own terms outside of my family. My paid work that summer was temping as a receptionist in the financial district, a stark contrast from my volunteer work at Global Exchange. One day, Charlie from the mailroom invited me to Puerto Alegre, a block up from my internship. I had my fake ID just in case, the one my friends and I all got from an ice cream shop on Market Street in high school that worked at most bars and clubs in Chicago.

Puerto's clientele twenty years ago was not the New Valencia that can be seen today. All those cheese and chocolate shops were nowhere in sight. Nor the clothing stores with must-have dresses for toddlers starting at $100.

Back then I soon became a regular, finding out how deep their roots were in the Mission. Willy, who co-owned Puerto Alegre with his siblings, told me his grandparents had opened the family business; now one of the oldest

Mexican restaurants in the city. Their secret margarita recipe, and a framed photograph of the founders above the bar, are still part of the establishment today. Willy often stood behind the bar and worked his multi-tasking magic stirring and shaking here and there, pouring just the right amount of tequila, salting the glasses, refilling the pitcher. The smell of agave azul, grilled shrimp tacos and fried tortilla chips filled the restaurant.

Norma, who also worked there, had a voice just as powerful as Ana Gabriel's. She would sing mariachi impeccably after the restaurant closed and the jukebox was free-range. She also used to be one of my father's students at Everett Middle School. Part chola, one hundred percent chingona, her smile was bright and bold. And then there was Antonio, in his mid-seventies, a chunky Afro-Rican transplant who wore a cringe-worthy blue t-shirt that said "Viagra Works." Despite appearances, he had a lot of wisdom to share about his years between Puerto Rico, New York and San Francisco.

"Ten cuidao, mamita," he'd say to me. "These cabrones out here aren't worthy of you." His murals covered the walls below the picture of Willy's grandparents. I knew Puerto had really become my Cheers when I made the cut on one of the murals Antonio painted of all the locals at the bar. I had found my people.

Many years later after having spent time away from San Francisco, I found myself back in the Mission, this time working at the Women's Building as the Political Director for Mujeres Unidas y Activas (MUA), a Latina immigrant and domestic workers' rights organization. My mornings started with walking past the mural that covers the building: Rigoberta Menchu's outstretched arms, Audre Lorde's writing on ribbon for future generations, and Puerto Rican freedom fighter Lolita Lebrón, alongside other women from Palestine to South Africa, singing songs of resistance. On good days I stopped, breathed in the gratitude and remembered how they are holding us. I would also remember how circular life could be.

My maternal great-grandmother, Karin, was a domestic worker too. She migrated from Sweden to San Francisco and worked for 30 years for a family on Russian Hill. With grandmothers from both sides of my family having migrated to this country to do the often invisible and invaluable work of home care, I was drawn to work that honored the dignity and value of immigrant women and domestic workers of today, resisting and building power within a new landscape in the city.

At MUA I found my political home. We fasted together to fight for just immigration reform, and got arrested to stop the deportations. Many of my friends risked so much more in these acts of civil disobedience. My U.S.

citizenship allowed for protections not guaranteed for most. They taught me what bravery looks like and the true meaning of resilience. I met women with ankle monitors who survived months of detention and were still waiting for the final proceedings. They held their children tight at night, forced to figure out emergency plans should they not come home again. These mothers shared their stories to the media hoping that maybe another domestic violence survivor who immigrated to this country wouldn't have to go through what they did when they called the police afraid for their lives, and ended up instead f inside a patrol car.

Several years ago Galería de la Raza on 24th Street—a street I now visited frequently instead of peering out towards it from the bus—put up a mural on their Bryant Street wall titled "Por Vida" designed by the Maricón Collective. The mural depicted Latinx queer love and was intentionally ruined several times, with no suspect in sight. I felt like a part of myself was scarred too. I looked at the damaged wall, studying the burnt marks and the images that showed a transman, two women, and two men in loving embraces. As I held my partner's hand, I wondered if the people who did this were staring at us now, and if they wanted to burn us too. The mural was created in honor of SF Pride. Someone wrote online, in response to the vandalism, how the artists should have kept that type of thing in the Castro. And what if we, as queer Latinxs, never felt like we belonged there either? Where could we go, the others of the others living in the intersections, to feel like we had just as much right to claim San Pancho as our own?

It was my friend Chuy who pulled me out of my solitude when she encouraged MUA members to show up to the vigil that Galería de la Raza was holding to support the queer Latinx community. In the months that followed, Chuy would take the lead in ensuring San Francisco stayed a sanctuary city.

Today when I visit the city, maybe it's because I'm holding 100 years of San Francisco history in my own DNA. I can feel a nudge, a whisper, to stop staring at the new condos, and cussing under my breath, and instead pay attention to who and what is still here, and is being created.

Now I can see more. Appreciating the times I took a Zumba class with my friend in a tiny room with a disco ball hovering above a laminated floor in the back of a laundromat, where little girls joined their mothers in a bachata cooldown. Or the other day heading towards BART, I heard a classic early eighties Hip Hop song, "The Breaks" by Kurtis Blow, and I couldn't help but smile. It was coming from a mini-boom box a street vendor was selling on Mission Street. I remembered how my friends and I used to write down the lyrics of songs, press play and rewind on our cassettes, as I got exposed to my first poets and the power of words.

Other days, it's recalling having coffee in the Excelsior with Charlie, a community organizer from Poder, hearing about a new space they opened to find solutions to displacement and the housing crisis. They are creating new possibilities of economic justice and solidarity economies with urban campesino gardens and cooperatives.

Or walking past El Rio and remembering when I first went to Mango, a party held there for mostly queer women of color back then. I had been to more clubs than I could count before that. But they were either straight or gay male clubs. Mango, like Backstreet in Potrero Hill, was a club full of women and gender non-conforming folks and felt magical. I couldn't stop smiling, my body at ease after I entered and allowed myself to feel, observe and breathe it all in. Those days, I was still convinced I was a down ally for the queer movement.

Peering in at El Rio, to the pool table and back patio, took me to a more recent memory, over a decade after my first visit. Divorced from my ex-husband and fully out in the world, I went back to Mango and met my future wife there, in my beloved city. She walked through the front door with her white Kangol tilted to the side with so much swag and a smile reserved just for me.

For those of us who grew up here and have seen or experienced so many displaced and pushed out, especially people of color, we are often filled with stories of mourning. I've written and felt them myself. But I need to also remember what the city has given me, what keeps me coming back whether in person or on the page.

El Rio, a welcoming LGBTQ+ bar on Mission Street, 2017. Shizue Seigel.

My identity as a queer Xicana came full circle here in San Francisco. Xicana identity is still associated with place for me. It's just more fluid than before, ample enough to fit outside the boxes. Maybe I never was on the outside looking in. I just needed a broader understanding, one beyond a single narrative. Today, I can't imagine my life not shaped by this city and I'm thankful for the fateful day my parents found a tiny church, on a street in San Francisco, and lit a candle for me.

Karina Muñiz-Pagán is a queer Xicana writer from San Francisco. She has taught community-based creative writing with Latina immigrant and domestic worker leaders in the Bay Area, founding the group Las Mal-Criadas. She is an alumna of Voices of Our Nations Arts Foundation (VONA) and contributing writer for the online journal, *Race, Poverty and the Environment* (RP&E) and Collaborative Liberation Arts Workshop Series (CLAWS). She holds Masters degrees in Urban Planning and Latin American Studies from UCLA and an MFA in Creative Writing from Mills College. She lives in Long Beach and works for the National Domestic Workers Alliance.

Valentine's decorations at Nancy Chárraga's Casa Bonampak, a Mission District business and community mainstay for over 20 years, 2016. Shizue Seigel.

Thanksgiving
Kimi Sugioka

Chestnut & sweet rice flour pie crusts
Roasted pumpkin
Allspice ground with mortar and pestle
Juiced lemons
Cardamom coffee
Heritage turkey
The eminent domain of flavor
Extracted
Pressed
Massaged

Metered interlocutions
4/4, 3/4
Staccato interjections
Tectonic shifts of socio-political
And psycho-social paradigms
An insistence to examine
The labyrinthine interplay between
denial, tolerance and rage

The table is laid
With Mexican & Italian ceramics
And the once prized china
Of relations born
To tin bowls and factory enslavement

Assemble are assimilated
Mongrel Africans, Chinese, Japanese, Europeans
Progeny
Of the eager or desperate or forcefully displaced
Without complacency
With the experienced and erudite conviction
That ultimately we must all
Face the blind trajectory of bullets
From the xenophobic supremacists gun
By rising from bus, train, plane or theatre seats
As the righteous many
Against the pernicious and cowardly
Few

For Kimi Sugioka's bio, see page 242.

2

sanctuary
& opportunity

Eduardo Aguilera, *Labyrinth at Land's End*, 2011

Eduardo Aguilera built this sacred path on public land in 2004, modeling it after the ancient design at Chartres Cathedral in France. Originally built without park service approval, it has been destroyed by vandals several times and rebuilt by volunteers for whom the site has become a local treasure. Aguilera is a San Francisco resident originally from Baja California.

Permit!
Iran, Tehran 1984.
Anahita Miller

Neda's desk began to rattle. The whole classroom shook. The glass windows imploded, despite the heavy-duty duct tape X'ed across them and a million pieces of shattered glass showered them all.

Even though they had practiced maybe hundreds of times over and over, Neda was still not fast enough to get under her desk in time. Flustered by a sudden sharp pain on her right cheek, she noticed a gush of blood. With a shaking body and trembling hands, she finally managed to get under her desk.

The deafening sound of heavy explosion still echoing in her ears was now mingled with the shrilling sound of the alarm they all knew well. She covered her head with both hands to protect it. Yet, somehow in that craziness along with the ringing in her ears, she could hear her own heart beating. That moment felt like an eternity of numbing fear.

A hand touched her back.

"Are you OK, Neda?" Her teacher Mrs. Zand said in a shaky voice. She left to check on someone else—without waiting for an answer.

Neda lifted her head. Her ears were still ringing. She slowly brought her shaking hands down and noticed fresh, red blood all over them. Where was she bleeding from? She wasn't sure if her hands were wounded or the blood was from her cheek. At this point, it didn't matter.

The air was packed with dense dust. She couldn't see clearly and breathing was hard. Everyone was coughing. Through the dust, pieces of rubble and glass, her friends and classmates were slowly coming up from under their desks. Some started crying. Some looked shocked and numb. Some were screaming.

Blood mixed with dust was everywhere.

Oh no! Fariba! Her best friend Fariba! Where was she? She had been at the board writing when the bomb landed. Neda tried to get up, but her legs were too shaky to bear her wait. Covering her nose with her sleeve while coughing, she tried again and slowly stood up looking around for her friend. Fariba was standing at the other side of the room crying and bewildered.

"Everybody! It is OK. We are OK. We must get out fast. Help your friends up…." Mrs. Zand's voice was interrupted by yet another shake. A second bomb had landed. Even though this one was farther away, the building still shook badly and pieces of rubble started falling. Suddenly everybody started to run outside as if the second bomb had woken them all up somehow.

Outside in their huge schoolyard, Neda saw her classmates running around and some falling down trying to get back up. Everyone was running towards the underground shelter which was still under construction. She had always wondered how all 3000 of her middle-school classmates would be able to fit into the small and still unlit underground haven.

Looking around, Neda decided to walk in the opposite direction and just leave the school. Even if there was to be room in the shelter, there was no way she could reach it in time. Besides, she doubted that the Iraqi planes would bomb the same place twice in such a huge city.

The shockwave had been pretty strong, so she knew the bomb must have landed somewhere close by. Robot-like and numb, Neda started to follow the crowd. The firefighters were finally arriving and a wave of people running pushed her in the direction of the impact. Everyone was rushing to help, hoping to get to the victims quickly. They were desperate to find and help the survivors, if there were any.

As Neda neared the impact point, the destruction around her grew worse. She must be close, she thought. Then she saw the impact area. People around her were yelling and running covered in dust and blood. Some who had already arrived were removing the rubbles and looking for survivors. Neda knew that there was a very low chance anyone had survived. The house was completely destroyed.

OH NO! She suddenly noticed where she was!

That is the house! That is the big, beautiful house they wanted to buy!
The house with a huge backyard, and a swimming pool!
The one with a running natural stream passing through!
The house they had tried so hard to get!
The house where Neda and her brother had already chosen their rooms and her mother had talked to interior designers about how to make it homey and cozy for them.
The house that was perfect because of its proximity to their schools!
The house they had visited so many times, they got to know the owners.
The house that seemed like an unattainable dream
That very house was now gone.

They had cried for that house when her father, an engineer, announced that they would pass and not buy it.

"I know all of you are sad—and possibly you hate me. The reason we are not going to buy the house is this. No matter how hard I tried, I couldn't get the permit for the bomb-safeguarding modifications I had in mind. The house wasn't built to handle earthquakes or bombs. Without reinforcing and modifying, I have an uneasy feeling about it," her father had said sadly.

The house they had remembered wistfully as "The No-Permit House"! Yes. The No-Permit House was now completely gone. She now knew that no amount of modifications would have saved the house or anyone inside.

Anahita Miller is a mother, wife, and a medical professional. She is an Iranian American who has lived in four different countries on three different continents. She thrived and progressed while surviving childhood depression, a narcissistic parent, revolution, war, immigration, and years of living in an ex-communist country. She is a writer who has many stories to share—stories about her eventful past and her winning battle with depression. Her favorite story is her sci-fi novel set in an imaginary utopian future.

Bao
Shirley Huey

It was in our kitchen with the linoleum floor and the stove from Sears that my grandmother told me about that time in China—that time she had to flee on foot from advancing Japanese troops—soldiers that everyone feared, men who had engaged in horrific acts of violence. She was just talking, telling stories while making me a snack—the way she always did on one of the many days that she babysat me. This was back when we all lived in the same house—my grandmother, Ngeen-Ngeen in Toisanese; my uncles and aunt; my parents; my brother; and me.

In this story, people ran for their lives, carrying all their belongings with them, their children struggling to keep up alongside or carried on their backs. Some babies sat by the side of the road, no mother or father in sight—abandoned in the desperate, long trudge to what people hoped would be safety. Listening to Ngeen-Ngeen, I wondered about the weight of a baby on such a long journey—how hard it might be to carry a baby for miles and miles, what it would be like to have the heavy burden of all one's worldly possessions carried on your back, hidden in pockets, in your socks, in your shoes. I wondered about the weapons that people secreted on their bodies, imagining what the worst thing the need to survive would demand of them.

As I munched on faan jiew, crackling crusts of rice from the remnants of last night's dinner, my grandmother told me about the pity she felt for one child left by the side of the road. The baby was crying. Ants crawled on it. I didn't ask whether the baby was a boy or a girl, but I listened closely—this was a world far, far away from the kitchen of our house next to a gas station on a large, noisy street in San Francisco.

In her Toisan dialect, one that I would always listen to and understand but never speak, she told me that she was moved by the sight of this baby to stop. She reached into her pocket for the piece of bao that she had saved for herself—food was scarce in wartime, she emphasized. Nevertheless, she walked over to the child, and put the bao in the child's hand. I never asked her how old the baby was—whether it was old enough to eat solids or whether the baby ate all or any of the bread. From what I remember, my grandmother stopped for just one moment and, in that split second, gave the child food before continuing on her way, another dark figure merging into the surging flow of hundreds, thousands fleeing the anticipated onslaught.

*   *

We do what we can to help others in need. This I learned from my grandmother's story. We frequently cannot know, comprehend, or predict the full impact of the actions we take. Ngeen-Ngeen's life spanned decades, oceans, and continents. She was trying to teach me something about the good fortune I had to be born in America, where food was plentiful in our household—to be grateful and not to take what we had for granted. I was an eager listener, drinking in the stories of far-off places filled with drama and intrigue, despair and urgency—all the while sitting at a little brown Formica folding table in our San Francisco kitchen.

* *

My grandmother is now gone. I conjure her up in my imagination these days, filled with love for her children and grandchildren and also an ever-present fear of hunger, manifested by hoarding crackers, candies, and American foods that she would often never even eat herself—giant tubs of peanut butter, bright orange blocks of cheese—because someone was giving them away.

"What a country to live in," she'd say. "What a land of plenty."

"Bao" was posted at www.shirlintheworld.wordpress.com, April 26, 2016.

Born and raised in San Francisco, Shirley Huey is a storyteller and writer. She has read her work at the Oakland Asian Cultural Center, the Bay Area Generations reading series in Berkeley and Oakland, Liminal in Oakland, and Book Passage in San Francisco's Ferry Building. She is a VONA/Voices alum in travel writing and memoir, and writes about arts and culture and social justice issues. She is also a facilitator, researcher, and consultant who works on community building, organizational development, and transformational social change projects.

My grandmother and her family incarcerated at Poston, Arizona, 1945.

Baachan Grandma
Shizue Seigel

Baachan. Grandma. Of you I know mostly facts, not feeling.
Your eyes were like jet—brightly opaque.
They saw all without a hint of weakness.
Gaman. Endure. Persevere beyond hope.
Kichinto shinasai. Do it just the right way.

The year before you died in 1981
you thought you were a little girl again, back in Japan.
You dreamed you died but the gatekeeper sent you back
because you hadn't suffered enough.
They say Nirvana, the Pureland, awaits
anyone who says three times from the heart
Namu amida butsu. Namu amida butsu. Namu amida butsu.
I put my faith in the Buddha.

In 1913, you put your faith in a man who called you to California
He sparked the wanderlust born into your blood—
The seed of disappointment and the egg of hope conjoined
in some Hawaiian canefield that your parents endured just long enough
to serve out their contract and drag themselves back home.

But you could not be contained by two-acre rice plots in a mountain village.
When the man from the next village called you
to join him in California, you went.
He was plain but sturdy—courted you with photos of horse and plow,
haystack and wagon, wooden irrigation flumes,
and a Japanese woman in a billowing shirtwaist and a long Western skirt.
So you packed your best kimono, steamed over the long ocean to the big land
where he bought you a hat with ostrich plumes,
and a jacket with muttonleg sleeves.

You placed your faith in this man, this life, this land
and it was good—though children died and crops failed.
You prayed to the Buddha in the dining room and Kamisama in the kitchen.
When plows turned up arrowheads, you brought a Shinto priest 200 miles
to placate the spirits who'd roamed the land before you.
You and your husband were kigyo shin, enterprising spirits.
Isshoni, together, Issho ken mei, you worked together, with all your might.
Worked around the alien land laws, shipped your produce to L.A.,
dressed your sons in sailor suits and your daughter in silk stockings.
You bought property in town near the Buddhist church
that became San Luis Obispo's mini-Japantown,
with a Nihonjin barbershop, fish market, pool hall, hotel and gas station.
You planned to populate your own little community—
your kids would become the pharmacist,
the seamstress, the garage mechanic….

Where did your faith go in 1933 when your husband
drove into a telephone pole? A silly little accident
until his stomach filled up with blood. The hospital would not x-ray.
The insurance company would not pay double indemnity for accidental death.
You said he might not have died if he'd been white.
You said it only once out loud, but your children say after that,
you often walked to cliff edge and stood for long moments
looking west across the sea towards home.

Gaman and ganbatte. Suck it up. Never give up.
Put your faith in 140 acres and four children.
You made your 13-year-old learn to drive
so you could keep up the mortgage on your Japantown property.
Throughout the Great Depression you visited tenants who often said,
"We can't pay this month; business is too slow.
Yoroshiku onegai shimasu. We are forever in your debt."
Long after the war, Issei ladies bowed and you bowed back.
I was too young to notice who bowed deeper.

You hired a new foreman to help manage the ranch.
Lettuce, peas and cantaloupe thrived in the moist sea air.
Then a white man bought the land out from under you,
plotting to turn a profit by doubling the lease.
But you told him no. Moved off the land and up the hill. Built another house.
You put your faith in your community. "Let's all tell him no!"
For a full year, no nihonjin leased in your place.
The land lay fallow until the landlord knuckled under
and let you come back at the same price.
That kind of Jap conspiracy does not go unpunished.

In 1942, Pearl Harbor forced you from the coast
You moved outside the curfew zone—five miles east, then 100 miles more—
fleeing the barbed wire until it finally snagged you just outside Fresno,
and cast you east of the Colorado River
where—against the wishes of displaced Indian tribes—
you were imprisoned with thousands of others in the searing desert,
trapped amid tar-paper shimmering like a mirage that would not dissolve.
Tucked inside your shoe was all that remained of your previous life.
A clipping: "Jap house burns to ground." And cash from the realtor who
bought your Japantown, saying, "You already put $80,000 into it,
but you won't be able to pay the mortgage from behind barbed wire.
Let me do you a favor. I'll take it off your hands for two grand."
He even put his name on the hotel your husband built.

How many dollars did you have left when they let you out in 1946?
"Don't go come back to the coast," friends warned.
"They're shooting out our windows at night.
They won't sell us gas or fertilizer."
So you came north to start again—at 57 on your knees—
sharecropping strawberries in another tar-paper compound.
In ten years you saved enough to buy ten acres of your own.

Gaman, gaman and gaman some more. Persevere in the face of hardship.
Until it becomes shinbo—endurance as a way of life.
Maybe your soul wore away in pieces too small to notice
until all that was left was efficiency,
washing the rice, "goshi, goshi, goshi," scrubbing the grains three times firmly,
snipping your scissors in quick clips to make crepe paper petals,
combing black dye through your hair with a toothbrush,
mentally plotting the most precise way to live without wasted motion.
Chanto shinasai! Do it right.
How much suffering was enough?

Your cactus collection still grows near the garbage can.

What Were the Rules
Holman Turner

The year was 1950,
And all that I could see,
Were short-brimmed hats,
And Converse shoes,

And Whites singing—
Country songs,
And Blacks sang—
The Blues.

And as I walked
Home from school
I knew the rules,
As you approached me.

I was to look
To the ground—
Certainly
Not at you.

For if I did
I could be
Accused, of

"Reckless Eyeballing You"!

And what was the
Punishment for that?

Let me see,
It was—

Whatever you wanted it be.

Maybe you would say
"What are you looking at,
Nigger?"
And I would look away.

Or according to how you felt,
You might slap
The Hell out of me—
That day.

Or maybe
What you might do
Would be to tell the Cop
Standing next to you—

"This Nigger is—
'Reckless eyeballing me.'"
And that's all it would take,
For this cop to twist my arm

Until I thought it would break.

Holman Turner's Artist Statement

Shall I die as I was born, yearning to be free?
Free of what you ask?
Free of your hate or apathy for me.

Nine People
Holman Turner

As I sit at my desk
Thinking of you,
I can't help but wonder
What would you do—

If I went to an all-White
Church,
And killed nine people—
Who look like you?

Would you rush—
Right over,
And place a
Bulletproof vest
On me?

Or would you simply
Hang me—
From the nearest
Tree?

Let me see,
If I can draw
A picture—
For you.

I walk up to your mother
Place a gun to her head

And then, I shoot her—dead.

The blood from her brains
Flies all over me
And onto the lady
Standing next to me.

As people begin to scream
And call out the Lord's name,
They run from me, as
I fire again and again.

So, let me ask you, once again—

Would you rush—
Right over
And place a
Bulletproof vest
On me?

Or would you simply
Hang me—
From the nearest
Tree?

Great-Grandson
Holman Turner

As the great-grandson
Of a former slave
Who now lies quietly
In her grave

And the
Great-grandson of
Miscegenation
I'm still not free in this nation.

There's no doubt
She would be shocked to see
That I'm still fighting
To be free;

Free from what you call
"A way of life,"
As you fly your Confederate Flags
Of hate and strife

Flying it free for all to see
As you try to assure me,
That I'm already—
Free.

Free from what,
I might ask
Certainly, not from you
Telling me what I can, and cannot do.

But please forgive me, if I forget
It was you
Who built this country
Not me.

You plowed every acre of land
You could steal
And killed every Indian
You could kill.
You even say you built
The Whitehouse
All by yourself,
And then named it for no one else.

And here I come
Accusing you
Of things
You did not do.

So, I apologize
For all my lies
When you say
To me,

This is a flag of heritage
Not of hatred
And it has nothing to do
With you.

So, forgive me, I'm sorry
I guess I just forgot
I'm already free, and how do I know—
And I guess the one thing
I must now learn to do,
Is to pay more attention
To what you say—

And not what you do.

Everything I See
Holman Turner

Everything I see
Bothers me
From short-brimmed hats
To the Converse shoes

To country songs
And even the Blues.
To me it's all the same—
I'm back in the 50s once again.

Where red-necks
Get to choose,
Who will win
And who will lose.

Where now
There are
Suits
Instead of Sheets

And young people seem
More concerned
With "Me"
Than "We."

And people try
Very hard not to see,
That the thing that is
Killing me—

Will one day
Kill you.

For you don't
Have to die
To be
Dead.

You simply
Have to lose
All hope
Instead.

But you look
At me
And say –
I'm okay.

But
So were the
Jews -
In '32.

And if,
You are not careful—
The same could happen—
To you.

Holman Turner. I am an African American. I was born in Birmingham, Alabama, where I spent the first twenty-two years of my life. It was a tough and demanding place. The physical violence experienced there, daily, was equaled only by its psychological counterpart.

As a young person, you learned early on that the decisions you made outside of the home were every bit as critical as those that were being made for you by your parents. Your immediate and future chances for survival were directly linked to those decisions. It made for a brief childhood.

My dark skin, so much like my patients:
Sriram Shamasunder

In medical residency I trained at a county hospital in Los Angeles. Black and brown patients lay on gurneys in the emergency room and lined the halls on the wards. Our patients were mostly poor, often undocumented. The doctors were mostly white.

One of my Guatemalan patients told me that on the difficult, month-long walk into the U.S., contending with blisters and diarrhea, she'd learned that our hospital was the first place to get decent, free care.

As residents, we worked and lived in the hospital so many nights, it felt like home.

On one of my days off, in street clothes—jeans and a t-shirt—I went into the hospital to finish dictating some patient notes. It was morning. As usual, I went through the metal detector coming into the hospital. I collected my stale coffee from the cafeteria. Later that morning, I got stopped by a police guard

Federal Bulding/Rasta by Shizue Seigel was first published in *Whilwind Magazine*, No 6, 2015.

coming out of the bathroom, suspicious I might have been shooting up in one of the bathroom stalls. I presented my doctor's ID out of my jeans pocket, and immediately apologies flowed like water from an open faucet from the mouth of the police guard.

My dark skin is so much like my patients. I learned never to walk the hospital without an ID. Until then, the hospital had felt like home. Suddenly, it was not a home where I could move freely without question. It was no longer *my* home.

A few months later after a long on-call shift, I decide to drive to the ocean. Making my way to the water feels like making my way home. This is a habit of mine. The air by the water is fresh and clean and welcoming. **It** opens the lungs after 30 continuous hours in the hospital.

The neighboring cities of Redondo Beach and Hermosa Beach are beautiful, with strips of bars and flocks of white folks that flood them in the evening hours. It's 11 pm on a Thursday **and bea**ch-front parking is full. I want to bypass the crowds and the bars and go sit on the beach to clear my head.

As I circle for parking in my sister's black, beat-up 2004 Jetta, I can see a cop car eye me as I come around the block again in search of parking.

My black, beat-up car and my nearly black skin in this dark night.

My third time around the block, the cop starts to follow me on my parking search, a slow dance around a three-block radius. He pulls me over.

The cop is rude. He flashes his light onto the back seat, where he suspiciously eyes an ophthalmoscope and reflex hammer. He shines the light in my eyes and asks what the paraphernalia in the back seat is all about.

He doesn't give me a chance to answer. He asks for my driver's license and registration and proof of insurance, his voice finding its footing somewhere between irritated and angry.

I am nervous. I was living in New York on 9/11, and immediately afterwards I saw fear in older white women's eyes as they looked at me. It is a look I recognize in my dying patients—the fear—but it always catches me off guard when I look into someone's eyes and realize I am the thing they fear.

Back in the Jetta, my white coat hangs off the back of my driver's seat. My doctor's ID hangs off my white coat close to the drivers' side window. The policeman's flashlight catches the ID and he asks if I am a doctor. I say yes, at LA County a few miles away.

The pile of papers in his hand—driver's license, registration, proof of insurance—become like a lotus flower as he opens his palms and they flow back to me.

He apologizes and apologizes. He says he didn't realize I was a doctor. He didn't realize that I worked at the hospital, the trauma center that takes care of cops when they get hurt or shot.

My doctor's ID becomes a get-out-of-jail-free card. An "I exist" card.

I exist. I exist. Something to distinguish me from the black, the brown, the sick, the poor, the nameless, the undocumented—from my patients.

What if I had been a plumber, looking for the sea after a hard day's work? What if I had been one of my patients, black and brown and nameless?

I remember taking care of an undocumented Mexican man who worked and worked for four decades in the vineyards of Napa. He never had health insurance.

I saw him in the hospital when his bone marrow finally failed, exhausted by decades of field work. His body was announcing its existence the only way it could.

If the soul is ignored long enough, the body rebels. A mass in the throat rises to the surface of the skin. A cavity in a lung riddled with tuberculosis starts to bleed. The body announces its existence.

Sometimes when I fill out death certificates I wish I could write the cause of death as poverty. Or American racism.

As a doctor, I am looking to make common cause with a Navajo woman. Uranium mined from the earth and left bare for Navajo folks to fall ill. The uranium in the earth rises as a lump in a Navajo woman's breast.

As a doctor, I am looking to make common cause with black boys stopped by the police, shot by police without a doctor's ID to protect them.

With my patients where we work in Liberia, I am looking to make common cause with the 11,310 black bodies who died from Ebola! They came into our awareness only in sickness and in death.

Before blood flows from every orifice, can we note their existence?

The 109 black bodies killed by the police this year.

May we learn their names in life? They exist.

As a doctor, I aim to stand with them before the beautiful fire of their lives becomes ash.

In this country, the only way I know home is through them.

I want to reclaim a space for home for the black, the brown, the nameless, my patients, myself. I try to find my home through them.

Dr. Sriram Shamasunder, a poet and doctor at UCSF, has spent the better part of the last 10 years working in Burundi, Haiti, Rwanda and India. He is interested in health equity and narrative equity, working towards a world where lives are of equal value, both in the health care we deliver and the stories we highlight.

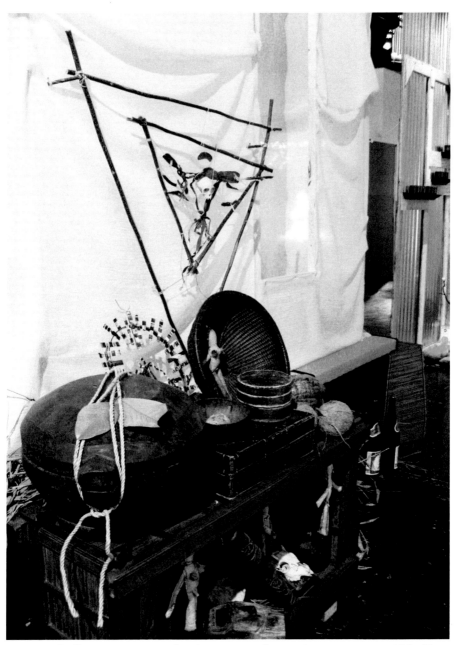

Detail of *Al's Tea House*, an altar honoring Filipino American poet Al Robles created by Russell, Ray, and Fredda Kaplan Robles with the extended Robles family as an installation the 2009 Día de los Muertos exhibition curated by Rene and Rio Yañez at the SOMArts Cultural Center. Shizue Seigel.

the youngest
Simeon Alojipan

June 2006. My mom tells me she's the youngest of her siblings.

February 1984. Her little brother, 22, kills himself in the basement
of their house on 13th Street, San Jose

Did you use Clorox
to scrub the mattress?

Did you wear gloves?
Or not, because touching the rust
was your way of holding
his hand again?

if only you had given him
a touch of love
to stop his finger from pulling

Were you the first
to feel his skull shatter
his brain dribble?

Not because your feet felt the
     —bang!
and his corpse crack the air under you

but because you were
the second youngest
and now the first—

his life splattering onto yours
before theirs

Do you remember the last time
he called you *ate*[1]?

Do you remember the day a bullet
revoked your title
& anointed you another?

Did Lola cry? Did Pina?
Did you?

When I come home from school,
you're in the bathroom
bleach-bloodied from scrubbing
your crimson-cursed number.

Mom, tell me.

How does it feel to become
  the youngest?

[1]*Ate* in Tagalog is a loving term for "older sister."

Simeon Alojipan Artist Statement. As Filipinos in the diaspora, the cultural silence surrounding the intergenerational trauma that we inherit prevents us from understanding our family's pain and thus our own history. As a child, I remember feeling silenced each time I would try to ask a question about something I wasn't "supposed" to talk about. My poems "the youngest" and "in the place of memory" use this act of questioning as a way to disrupt silence. They represent a way to discover the emotions experienced by my mother and Lola ("grandmother" in Tagalog) during two traumas they experienced in their lifetimes. In this way, I aim to impart that in order to learn and heal, we must explore our heritage using our imaginations; and in doing so, we not only heal ourselves, but our families as well.

in the place of memory
Simeon Alojipan

for Antonia Serafica

Imagine a world where I'm loved by you.
Imagine in the place of memory, and remember that memory is but
    imagination.
So imagine.

Imagine Bobby was still alive, that yes, it was he who visited you in your room
    last night.
Imagine your parents as if you knew them. Imagine a world where they knew
    you.

Now imagine the man who you loved in their place. Pedro.
Imagine him waking up at midnight. His muscles imagining a war.
Imagine hiding my mom from the gunfire. First in her room, and then in
    America.

Now, imagine America,
imagine your funeral.
Imagine the coffin as a creaking mattress, the soil a warm quilt.

Imagine Pedro lying next to you. How you share a bed with him again.
Does he care about your lack of memory? Has he spent the years like you,
    imagining in the place of memory?

Imagine how love is sharing the Earth with someone you once remembered.
Imagine how love is just the act of remembering.
But now you can no longer remember him. So imagine.

Then when you're ready—and only when you're ready, Lola—imagine
    Heaven,
and be free.

Simeon Alojipan was born in San Jose, California, and lives in San Francisco.
He is currently pursuing his BA in Asian American Studies with a Minor in
LGBT Studies at San Francisco State University, where he is a Peer Mentor for
the Asian American & Pacific Islander Retention and Education Program.

Talayee/Like Gold
Dena Rod

golden channels,
soft as fine white sand
warmed by the sun.
latticed together,
bound by duty

hala famil eh moh hasten
families married, threaded
soft gold veins run through
this family tree,
gilded ochre tendrils
reach to bind hands
to hold

the seat belt stretches as she
pulls woven threads
of gilded flax and honey,
catching on brown knuckles
and gently drops sunshine
into mother's softly lined palm

tashakor, gratitude
the thankfulness of acceptance
bringing daughter to breast
to nurse and nourish
inheritances

doktar-e-eslami
worn fingers, curled up cuticles,
red and ragged,
peel back layers,
rivers of decadent fabric
silk, satin, charmeuse

yet cotton reigns king
once more, placed gently
on baby's furry brow
veiled to a free country
heritage unforgotten
Gom sho

golden channels,
soft as fine white sand
warmed by the sun.
latticed together,
bound by duty

Maman bozorg,
where are you now

now that veils are gone

Dena Rod is a 29-year-old writer born in the Bay Area to parents displaced from Iran. Dena and her wife lived in San Francisco until recently, when they were displaced across the Bay. Dena enjoys long city walks in search of street art, community connections, and dogs to pet. A graduate of San Francisco State University, she has a Master's Degree in English Literature. You can find more of her work in CCSF's *Forum Literary Magazine* and the upcoming anthology *Iran Musings*.

as it happens

day

to

day

Shizue Seigel

Chinatown USA series
Photography and poetry by Leon Sun

Leon Sun, untitled silver gelatin prints, 8.75 x 13.5 in., 1992 and 1993.

Artist Statement: These three photos are a small sampling of images taken over a period of about three years, from 1989 to 1993, as a self-directed project to capture life on the streets of San Francisco's Chinatown. Most were shot "off the hip" with a 35mm SLR film camera. My intent was to make visible the humanity and complexity of the Chinese American community, which has been largely ignored and, in that way, disrespected by so-called "mainstream" media and society.

Ah Mo's

Sweaters smell of old wool
And White Flower oil
Secret pockets hide stash of
candies and mui
waiting to be liberated
by the eager little hands
of grandchildren

Boy in New Land

Hand hold onto China
Feet stand on American ground
Eyes on Chinatown

Chinatown USA series
Photography and poetry by Leon Sun

Chess Players

Cooks, waiters and writers
Become generals and foot soldiers
Old men and young boys
Invent plans and strategy while
On the move

Together
With horses and canons
They cross rivers and streets
Centuries of struggle and contention
Played out on a slab of stone

Little round pieces armed with words
Defy the barbarians' towers
Little round pieces etched
With character
Strike deep
into alien territory

Leon Sun. I was born in China and grew up partly in Shanghai and Hong Kong, which was still a British colony at the time. I came to the U. S. in 1966. By the 1970s I was involved in the Asian American Movement, as well as Peace and anti-Imperialist activities. From the early 1980s until the mid 1990s, my work was always based on the premise that art served politics. I worked as a photographer and graphic designer for *Unity Newspaper* and Art Director for *East Wind Magazine.* In addition, I did some self-directed projects in editorial

Leon Sun, untitled silver gelatin print, 13.5 x 13.5 in., 1989

photography, such as the *Chinatown, USA* series. I also freelanced for a few small businesses and for the non-profit, social service sector.

In 2000s, I began studying and practicing Buddhism. After I retired from the City of Richmond as a graphic artist, I began to pursue a more personal art, inspired by nature and animals and by traditional Chinese and Native American art. I work now mostly in screen printing, with some painting and photography. Occasionally I apply my art to environmental justice work, such as the struggle against the Dakota Access Pipeline.

Midnight Shift 1969
Roji Oyama

The stream of bodies passing by City Lights bookstore on Columbus Avenue became a blur by midnight. I managed to clear out the last customers from the basement and the loft upstairs, except for one.

"Bob, Bob! Lights out, time to go!" I had to get a stool and reach over the low toilet door with a coat hanger to release the latch from inside. Bob was passed out, sitting on the toilet. He had pissed in his pants. I stared at this beautiful broken man, a bag of bones with a quickly deteriorating mind. His beautiful words graced all of his books. Now he stole them back to be able to eat. He stirred and looked up at me with watery gentle eyes. He nodded and walked past me without a word. I followed him upstairs to keep track of how many books he would leave with this night. Tonight, he left peacefully with four of his own books stuffed under his moth-eaten sweater.

Back in 1969, City Lights Bookstore gave me a job when I needed it. The odd hours worked with my school schedule. I locked up and slid across the alley to Vesuvio's Bar for a nightcap before my next job. The regulars were pasted to their regular spots along the bar reminiscent of abstract sculptures, motionless and stoic in a state of immobilized inebriation. It was like that most nights. Outside, North Beach was still abuzz with revelers, but inside Vesuvio's, Dexter Gordon's tunes and a double shot were a warm and fuzzy blanket late at night.

The funky, colorfully painted bar was a refuge, across the alley from the bookstore. I would regularly order cocktails by phone and pick them up in a paper cup to make a slow shift at the store pass by. I worked the cash register and did stock work. I had many great conversations with all the North Beach writers who would pop in regularly. Some of them, like Bob, were so down-and-out they stole their own books, plus a few more, and pawned them down the street at Discovery Books. It was the City Lights' unofficial welfare system. The Discovery clerk would simply call me to retrieve the books. The two bookstores had an agreement as to how much cash to keep this welfare going.

A battered '66 Plymouth pulled up outside Vesuvio's. It was Buzz, who was going off shift and he was here to pick me up. We both drove for Red and White cab company. This cab had seen better days. With a large number 15 painted on both doors, it had the appearance of an American stock car that had been put out to pasture. The "Jesus Saves" sticker on the windshield gave it some respectability.

We made our way down Columbus Avenue towards Bay Street. Buzz would end his night at an hidden dive down near Fisherman's Wharf which would lock its doors at two so you could keep on drinking. It was Buzz's second home. He was a quiet reclusive drinker who preferred to live life in the shadows. Stella the bartender was the only bright spot in his life. Too bad for him as she was a lesbian, but he never gave up hope.

The summer fog was coming off the bay like a sinuous white serpent winding its way through the streets and alleys of North Beach. My dispatch radio was silent. It looked as if it was going to be a quiet night.

I drove up to the top of Montgomery Street and parked at the top of the hill to take in the view of the Bay Bridge. I flipped open the glove box to find our stash of bourbon and Pall Mall cigarettes. Gazing out at the night, my only company was great late night jazz on the radio. Sonny Rollins was taking me to a nice place with his horn.

I zoned out reflecting how I ended up back here in San Francisco. A couple of years earlier, I'd been involved in the student strike at San Francisco State College. After five months of demonstrations and teach-ins, the administration agreed to create the first ethnic studies department in the United States. It was truly a revolutionary moment, but then they closed the school. The momentum of the strike—and of my freshman year—were derailed.

Our group of Asian American activists went our separate ways to continue our quest for meaning in our lives. I sold my car and bought a one-way ticket to Europe with a pack on my back. I had plans to go all the way around to Japan, through the Middle East. Even though my journey was aborted by being called up in the draft for Viet Nam, it was the most amazing time of my life. I learned how to survive using my own wits. I made it as far as Istanbul before having to return home to avoid being arrested.

Once home, I began to fight my draft status with the best academic paper I had ever written. After my induction physical, I had my hearing before the draft board. When I was about to present my case against violence and war, one of the seated board members informed me that my presentation was not necessary. I had been rejected from the draft because of my allergies. I had beaten the draft, but not on my terms. I was relieved not to go, but I felt guilty about how I got out of the draft.

I managed to get into art school and ended up in North Beach. I realized after everything that had occurred up until this point, I still did not know my ass from a hole in the ground. I was not even sure about the path of being an artist. The fog had thickened enough to blot out the view. Expecting a slow night, I lay down on the bench seat and turned up the radio, letting jazz take me away somewhere, anywhere, from my miserable life.

"Pick up needed at Lombard and Columbus." The dispatcher's voice jolted me awake. I took another swig of bourbon and made my way over the hill. As I approached Columbus Avenue, I saw an apparition flailing its arms. As I got closer, I saw a tall woman in a dazzling, skintight evening gown and some kind of fur wrap. Her hair was a mile high. The sparkling sequins made her appear as some kind of exotic mermaid.

She flung open the door and jumped in. "I was waiting forever and a day, where were you?" She exuded a blend of booze, perfume and sweat. "Where to?" She flipped on the dome light to adjust a false eyelash and started to apply powder to what appeared to be a five o'clock shadow.

"48 Mason Street and step on it!" I caught myself staring at her. "What? Wanna take a picture?" Her exaggerated eyebrows gave her a look of constant excitement.

"Naw, I was just admiring how beautiful you look tonight." She smiled. "You're sweet. I needed to hear that!"

We headed down Mason Street towards the Tenderloin. "That Tony Balazzo stood me up for some other bitch tonight and I'm going to find out who he's with right now!"

"Maybe there was a misunderstanding; maybe Tony is alone. Try to stay calm 'til you get his side of the story," I advised.

She gave me a teary look. "Hey, you got any booze?" I reached in the glove box and handed her the bourbon. She took a long swig and handed it back to me. "Here's a twenty, keep the change. You are a sweet guy. You're right, I love Tony too much sometimes."

She threw me a wink and got out of the cab, somewhat calmer. I hoped for the best.

"Got a fare at 860 Taylor, he's waiting outside." I headed around the block. Chet Baker was blowing sweetness from the radio, putting a smile on my face.

I pulled up to see a very ordinary looking guy standing at the curb. He had the appearance of an insurance salesman, quite innocuous and totally unassuming.

He got in with a smile. "Where to?" I asked as I glanced back at him. His thoughts seemed to be elsewhere as he gazed out the window. A snarling cat and the clatter of a bottle rolling down the street broke the silence as I sat there awaiting a response from him.

"Excuse me, what did you say?" He finally turned his attention to me.

"Where to you want me to take you?"

He pondered the question for a minute and replied, "Take me to the Golden Gate Bridge, the place where you can see the whole city." I looked back at him as we made our way across the city. He seemed fixated, staring out of the window.

"Pretty foggy tonight; there may not be much of a view." He just kept gazing out into the darkness in silence.

We arrived at the vista point which was in total whiteout without a sign of life anywhere, only the low rumbling of the foghorns. A few dim lights barely illuminated the guardrail.

"I was here last night, just over there, on the path up to the bridge. I was on my way to, …" he paused for a moment "… 'the end.'"

I didn't like where this guy's thoughts were heading, especially when he said, "Have you ever considered the afterlife?" It wasn't really a question. I already knew what he would say next: "I was ready to get there last night."

He was now leaning forward with his chin on the back of the front seat staring deeply into the white of the night. "It's like I thought my time in this life was over. I felt my life was without direction and meaning."

I felt a shiver at the familiarity in what he was saying. I'd felt the same more often than I wanted to think about. "The idea of going into the next world took over last night and brought me here."

His words immobilized my body. He now had turned his face towards me. It was a bit unnerving, so I kept my eyes forward. My throat felt so dry I had to force the words out. "What made you feel bad enough to come here?"

"Work sucked, my private life sucked, my love life sucked. I felt I had nothing left to live for."

Those same feelings had crept into my mind now and then. I studied his face in the rear view mirror. Then I forced myself to turn and face him. I had to ask, "What stopped you from jumping?"

"Nothing dramatic. I didn't hear voices or see any visions before my eyes. I was simply overcome by a huge wave of shame and cowardice. That was enough to stop me."

He gave a short laugh, "You know, I hit rock bottom last night—a life of one failure after the next. I realized I had even failed to kill myself. It was time to stop fleeing and face my own weaknesses. I realized acknowledging weakness did not make me less of a man. It would make me more of one to confront them—all of them. At thirty-seven years of age, I was ready to give up. I had to admit to myself I had fallen into the abyss of misery due to my lack of trying in life. How pathetic is that?"

I lit a cigarette and pondered his words. He sat back and took a deep breath. I ground out my cigarette and took my own deep breath. "You know, I am a lot younger than you and yet I know what you felt last night."

The early glow of dawn lightened the sky as a lone maintenance guy started to sweep the walkway in front of us. We sat silent, each of us thinking of our own waywardness.

"You can take me home now."

As we rode quietly back to the Tenderloin, I glanced back at him. He seemed so serene and content that I was a bit envious. I was still shadow boxing with my own personal turmoil.

"That will be twenty bucks."

"Is that all?"

I turned around to look at him. "I shut off the meter when we stopped to talk. Your story made me think a lot about my own life. Thanks! It was really cool how honest you were about courage, shame and all that. It really defined what it means to be a man."

He put his hand on my shoulder.

"Don't waste time being afraid of failure. It only keeps you down and out. Keep trying; keep experimenting. Don't wait until you are my age."

He disappeared into his drab apartment. I parked for a moment to reflect on our conversation. I shut off the radio. In the silence, I felt new sense of calm and renewed courage. The need to keep running for something subsided. For once, it was enough to be me in my own skin.

Roji Oyama was born in Japan to Japanese American parents. His family returned to the U.S. when he was 8. He became a student activist at San Francisco State in 1968 as a member of Asian American Political Alliance, which helped form the first Department of Ethnic Studies in the United States. He earned a BFA in filmmaking from the San Francisco Art Institute. He lived in Japan in the 70s, and now lives in San Francisco. He volunteers with Japanese diasporic community groups in San Francisco and in Latin America. He had a supporting role in the 2014 film *East Side Sushi,* and is a craft carpenter who often works with traditional japanese tools.

To greet the New Year, Oyama creates pairs of traditional kadomatsu gate pines to place in front of homes and businesses to honor the ancestors and invite a bountiful harvest.

Shizue Seigel

Do You Recognize Me?
Susan Kitazawa

We were six young adults, starting out on our own in the early 1970s. We were pleased when we found a run-down rental home in an unincorporated part of town, along Highway 101, about 30 miles south of San Francisco. The area was home mainly to working African American neighbors who, like us, quietly kept to themselves.

Having recently met through a housing bulletin board, the six of us had been brought together by financial necessity. Liz and her husband Paul hailed from the Midwest. Blonde Bob was from a beach town in southern California. My boyfriend Jeff worked on the line at a nearby bottling plant. Tim was a pale, rather sheltered photographer, pleased by the novelty of living among people of color.

Indeed, he was even living in the same house with a person of color, since I was Japanese American. Tim had said that I was "almost white," not quite but almost.

Our home in this quiet neighborhood was some miles away from a well-known private university medical center. There, unrest was growing. The lowest-paid staff had begun to organize under the leadership of an intense African American man, who was always seen wearing his signature beret. He was the friend of a Jewish activist friend of ours from the bottling plant.

One evening well after dark, someone knocked on our front door. Tim, the photographer, opened it a few inches

A deep male voice said that they had come from a local charity. He asked Tim how many people lived in the house. Tim replied that there were six of us. The voice asked if they could come in to chat.

Not wanting to invite strangers in after dark, I went to the door and said that we were just about to eat dinner. I asked if they could drop off a flyer about their work. Then I said goodbye to them and gently closed the door.

Tim said that I didn't need to be so rude to people who were doing good work.

We shifted our attention to getting dinner on the table. As we sat together, eating spaghetti with stretch-the-meat-as-far-as-it-will-go sauce, a salad that was only lettuce, and some sourdough bread, we talked of the news of our day.

A loud bang and the sound of breaking glass exploded into our conversation. Three lean, very dark-skinned men stood by the kitchen table. Each one held a handgun, pointed at us.

"All of you! Get on the floor!" It was the man who had come to the front door.

My five housemates hit the floor, face down. Tim started crying.

I sat at the table, fork loaded with spaghetti halfway to my mouth. I stared at the men and their guns, stunned.

The youngest one said gently, his gun pointed at me, "Sister, you need to lie down, too." I apologized and slid to the floor.

He and I looked at each other in recognition though we had been strangers until this moment. We both understood that I was not "almost white." This quiet man and I were both fearful of the situation we were in, but we weren't afraid of each other.

Then this same man said softly, "Sister, you're not supposed to look at us." I apologized again, turning my face away.

Leaving him to keep a gun on us, the other two frantically searched the house. "Where are you keeping the stuff?!"

We knew they meant drugs. The problem was that we didn't have any drugs except for part of a bottle of cheap red wine. We didn't have much cash either.

Finally, they settled for Tim's Nikon, two purses, my guitar, and a glass jar of dried oregano, grown in our backyard. They left.

We called the county sheriff's department. Two officers arrived, looking tired, as if they'd rather be at home.

Having clearly seen our surprise visitors, I told the officers that the men looked to be in their 20s, all of them tall, quite thin, and very dark-skinned, with closely cropped hair, all clean-shaven.

For the next two hours, the officers brought us a series of suspects, hand-cuffed. None of them matched my description at all, other than being black men. There was a guy with a beard, short men, a chubby man with graying hair. They stood them outside in the harsh beam of the patrol-car searchlight. One at a time, they un-cuffed the men and let them go as we insisted, "No, not him."

Last, they brought a very light-skinned man who, unlike the others, looked very sad.

Under growing pressure from the officers to identify suspects, Tim said that maybe this last man was one of the men. I protested that this man looked nothing like the men I had described.

Then one of the officers said, abruptly, "What about the one with the beret?" We told him that none of the men wore a beret. The officer asked Tim, "What about the one with the beret? Did he have a gun?" Tim re-asserted the truth: that none of the men had worn a beret. Even he realized that the officer was hoping to frame the man who was organizing the university hospital workers. This weary officer was hoping to make his evening worthwhile, hoping to become a man of importance.

Setting this last man free, the two officers left, clearly frustrated that we had wasted their time.

The next day, back at work as a recent hire at the nearby county social services office, I welcomed a man who came in to apply for General Assistance. We both stared. He was the light-skinned black man with the sad eyes who had stood hand-cuffed in the beam of the patrol-car searchlight, the last man of the night.

"It was so good that you said that I didn't rob you. Thank you."

"You don't need to thank me. I just told the truth. That's all."

I helped him with his application for aid and said he would hear from the county.

Later, he returned to the office, accompanied by a stout, elderly woman. "My mother wanted to meet you." Softly crying, his mother handed me a paper plate piled with sugar cookies.

"I baked these for you. Thank you for saving my son.

"He just got home from prison. Five years ago, somebody with a gun grabbed an old lady and took her purse. The sheriffs took him to the lady, just like they brought him to you and your friends last night. The old lady said it was him. She said that my son robbed her with a gun. She was probably so shook up, she didn't even know who it was. She did a terrible thing to my son, but she didn't know."

Her words echoed my Japanese American mom's words from years earlier: "They didn't know who we were. They got us mixed up with the people who bombed Pearl Harbor, so they put us in prison camps during the war. They were afraid. People who really didn't want us here stirred up fear in other people."

Her son had been imprisoned, just like my parents and grandparents, because other people thought they themselves would be safer if people unlike themselves, people who they feared, were sent away, were locked up.

Sadly, this is still happening. Every day.

We need to see each other. We need to recognize one another.

The mother of this sad-eyed man and my mother both understood this. They both saw through to the fear, the deep fear and unfamiliarity that keep us all from recognizing each other. His mother and my mother had both found a way to move beyond bitterness, to clearly see the wrongs, to stand against injustice and yet still have compassion for people who made mistakes, for people so damaged that they couldn't recognize others as fellow human beings.

More than forty years later, I still have not grown into the deep compassion of these two mothers, mine and his. The instruction to love even our enemies has not fully taken root in me, even though I understand that this does not mean that we need to love what lost and damaged people often do to others.

Before we can love someone, anyone, we have to be able to see them, to recognize them as our fellow beings. Perhaps we could all help each other move toward this. It could make a real difference.

Having grown up in a series of smaller towns on the East Coast, Susan Kitazawa has made San Francisco her home for over forty years. Living with significantly decreasing eyesight, she continues making art, writing, dancing Argentine tango, singing in a community choir, practicing Braille, and meeting a fascinating array of people during many hours spent riding San Francisco Muni buses. Susan believes that we have extraordinary ability to heal and transform ourselves when given even half a chance. She saw this happen many times in her twenty-five years as a registered nurse in San Francisco. Now retired from nursing, she hopes that her writing inspires at least a few people to have faith that self-healing and transformation are possible, even when the odds seem to be stacked against it.

Shizue Seigel

Poetry in Chinatown
Clara Hsu

Five/five
the fifth of May
paddle the dragon boats
eat zonzis by the bay.
The poet had sunk
to the bottom of the river.
  nothing is sadder ah than separation
In the town of funky old lanterns
and alleys littered with cigarette butts,
Li Po is but a cocktail lounge.
Heightened thoughts dissipate in the porridge steam,
duck grease drips down windowpanes.
The moans of China's progeny—
their tired backs
their blood shot eyes
weariness squeezes the minds dry.
Children open their mouths and cannot sing
Grownups hiss and spit in their streets.
  the heart is heavy ah unsettling

A man treaded gently up the hill. Illness had made him gentle. He found the
mail slot at the corner of my building and was about to shove a book through.
I opened the door.
  "Hello!" breathless, his eyes looked even wider behind the huge glasses.
  a bit of rouge
we had met the day before
  into a smear of blood and tear
I gave him my book
  swaying in loneliness
a window into a stranger's mind
  that derives from a thousand years of sorrow

  don't ask the blossoms and their leaves about emotion
  let's just carry the hangover
  and stagger in a carmine reverie

He told me he had a few essays to write and left. He sent me the finished
work by email. But the poet has blurred into the streets of trinkets and meat
markets.

Sometimes brutal, sometimes gentle
  How bright, the moon

we are being cut down by age,
    Ask the clear sky with wine in hand
becoming the old poets of Chinatown
    not knowing in the heavenly palace
    what year is this night
live, laugh, cry, die among the sound of mahjong
    I would ride the wind and depart
mouths and bodies yearning to be touched
    but I fear the bejeweled jade dwellings
    the cold in high places

At Chinatown's One Day Sidewalk Sale I put a table out on Waverly Place with
my books and broadsides. Genny Lim dropped by the day before and gave
me her chapbooks. Francis Chin arrived with her memoirs in a suitcase. It
was a warm and sunny day. We hung out in front of Clarion. Frances met a
fan of hers and struck up a lively conversation. Nellie Wong came a little later
with her books too. Earlier in the day the youth community across the street
brought over some helium balloons. I tied them on the handle of a poster
board. Fidget spinners were selling by the bushel down on Grant Avenue. At
least that's what I heard.

Pedestrians hastened their speed when passing our table. A few brave ones
turned their heads toward the books for just a second but inevitably looked
the other way.
    to
        catch
             an
                    eye
    or a smile
    to catch the attention of someone
    not interested
    POETRY IS SUNNING IN BROAD DAYLIGHT
    not interested
    VIBRANT AND THOUGHTFUL WOMEN ARE READY
        TO CONVERSE
    not interested
    Are we as obscure as creatures from Mars?
    those creatures might be more interesting than poets!
    Don't be afraid. We are here to stay

in the town that sells everything
    the five colors blind the eyes
in the town where all languages are spoken
    the five tones deafen the ears
in the town that relishes food

> *the five flavors coy the palate*
in the town where conversations
wind around the wooden stools of Sam Wo
where Xing Chu Wang and his wife Gimmy
recalled reading love poems to each other
on their wedding day

—twenty roses blooming spring eternal—

At midnight, I scribble to the bells of the Old St. Mary's
drink paper wine
becoming intoxicated …

Notes:

1. Five Five/The fifth of May in the lunar calendar is the date of the Duanwu (or Dragon Boat Festival). The festival commemorates the ancient poet and politician Qu Yuan (340–278 B.C.), who committed suicide by drowning. He was so beloved by the people that they wrapped sticky rice with lotus leaves and threw them into the river for the fish to eat so they wouldn't touch Qu Yuan's body.

2. Li Po (701–762) was a Chinese poet in the Tang Dynasty.

3. "nothing is sadder …" and "the heart is heavy …" are lines from Qu Yuan's "Nine Songs."

4. "Azalea" by Bacon Hui, originally written in Chinese.

5. "How bright the moon … the cold in high places" lines in italics by Su Shi, an excerpt from his poem, "Water Melody—Source of Song."

6. "The five colors blind the eyes … coy the palate" excerpt from the *Tao-te Ching*, passage XII, by Lao Tzu.

7. Clarion refers to Clarion Music Performing Arts Center at 2 Waverly Place.

8. Sam Wo is a Chinatown restaurant since 1907. It is still in business today although the location has changed from Washington Street to Clay Street.

9. "twenty roses …" by Xing Chu Wang from his poem, "The Mood of Twenty Roses." Originally written in Chinese.

7. All translations in this work are by Clara Hsu.

Clara Hsu is a mother, piano teacher, director of Clarion Music Performing Arts Center, traveler, translator and poet. Clara's first book of poems, *Mystique*, received Honorable Mention at the 2010 San Francisco Book Festival. Other works include a book of short stories, *Babouche Impromptu and Other Moroccan Sketches*; a second book of poems, *The First to Escape*, and a third book, *Lao-Tzu Tao-te Ching, Translations and Infusions*. Clara's poetic activities include her unusual performance combining Chinese poetry with Asian traditional instruments. clarahsu.com

Soul Medicine
Tony Robles

Barbeque and corn bread and greens made by black hands. Adobo and rice eaten with thick brown fingers. A handwritten love note with a #2 pencil. A street sax blowing colors across the sky. Tortillas and rice and beans and abuelitas' voices rising through rooftops. Murals on our skin, wet with our stories, our lives, our revolution. Palleteros pushing cool cool cool flavors that paint the tongue a picture of community, finger-painted portraits of our dreams. Grandpa with a wrinkled racing form, transistor radio broadcasting voices of spirits dancing, splashing like flowers in the throats of babies. Wrinkled photos and longhand notes written illegibly legible on the palm lines of leaves. A belly full of pork noodle soup. Familiar faces on Frisco streets. Terry on the corner of 7th St selling slow jam CD's—Delfonics, Isley Brothers, Dramatics. Nella planting collard greens and kale and everything that is good, her brown Filipino hands offering her gifts from the soil in the Tenderloin. Stories written in Russian rye bread. Rice noodles whipping around block after block of the TL. Dreams fermenting on the corner of Turk and Larkin. Black voices that never die. Samoan church food passed from hand to hand, elder to child, heart to heart. Sacks filled with Chinese vegetables. Fish eyes looking through tanks as rivers flow down Chinatown streets. My grandmother's cane that kept our unstable world stable as she walked to and from St. Patrick's Church on Mission. Mission Street palm trees that tell us home isn't too far and can be heard in the conga drum that dreams of freedom from the pawn shop. Fog horns moanin' wetness as the sun breaks though for the first time over and over again in my city.

Rio Yañez's billboard "Ghetto Frida's Mission Memories" on the outside wall of Gallería de la Raza, 24th and Bryant Streets, 2009.

The Royal Baking Company in the Excelsior was founded by Italian immigrants. When they retired, they sold their business to a long-time Chicano employee, whose son now operates it. Photos on both pages: Shizue Seigel.

Rio Yañez - Untitled Images

From the moment he was conceived in an artist's studio, Rio Yañez' fate as an artist was sealed. Born and raised in San Francisco's Mission District, Yañez is a non-profit worker and artist. He has been curating art exhibits together with his father, Rene Yañez, since 2005. Rio has exhibited in cities ranging from San Francisco to Tokyo. His work examines the intersection of pop culture and Chicano icons and aesthetics. Rio is also a founding member of The Great Tortilla Conspiracy, the world's most dangerous tortilla art collective.

Artist Statement. My primary interest, as an artist, is in combining the icons and mythologies of Chicano culture and popular culture. Growing up as the son of two Chicano artists, I was often frustrated that Chicano art and iconography rarely intersected with my personal mythologies of comic books, pro wrestling, music, and Godzilla movies. My images bring together my

heroes, friends, neighborhood stories, and childhood fantasies with Chicano aesthetics, traditional images, and politics. They are a fulfillment of my childhood yearnings and an exploration of my relationship to the worlds I walk between.

As a native son of the Mission District, I've seen the city change over four decades. As a teenager I was obsessed with photographing the five movie theaters that lined Mission Street between 22nd and 20th. They were the social epicenters of the neighborhood's Latino residents and their closing in rapid succession changed everything. I took photos of what remained of them as towering altars dedicated to the neighborhood I once knew. As my work as an artist matured, I began to create work that told more narrative stories about the neighborhood, starting with images of Frida Kahlo having misadventures in the Mission of the 80s and 90s and culminating in a series of prints chronicling an average day of twin sisters living in the neighborhood. The Mission District and its ever-changing faces have remained strong influences in my art.

Mission Street Theaters

The Grand, Latino, El Capitan, Tower, and New Mission theaters have dominated the Mission District landscape for generations, morphing from movie palaces

Photos 2010, except El Capitan 2017.
Shizue Seigel.

to pigeon palaces—to dollar stores, SROs and parking lots. Mission Street went from a place to see Jean Harlow movies to a place to buy Harlow-syle, movie-queen beds for a few dollars down and a few more every month. Who knows what the future will bring to this street of dreams and dreamers?

—Shizue Seigel

Endangered People and Places

In a walker's town like San Francisco, it's possible to enter a new world by turning a corner, and to meet the most amazing people on the street or at a bus stop. San Francisco seems to attract people who think they can actualize their dreams—whether as a one-man Mardi Gras Float at the Juneteenth Parade, a cool dude at the Nihonmachi Street Fair, or a girl in pink simply enjoying a day without harrassment.   —Shizue Seigel

Gentrification eradicates businesses, too—those tiny holes-in-the-wall we take for granted until they disappear. At Eco Jewelry. barely eight feet wide, Jose Junio Campos from El Salvador has been in business for 15 years. The store's chandelier as bright as the smiles of the staff. Go to Nueva Libería México for embroidery thread, saints and Spanish-language magazines.

A Chance Encounter
Francée Covington

Mildred was walking home along Laguna Street from a Wednesday evening at the opera when an aggressive panhandler accosted her.

"Spare change!" he demanded—his voice a high demented tenor.

"I don't have any money," she protested, scurrying down the empty street with him close behind.

"Yeah you do. I can tell you have money," he shouted then moved in front of her, blocking her path. "Spare change!" The strong stench emanating from him assaulted her nostrils, causing her to turn her head away from him. He spread his legs, making his body a toll booth, and thrust his open palm toward her purse. She clutched the handbag to her chest with both hands and backed away a step, then two, when a low loud growl punctuated the darkness.

"Hey! Leave her alone. She's not bothering you!"

Mildred and the panhandler turned towards the dark wiry man emerging from the darkness. He stopped in front of them, standing taunt and straight, his hand full of rumpled *Street Sheet* newspapers. The panhandler growled low, "Mind your own business." His voice promised violence if he wasn't obeyed.

"This is my business," bellowed the man in a commanding baritone. "Now go AWAY!"

The panhandler stood his ground. "You know who you messin' with?" His eyes narrowed to slits. "I seen you before and I'll see you again."

"Not if I see you first," the wiry man retorted, jutting his sharp chin out for effect. The panhandler looked the interloper up and down menacingly before moving off down the street, grumbling as he went. The man turned to Mildred.

"Where you going, Ma'am?" His voice was matter-of-fact, like a cabdriver asking his fare's destination.

"Home—just a few blocks away," she replied in a voice more like a soprano choirboy than a middle-aged woman of the world. She'd intended to sound stronger than she felt.

"I'll walk behind you to make sure you don't have no more trouble." He waved his open palm toward the sidewalk to encourage her to resume walking. It was a Sir Galahad move.

She hesitated, weighing if she should thank him, be silent, or tell him that she'd be fine alone. Unsure of herself, she began walking and after a few steps turned and said, "Please walk beside me."

He was surprisingly fast on his feet and covered the space between them in one long, quick stride. "Perhaps he's an ex-prize fighter," she thought. "Or, maybe he's in cahoots with the panhandler, and they're playing good vagrant, bad vagrant when in fact they're both bad guys." She walked the rest of the block with her ears strained for footsteps behind her. She adjusted the red silk scarf under the collar of her Chesterfield coat, making sure the strand of large pearls was concealed. She wished she'd worn her costume pearl earrings instead of the inherited South Sea Mikimotos with diamonds. At least her cashmere-lined leather gloves hid her diamond rings.

They covered half a block without speaking. An uneasy silence hovered between them. She noticed that he had a slight limp. He noticed that she was wearing low black heels, which brought the tip of her head just to his shoulder. He spied the opera program in her hand.

"Why do most people wear black when they go to the operuh?"

"Tradition. And so as not to be a distraction to the cast, the orchestra, or other opera patrons," she was happy for the distraction of conversation.

"I always wondered about that." He walked with his head down, studying the pavement, then looked at her. "What about the orchestra? Do they dress up in tuxedoes like they do in the movies?"

"Yes. And the conductor usually wears tails," she answered, sounding proud for the conductor.

"No shit!? I'll be damned!" He chuckled, then ducked his chin into his chest. "'Scuse me. I didn't mean to cuss. Not supposed to cuss in front of ladies."

"It's okay. Believe me, at my age I've heard worse," she replied, trying to put him at ease. In fact, it had been many years since anyone used profanity in her presence.

She took note of his worn, faded black sweatshirt, at least two sizes too large, and his shoes were so big he was forced to shuffle to keep them on. "He must be shrinking," she thought. "Everything on him is too big, from his clothes, his nose and ears, to his impossibly large lips. His lips are large even for a black man, and he's as black as the moonless sky above."

He spied her jet-black pageboy hairdo, hair too black for a woman of her suspected age, the bangs too large for her small face. A full-figured black woman the color of the deep golden hues of sunset. He imagined, "She's probably married to a doctor or lawyer, a respected man sitting at home in a big easy chair in front of a cozy fire on this chilly San Francisco night listening to cool jazz on his stereo." He eyeballed her tailored coat and designer purse, the same the panhandler wanted her to open and give him its treasure.

Suddenly his arm shot out. Her heart stopped. He pointed to the ground. "Watch the sidewalk," he said. "The cement ain't level right there."

She stepped carefully over the uneven pavement, and tried to settle nerves jangled by the sudden thrust of his arm. She turned to him.

"What is your name?"

"Bartlett."

"Bartlett? Really? What a lovely name. I've never known anyone named Bartlett. How did you get that name?"

"My momma craved Bartlett pears when she was pregnant with me. You know, the ones that come in a can?"

"Yes." She didn't really, but she assumed that pears could come in a can.

"My father said she ate so many he was sure she was gonna give birth to a big ole pear, and was relieved when it was a boy!" His laugh was rough in his throat and brought up some phlegm which he immediately spit into the gutter.

They waited for the light on the corner as a young man in a tight black jacket and jeans crossed their path, head down, texting. Mildred tried to catch his eye, but he never looked her way.

"What was they showing at the operuh tonight?"

"Oh, it was *The Flying Dutchman*. A wonderful production."

"The what?"

"*The Flying Dutchman.*"

"Ain't that a insult? To call somebody a Dutchman?"

"No. Why would it be? This is a very old and celebrated opera." There was an edge of defense in her voice.

"Well, if you call a Chinese person a Chinaman, that's an insult, so why ain't it a insult to say Dutchman?"

She stopped dead in her tracks. He stopped too, and looked around warily, searching for a threat.

"I really don't know!" She answered, a hint of panic in her voice. He stared at her, checked to see if she was okay. She looked as if she'd seen an apparition. Her mind raced. Had she all these years been using an epithet? How horrible that would be.

"You don't know if Dutchman is an insult?" He shrugged. "It's okay. You can ax somebody like um axing you. Just don't ax no Dutchman." He laughed heartily at his own joke. Her legs began to move again, slowly then regained their former speed. They walked on quietly as he stole glances at her, not knowing how to revive the conviviality they'd shared, wondering what to say next, annoyed with himself for having upset her.

Finally she spoke, "That man who tried to get money from me, do you know him?"

"I seen him 'round but don't actually know him. Usually, he ain't so bad.

He must be off his meds or somethin'. Usually he cool. He shouldn't ah scared you like that."

"Maybe he's one of those veterans I read so much about."

"Naw, he ain't no vet. Most guys say they vets, they's liars and cheats. Now me, I'm a vet!"

He stabbed his chest with his thumb. "Desert Storm, 1990, first wave goin' inta Iraq."

"Will he try to get back at you for stepping in?"

"Him? Nah. Next time I see him he won't even 'member what happened. He like that." He paused. "Your operuh friends probably home by now. Why they let you go home alone? I know some of them must drive big 'spensive cars."

"I always walk home alone, but I usually go to the opera on Friday, not Wednesday. On Fridays lots of people clog the sidewalks of Hayes Valley and things are quite safe."

"Yeah. They be jamming the streets hereabouts nowadays. Hayes Street useta be empty twenty years ago. This place done growed up real big." He shifted his clutch of *Street Sheets* from hand to hand. "What 'bout your family? Why they ain't with you?"

"My family likes other kinds of music—not opera." She left out the details of her life: that she was a widow and her only daughter lived in Seattle. The big house would be empty, with only the porch light to greet her.

They'd passed the botanical alleys—Linden, Hickory, Ivy—and were approaching the corner of Page Street when a young man turned the corner at a fast clip, almost bumping into them.

"Mildred!" Her next door neighbor, a tall young man with a ruddy complexion and light-colored, clipped beard greeted her warmly. Smiling, he bent to touch his cheek to hers, his eyes shining at her, laughter in his voice. "I see you're out late tonight."

"Yes, Mark. A little too late," she answered.

Mark stepped back and shifted his glowing gaze from her to Bartlett, taking in his unkempt hair, tattered clothing and well-worn face. She watched as the shine left Mark's eyes and his expression turned cold. Her stomach churned. She thought, "What must life be like when people look at you that way?"

"I'll walk you to your door," Mark said firmly.

"Why thank you, dear."

She turned to Bartlett, withdrew her hand from her pocket and extended it toward him.

"Thanks so much for your help this evening." His eyes widened when she put her gloved hand in his.

"No problem," he said. When she released his hand, he shoved his fist deep into his baggy pants.

"Oh. And I'd like to give you this. It's tonight's program."

"Thank you," he said glancing at the cover of the *Dutchman* in the dim of the streetlight.

He looked into Mildred's face, nodded, then turned and walked back the way they'd come.

"Who was that?" asked Mark.

"Oh, that was Bartlett, my military escort." She hoped Bartlett overheard her. She smiled to herself, satisfied that the $20 bill in her pocket had been transferred seamlessly into his hand and that she'd given him the only program that would be missing from her twenty-year collection from the San Francisco Opera.

Francée Covington. During a successful TV career as a producer, director and writer of news, documentaries, public affairs and magazine shows, Francee Covington worked at television stations WCBS in New York; WBZ in Boston; and in San Francisco at KGO, KPIX, and KQED. She later formed her own video production company and led it for more than twenty years. Her clients included numerous Fortune 500 companies, the *Oprah Winfrey Show*, and city and state agencies. Active in the community, she currently serves on the San Francisco Fire Commission. She's retired, lives in San Francisco and is working on a collection of short stories. store

Teri's Creation & Boutique, a Fillmore hatmaker and clothing store, was a peaceful haven of African American pride and creativity that closed after the owner's death in 2017. Shizue Seigel.

San Francisco: Live Up To Your Name
Thomas Robert Simpson

It was a very nice day in San Francisco on August 10, 2013.

That morning my theater company, AfroSolo, hosted a community health fair to help underserved youth and families of the Western Addition prepare for the new school year. This San Francisco neighborhood has had a difficult past. Every year since 2006, Mo' MAGIC, a collaboration of neighborhood-based nonprofit organizations, holds a back-to-school celebration at the Ella Hill Hutch Community Center, an oasis for the youth in the area.

To reward myself for weeks of hard work organizing the health fair, I planned to attend a concert that evening presented in conjunction with the America's Cup Yacht Race being held in San Francisco. At about 6 o'clock I began walking towards the Fisherman's Wharf to attend the concert. I was in a great mood. I'd had a great day. I'd had a good nap and showered; I was excited to attend the concert.

Knowing that San Francisco would be chilly that evening, I wore a fedora, turtleneck sweater, cashmere scarf, soft black leather jacket, dress pants and my Chelsea leather boots—all black in color.

I was looking forward to a real treat: the soulful rock group War was headlining the concert, with the comedy team Cheech and Chong as special guests. Walking down Market Street I began humming War's big hits, "The Cisco Kid," along with "The World Is A Ghetto" and "Slipping Into Darkness." I could hardly wait.

As I neared the foot of Market Street, I luxuriated at the sight of San Francisco's iconic Ferry Building, the historic Hyatt Hotel and the impressive Embarcadero Buildings. I turned left off Market onto Davis Street. Moving towards Washington Street, I saw (or glimpsed) the slight figures of two people.

Getting closer, I saw the two figures were a young white man and women. They looked to be in their late teens or early twenties. It appeared that they had been traveling for a while. They had a couple of rolled-up sleeping bags and a few plastic bags stuffed with other belongings. I didn't see a cup or a sign asking for money.

Walking by them I tipped my hat with a friendly "Hello!"

By then, "Why Can't We Be Friends" was playing in my head. I kept walking.

About a hundred steps past them, I thought I heard "…gerr." Focused on the music and excited about the concert, I thought I was hearing things.

Then I heard, *"Nigger."*

Denial and hope can do strange things. I said to myself, "No, you didn't hear that. This is San Francisco. Get to the concert."

A few seconds later I heard, *"Nigger, go back to where you came from."*

Wow, there was no escaping it now. I heard what I heard. I could not ignore or deny hearing it. He was yelling at me. No one else was around. First came fear. Is he going to attack me? Shoot me? Or what?

Then I heard, *"You ought to kill yourself! If you don't, I will!"*

Then came the anger. Who was he? Why was he shouting this to me? He didn't know me. I didn't know him. His verbal attack made me furious. All of a sudden, LL Cool J's song "Mama Said Knock You Out" pounded into my head.

I turned around and headed back to confront him. He was looking straight at me. We were about one hundred yards apart. My steps picked up speed. My heart started beating faster. My eyes glued in on his. *"Knock you out. Mama said knock you out"* grew louder and louder in my head.

All of a sudden, another voice invaded my mind, "What are you doing?"

I responded with, *"I'm going to knock that sucker out!"*

"What are you doing?" came again.

"Going to fight," I responded.

"No, you're not," the voice said. "Look at him! Where will he be sleeping tonight? What will he be eating? You've got too much to lose! Get over it. Let it go!"

"Turn around," the voice ordered. I didn't.

"TURN AROUND!" came again.

Reluctantly I turned around and headed towards the concert. But my steps had lost the easy flow they had before the insults. My movements were sharp, quick, and agitated. My jaw was clenched. My eyes suspiciously surveyed my surroundings. And, although it was chilly, I had to open my coat to cool off. Gradually, the guy withered into a bad memory. "Mama said knock you out" faded away.

Within ten minutes, I reached the venue. A long line was waiting to get in. They were young, old, male and female, Black, white, Latino, Asian, along with other ethnicities. I saw people in tie-dye t-shirts, people in leather, and people even in fur. Fans came in tennis shoes, street shoes, and high-heel shoes. I saw Gucci, Valentino, JD Crew, and labels in between. "This is the real world," I said to myself.

Smiles were everywhere. It was like a big family reunion. People greeted strangers like long-lost friends. One couple said they'd been to forty-three War concerts. Others mentioned 30 times, 19 times, 10 times. This was my second War concert, but I felt right at home.

When the lights went down, the smell of reefer swooped up. Joints were passed around freely. When the first few riffs of "Low Rider" blared through the speakers, the crowed went wild. I went with them. The blending of jazz, rock, soul and Latin music mesmerized us all.

While they were playing "Spill The Wine," I had a flashback from what the white guy yelled at me, "Nigger, go back to where you came from." I followed the voice inside me, "Just let go." The concert was too thrilling to let that jerk spoil it.

When War began playing "Slippin' into Darkness," the crowd went insane. Plus, more reefer inhaling ensued. I passed it on. In the middle of "Slippin..." the nasty incident flashed through my mind. I willed it away! War played all the songs I wanted to hear, plus more.

If my memory serves me, they finished the concert with their anthem, "Why Can't We Be Friends." To me, it proved to be a wish, a prayer, and a call for sanity.

When the concert ended and all the bows had been taken, everyone seemed content.

I certainly was!

I saw people gathering. Hugs and kisses were being exchanged between strangers. All in all, the joyous, homecoming atmosphere present at the beginning of the concert continued until the end.

Joyfully, I stepped out onto the streets of San Francisco and wondered what might greet me around the corner.

Thomas Robert Simpson, actor, director, producer, and writer is the founder and artistic director of the award-winning AfroSolo Arts Festival, now celebrating its twenty-fourth season. Noted for his acclaimed one-man show, *Still Headin' fo' da' Promise Land*, Simpson writes and performs solo works about the African American black male experience. Recently he has been performing biographical works based on the lives of black men. He strives to give voice to these men by portraying them as three-dimensional individuals choosing to live to the height of their ability. For more information, visit afrosolo.org.

In the Midst of It All
Venus Zuhura Noble

Multi award-winning singer Yolanda Adams' statuesque frame was on the stage when I flipped on my television. She skillfully began with a smooth, steady tone, "I have come through many hard trials …" My eyes closed, entranced by the melody. The lyrics tugged at my soul, causing my toes to start tapping to the synchronized swells of the background vocals, "He kept me in the midst of it all." Before I knew it, a precipitous flow escaped and ran onto my cheeks.

The stirring ballad took me way back. Back to my first year of college, when I experienced my first authentic relationship beyond puppy love and became pregnant. My mind continued to traverse several challenges that required tenacity to overcome.

Following my eldest son's birth, I did not want to remain on public assistance. The all-consuming desire to be with his father superseded logic. I moved in with my sweetheart, and found several temporary positions to help support our little family. Over a five-year period, our brood continued to grow. I had four children in five years. In addition to raising a family, I matriculated through several night and weekend courses. I was determined to complete my goal of higher education.

Throughout my fourteen-year journey to obtain my bachelor's degree, I encountered others that shared my zeal for information. It was empowering to meet other young parents that were attempting to escape the disorder that miseducation and poverty produces.

In 1991, long before Black Lives Matter was founded, I became involved with the non-violent/anti-police brutality movement. The brutal beating of Rodney King by Los Angeles Police officers caused uprisings all over the country. It was the first time that I got a glimpse of a modern-day lynching. I'd seen photographs with the likes of Emmett Till's maimed body and the strange fruit of Black bodies dangling from trees, but seeing the live video created an unrest in my spirit that I could not ignore.

With my three babies in tow, I went to protest rallies and joined a Speaker's Bureau for poor women. I had no idea that a few years later that fate would bring about first-hand experiences with Black Male incarceration. At the age of twelve, my precious son became involved in criminal activity that plagued the neighborhood in which we lived.

I was still swaying to the song when a recollection of standing in line at the Juvenile Hall came to mind. I remembered how carefully I had studied the beleaguered faces of both children and their primarily single mothers. I thought about how few men attended the visits. My son's father came because I insisted.

Facility personnel allowed guests to purchase vending-machine snacks for the young detainees. For an hour or two, we played board games and chatted gleefully until a buzzer rang to indicate the end of our time together. Each time I watched those youngsters file into formation, being herded like cattle back to their minuscule cells, a bit of my heart tattered.

Before my son started getting into trouble, I believed that a two-parent home would somehow shield him from the vicissitudes of living in the 'hood. In reality, I felt the identical pain as the other women who were forced to rear their children alone. Having a physically present partner does not equate emotional availability.

Over the years my son's behavior continued on a downward trajectory. For the next six years, I returned to locked facilities and visited him in more than one group home. I continued to observe mostly women visiting their sons. I wondered, how could I possibly be a mother of a child that was so troubled? Hadn't I loved him? Hadn't I modeled proper behavior? I needed answers as to why he was so drawn to destructive behavior. I later realized that I was not his sole influence.

I continued my education, researching and poring over statistics that spanned from 1972 forward. I found that the numbers hadn't changed in over a forty-year period. Empirical data concluded that there are more African American males in jail than in college. More African American children are being reared in single-parent homes. High percentages of teen parents are African American … on and on and on. I did not uncover a great deal of documentation lauding the resilience of people who are the members of what some consider a permanent underclass. Thankfully, there is more to the story than is being told.

I do not glorify my individual challenges, or demonize the shortcomings of my son or others. As Oprah Winfrey emphatically states, "What I know for sure, is this: people of color, whether gay or straight, poor or middle class, have success stories beyond the innumerable ordeals that are glorified in the media."

Pain equips its survivors. People of color, specifically Black folks, may be imperiled to alarming degrees, but many of us do not quietly go into the night of defeat. Tribulation fixates us not on the reasons we suffered. It encourages us to know that no matter what, we survive.

I still replay that powerful rendition that Yolanda Adams sang that night. Not everyone will enjoy the gospel genre as I did. Others may recite words about their experience through Rap. Some may express ideas in the form of prose or poetry.

There is one thing I am certain of however … No matter which roller coaster ride we are on, Black folks and other people of color continually rise. The resilience in our bones, and intestinal fortitude fuels us through hardship. What subsists in us is a dogged resolve that preserves us in the midst of it all!

Venus Zuhura Noble began her path to social justice following the savage beating of motorist Rodney King. She became a non-violence educator and poor women's advocate. In 2002 and 2005, tragedy struck, when her nephew and sons became victims of community violence. Despite the odds, she went on to earn degrees in Ethnic Studies, and advanced degrees in Social Work and Counselling. She is the mother of three grown children (one deceased) and three beautiful grandsons. Ms. Noble is a teacher, social worker, lover of the people and an overcomer.

Fillmore Jazz Festival, 2015. Shizue Seigel

The Art of Nannette Y. Harris

I was born and raised in Oakland, California, in the middle and late 1960s.
It was a great experience for an artist. There was the sound of music
and families in the neighborhoods. The air was clean and the sun so bright.
I would sketch whatever and whoever I could.

After graduating from the California College of Arts and Crafts in 1980,
raising a daughter, being a hair stylist, and
teaching high school special education, I found myself missing something—
my passion for art. In recent years, I have been able to
recapture my life-long dream of being
a full-time artist and art teacher.

I create my artwork using oil paint, recycled paint and acrylic metallics.
I am called the "Green artist" that paints "Blue People."
I have recycled my paints since 1993. I enjoy watching the paint grow into
mounds of hard color that I can sculpt into the hair of the characters I paint.
I help save our environment by never throwing away any paint.

After praying to God for a vision, a dream came in 2006 to paint people from
the inside out using primary colors Blue, Red and Yellow;
Blue represents trust, loyalty, wisdom, confidence, intelligence,
faith, truth and heaven.

Blue is the beginning of life.
Blue is the color of our blood before oxygen.
Red is the color of our blood after oxygen.
Yellow is for our aura and energy.
The universe which surrounds us, the sky and the water are blue.
I believe that black radiates when used with color.
I enjoy using the negative space, a touch of cubism, texture,
and geometric shapes in my paintings.

Text adapted with permission from http://nannetteyart.com

Nannette Y. Harris. In addition to her BFA, Ms. Harris earned certicates in special education and graphic design. Her artwork has been featured in one-woman shows at the African American Arts & Culture Complex and the San Francisco Main Library, as well in group exhibitions like the *Art of Living Black* and *The Black Woman Is God*. She was been written about in publications like the *Contra Costa Times*, the *Vallejo Times Herald*, and *Art Business News*. She makes her art available to ordinary people by exhibiting at festivals like the Fillmore Jazz Festival and Art + Soul Oakland, where local and out-of-town collectors have learned to seek out her artwork.

Nannette Y. Harris. *James Brown, 30 x 30 in., 2008.*

La TeKería
Sandra García Rivera

Bodies stand leaning
lining the interior of La Taquería,
coil around the inside perimeter,
spill out onto Mission St.
cast shadows down 25th,
contemplate picante/no picante
flour corn torta tortilla
taco quesadilla
crema carnitas
tamarindo pintos
negros chile verde
al pastor.

We turn the corner
approach hand in hand—
GIANTS boasts boldly
from his black hoodie
SF stretched broadly
across his chest.
He stops,
surveys the scene,
scowls under his breath,
"What the fuck!
Can't even get a burrito
in my own damn neighborhood…
Techies… Buses,"
burn his throat like
like acid reflux—
He sizzles by my side.

I tug on his arm,
continue our stride,
coax him towards 24th,
train rumbling under our feet
headed East, say
"C'mon baby,
let's hit up the taco truck
by the lake, or pupusas
at Plátanos, no wait."
His shoulders slump under
the shade of his hood.
We make our way.

It's an odd year in the Bay.

Seam Stress
Sandra García Rivera

She sits sewing like abuela
until her eyes say, No more.
Stitch by stitch
knuckles knees fingertips
thread and needle prick,
pins knots seams and hems
sleeves and patterns,
stitch by stitch
minutes woven into hours
hemmed into sunsets.
Salt spray tints time
mother worry wanders,
following the light.
Stitch by stitch,
joints jam, brittle back burns
years woven into generations,
memory threadbare
mechanized and forgotten.
Stitch by stitch,
she sews like abuela
until her eyes say, No more,
until I thread the needle
pierce the fabric
cut tug tuck fold iron
bone into steel
legacy into skin.

Sandra García Rivera is a Nuyorican poet chanteuse who has captured audiences throughout the U.S., Caribbean, and Europe as a spoken word performer and alongside Latin Jazz and roots music legends. She has penned two chapbooks: *Divination of the Mistress*, and *Shoulder High*, and her poems appear in numerous anthologies and journals including the *LA Review*. Her work elevates women and youth voices, Puerto Rican & Caribbean culture. She is the Host & Curator of Lunada Literary Lounge at Galería de la Raza, and performs as a singer/percussionist around the Bay Area with her band La Mixta Criolla.

4

in my own skin
seen
and unseen

Michelle Ibarra, *La Costurera*, pen, 10 x 8 in., 2017

Instructions on Bifurcation
Aja Couchois Duncan

Lesson Five

Pick anything, anyone. Make them into something greater than they are. This is a familiar activity. Remember when you cast that bastard as a revolutionary hero? Remember all that political rhetoric you used to swaddle your own heart?

The easiest solution is to make him her or her him. Some kind of biochemical transition. There's always that Lakota boy who knows enough about women to know they are not born as such; it is something they choose to become. Grammatically speaking there are two ways of being, some assignment the nouns take. But gender is as infinite as sound. Indonesian gamelan ensembles often include three gendér. Most heartbreaks involve three bodies. The best boys were once girls. That girl, the one who broke your heart, she was a boy once too.

* *

Seven Sides to the Story

There are seven bison remaining in California. They live on the slope of an excavated hill. At dawn they cluster together on the western edge of fence. There is no mountainside for them to hide in. White Buffalo Calf Woman gave the Lakota the sacred pipe. She was wakan and could not be harmed by arrow or bullet. The people had other weapons. She gave them seven sacred rituals and then disappeared into the white cloud of their disbelief. There are seven bison and 36,457,549 people in California. The largest terrestrial mammal in North America, the bison live in a paddock the size of a city block. Darkly furred and humped, bison can live for up to 20 years. In captivity their lives are more precarious; they suffer from alcoholism, poverty, a sickness of spirit. 60 million bison once roamed the grasslands of North America. There are seven circling their pen. There is only one way to tell you this. We are endangered. Current rates of depensation make it unlikely that we will ever recover.

Illustration by Kevin Parks.

Lesson Eight

Shem lived for six hundred years and was the progenitor of many nations. His son, a grandson of Noah, settled Aleppo, its old inhabitants. He is dead now; they all are. His name is not. It is the third day of charted time, the land between two rivers. Such fertile soil in which to people the newly cleansed earth.

The inhabitants of Benin and southeastern Togo practiced voodoo and spoke their name in tongues. When the land was divided into parcels too small to harvest another generation, the people migrated to concrete and steel. A landscape to disappear in.

In Yoruba, the story holds the earth in its gravity. She is called patron of the forest, that wild wind. To Hindus, she is he, a descendant of the sun god, a consort of nymphs. In America, she took her name for sex and her spirit for a neo Norse pagan, warrior of the Viking age. If she could, she would ravage her people with violent storms. She would whip the soil back into the sea.

*   *

Lesson Eleven

Call it superstition or projection. An obsession with the figurative. The sparrow's nest outside your front door. Or it was your front door, until you walked out of it with your hastily packed bags of clothes, shoes and books. The nest is still there. But the eggs have hatched; the chicks have died. The parents watch the house mournfully from the telephone wire. You could have told them that the nest was poorly built, the walls too low, the placement suicidal. New to procreation, they are still learning. They watched the first two fledglings fall, one by one, their bodies tiny and rigid on the porch. The third hatchling hid in her shell at the bottom of the nest. Weeks later, she is here to greet you. A white strip of feather across each cheek, painted for battle. You are uncertain which act would be the most brave: to leave or to stay. She is perched on the edge of a nest she has outgrown, weighing the odds.

*   *

Lesson Fifteen

A love poem will not save you. What can you do with a fleeting lyric, some hopeful rhyme scheme? Focus on other kinds of languaging. There is always the immediate satiation of propaganda. Take the cardiac transplant industry. They will tell you a new heart can save your life. But your body will see the transplant as an infection. That is why rejection medication is necessary. Every day you will have to swallow another pill. Some combination of cyclosporine, tacrolimus, mycophenolate, mofetil, prednisone, azathioprine. This makes you vulnerable to antigens such as thrush, herpes, respiratory viruses. You have a very short prognosis. After a transplant, men have a longer predicted lifespan than women. No one has bothered to explain this. Instead they describe different kinds of procedures, different kinds of hearts. Remember that guy at the party who had a baboon heart? He was drinking malbec in a lead crystal glass and channeling his dead primate. A few months later the man died too. The most successful patient survived 28 years. His heart was taken from the victim of a traffic accident. Blunt force trauma. When the brain dies the heart does not. Your own heart was removed in an orthotopic procedure, the great vessel transected, a portion of the left atrium excised. Before your chest cavity was closed, nothing was sutured to the remaining vessels. Nothing in fact was ever put in its place.

* *

Lesson Twenty-Three

Prairie voles live in the central grasslands. Highly social mammals, they have become the subjects of choice for scientists interested in the biological sources of monogamous pair bonding. This is not a popular activity. Only three percent of mammals engage in social monogamy. Voles are divided on the subject. The male meadow vole does not express the paternal devotion shown by his cousin of the prairie. This causes much family strife. The prairie vole has long repeating strips of DNA dangling like party streamers above a gene linked to vasopressin. This is the best explanation they have for the prairie vole's uncommon dedication to his mate and young. Vasopressin is released when a body is low on water, causing the kidneys to constrict, to hold onto everything they have. It is hard to imagine this as pleasurable, but monogamy does not always feel good. The meadow vole lives in moist open areas and will abandon his mate, his newborn litter for the dark call of night. But if he is injected with vasopressin, he will return home quickly, the nib of his tail tucked between his stubby legs.

Researchers have identified three neural chemicals associated with monogamy. Oxytocin is a hormone released after orgasm in both sexes and in women during childbirth. If you rub your nipples you may also trigger a rush of. Vasopressin is pressure and its absence. This too makes monogamy possible. Dopamine is that rush of excitement, the nexus of pleasure and repeat performance.

When we love we are fingering this microscopic string. Another mammalian experiment of. If the DNA snippets dangle just above, we are faithful. If the vasopressin is in short supply, or the oxytocin is depleted, we are more likely to wrap ourselves up in the nearest cotton sheet and waddle to the refrigerator for a late-night snack. Before departing, we will be sure to empty our pockets of everything that was sudden or elating. The night is its own intoxicant. There is a whole world yet to explore.

Lesson Thirty-Five

Somehow, without any warning, your desiccated heart has rehydrated, a bloated corpse in the center of your chest. People can smell it. Rather than being repulsed, they are drawn as if by a pheromone, the way boars detect estrus in sows. You had thought you'd be more desirable heartless, but animals survived by avoiding those among them who could not feel. Newly resuscitated, your emotions are black and iridescent, strange insects pricking the surface of your skin. You wonder if this is what people mean by wearing your heart on your sleeve. You had always pictured something red and bloody, like newly butchered meat. But the sensation is more brittle, as if sheathed in fractured glass. When the light hits you, you are kaleidoscopic. A million fragments of.

* *

Lesson Forty-Nine

Only the most irresponsible among them have recommended anything other than medication, several weeks of bed rest. But you have spent a lifetime attracting negligence. Gathering all the useless prescriptions and admonitions, you place them in an enormous bowl in the center of the room. They are like fish swimming around an empty glass. Such unhealthy things really. You wait for them to die one by one. It is not so bad to be alone in an apartment with a jar of dead ideas. It is the people, the ghosts that espoused them, who cause you the greatest concern. When they become too rowdy you slip out to the fire escape and watch the almost city draw to a close. It is not so different from all those nights you spent in the woods telling the stars off. Who are they really to look down on you with such bright indifference? The almost city lights obscure them. With your hands pressed against the metal railing, you search out another cosmology, some imploding luminosity to call your own.

"Seven Sides to the Story" was first published in *Restless Continent*, Litmus Press, 2016.

Aja Couchois Duncan is a San Francisco Bay Area-based writer of Ojibwe, French and Scottish descent. Her debut collection, *Restless Continent* (Litmus Press) was selected by *Entropy Magazine* as one of the best poetry collections of 2016 and won the California Book Award in 2017. When not writing, Aja works as a capacity builder and coach, supporting leaders, organizations and networks in advancing social justice. Aja holds an MFA in Creative Writing from San Francisco State University and a variety of other degrees and credentials to certify her as human; Great Spirit knew it all along.

To Love a Latina
Michelle Ibarra

A while ago I was at the bookstore
Browsing the shelves for histories and biographies
Running my fingertips along the spines
Currents running over covers,
Until suddenly they stop short …

Last year in 2016, a guy named Joe was able to publish a book called
"chica spotting: a 'field guide' to the different species of Latinas in the U.S."
To help men find/ "the right Latina to marry using user-friendly trait charts
    and promiscuity ratings."

To make matters worse, /This is then followed by a list of bad pickup lines to
    use on Latinas using broken Spanish.
It seems like our native tongue is too "spicy" for their tastebuds
If the Spanish language is chile setting fire to their gums
Our lips are ghost peppers, marinated with la lengua de nuestros antepasados.

I have written my own guide …

To love a Latina
Is to bite into ghost pepper lips
And wash her words down with milk.
It is not spitting chewed up dialect into the kitchen sink
Expecting her to clean up after you, and apologize for her spice.
To love a Latina,
Is to love her hips/ And trust that they don't lie.
It is not asking Shakira to twist her limbs,
Expecting her to break her bones into submission,
Apologizing for how they fit into her sockets.

To love a Latina,
Is to love her coffee colored hair,
Color de cafe.
To allow the curls to fall into place like sun rays through stained glass,
A cathedral of soft distorted light.
It is not forcing her to straighten out her kinks

Expecting her to burn out her fire,
Apologizing for coiled flames surrounding la Virgen de Guadalupe.

Loving a Latina is loving her eyebrows,
And when the hairs begin to reach out to one another
like the hands of god on chapel ceilings,
You *will* praise them as a work of art
Worthy of Frida Kahlo's blessing.

And when her eyes crinkle up at the corners when she laughs too loudly
Turning into wrinkles shaped like crescents,
Worthy of The Aztec Moon goddess.
You remind her that the spanish sun radiates from her eyelids,
A fusion of dusk and dawn.

However … / The skies in her eyes were not made for you.
You are not her conquistador.
You are solely an invader mining the pores of her skin
Trying to Extract gold,
In a desperate attempt to find the road to el dorado.

You will never be able to skim the surface.
Your thirst for precious metals and delicate gems will never be quenched
Because *Oro vive en en sus venas.*
Gold lives in Her veins
Forever embedded in the roots of Latin America soil.

To love a Latina is to love how her mestizo spine curves,
Running up and down her body
And don't you dare forget her bones were built from the leftover ruins of
    abandoned empires.
Forests growing from the cracks,
Leaving hortencias and cempasúchiles in their wake.

Loving a Latina means loving the chaos between dusk and dawn,
It is loving the way she paints frescos as love letters to the sky.
Eagle wings spread, ready to take flight …
Lista para volar.

Loving a Latina is loving the sound of colliding dialects
Being swished around in her mouth.
Spanish rolling off her tongue
Pressing against the corners of her lips.
For she is made of pyramids kissing one another,
Handing each other the remnants of flower wars.
Shrines to dying gods
And beating hearts.
Separated by war and rain
Huitzilopochtli [wee-tsee-loh-pohch-tlee] and Tlaloc.

To love a Latina **requires** sacrifice
… Maybe even human sacrifice.

"To Love a Latina" was published online by Whoa Nelly Press, 2017. http://www.
whoanellypress.com/to-love-a-latina.html.

Michelle Ibarra is a writer and visual artist who attends the San Francisco
School of the Arts. Her work has been featured in the *San Francisco Bay Area
Youth Poetry Anthology*, *Celebrating Art Book - Spring 2018*, Together We Rise
2017 National Women's Conference, and Art? or Politics? in London, England.
Her art centers around her experiences as a first-generation Latina growing up
around San Francisco and the rich heritage that surrounds her family history
in Mexico. She hopes to use her art as a tool to encourage others to stand with
Latinx immigrants in the face of political turmoil.

Michelle Ibarra, *Muñecas Muertas*, pen, 10 x 8 in., 2017.

Remembering Trayvon
5 years ago today
Amos White

when "hashtag" became identity
black parents banned hoodies
race became impolitic
black men caught blue leaded forties
with "one way" inscribed casings

when bias became M.O.
black students got body slammed
voice became scream
black staycations meant safer
with pressed collared shoulder glances

when grief became breakfast
black boys lost
hands up became protocol
black pools laid unmoved or covered
with no shroud on Canfield Drive

when 5 years ago became today
black lives shun apology
memory becomes a rose

black pews will gather dust
when the hearse idles weekdays

Black History Month

did you, too, fall in your dreams:
arms spread, black face down?

Maternal POV
Amos White

My mother doesn't get
my "itch"

the zing
in fresh mowed grass,
snug salt stained tees
hung like trophies in sunlight
or perennial bite
of new flats
that sear the moment
of time crossing

every spring;
or maybe it is time?

I have yet
to cross
the wide white chalk
laid out to measure
the end
of the race

to get
what she does
not

Amos White is an awarded American haiku poet and author, producer/director and activist, recognized for his vivid literary imagery and breathless poetic interpretations. Amos is published in several national and international reviews and anthologies. He is president & chair of the Bay Area Generations literary reading series in San Francisco and Oakland, founder and host of the Heart of the Muse salon for creatives, executive producer and host of the Beyond Words: Jazz + Poetry show, producer of the Oakland Haiku and Poetry Festival, and board director of Rhythmix Cultural Works. www.about.me/amoswhite www.facebook.com/amoswhitehaiku

Untitled
Nellie Wong

Oh, how can I write
A love poem
When I'm unsure
That I truly loved

When the idea of love or loving
Held me in its misty eye,
When I traversed clouds, flying
A bat not knowing
To hang upside down

Star-lit skies even in daylight lifted
My existence as I ran after beauty,
Lost, lost in reverie,
Imagination beyond dry skin,
Inflammation and heat
of parental scoldings, sighs

Typing and filing, writing
In shorthand, wondering
If Mr. Gregg would have praised
My skill, skating on paper,
Its shade of pale mint green,
A forest dense and far away

To tap dance and sing
In top hat and tails
My face smooth, body lithe, sparkling
An unreachable, an unreachable star

Blind to many angles
Of dreams and reality,
Drunk with notions of romance
And forever forevers, avoiding
The art and aches of loving

To reaching a pinnacle
Of age and experience, still chasing
Beauty no longer a gown of silk
And roses

Beauty's essence, its fragrance
Of camphor and mushrooms and ginger,
Tantalized this body, alone,
Writing a love poem
For breath and sky,
Walking the earth, chrysanthemums
In bloom.

An octogenarian socialist feminist activist, Nellie Wong has four books of poetry and work published in many publications, including *This Bridge Called My Back: Writings by Radical Women of Color*. Her poems are inscribed at public sites in San Francisco, including along the Embarcadero roadway. She's co-featured with Mitsuye Yamada in the documentary film, *Mitsuye and Nellie Asian: American Poets*.

Fighting back through the Freedom Socialist Party and community projects, Wong's words and actions for a better world means that making revolution is resistance. An Oakland native, she was honored in 2011 when Oakland High School students voted to name a campus building after her.

To Abide Being A Black Lesbian In Amerikkka
Kira Lynne Allen

I learn
to leave my home
simultaneously wearing two sets of clothes
The first is inside out
   so that the softest pieces of the fabric
   the parts without seams or hems or ragged strings
   sit next to my skin
The other is right side up
   so that I am presentable
   palatable
This kind of tangible code switching
   keeps me from scratching my own self raw
Prevents the hypervigilance
   from making me insane
Still the first two minutes
   in the shower
   feels like little blades cutting into my flesh

Until I start to relax
begin to imagine
breathing
without my very essence
being under attack

Until her soft cinnamon-chocolate skin
touches mine at the end of each day
and I remember nothing is as important
as our ability to love and be loved

Mommy, Is Grandpa in Heaven or in a Grave?
Kira Lynne Allen

As a mother
I crave the creative
ignite the raw unharnessed fresh of how

Have you ever seen a Redwood Tree
emit steam as the sun shines after spring rain
Redwoods make sunrays tangible
create whole worlds of sounds smells textures
How many shades of green live in a Redwood forest

How many complexions breathe in my family history
Inhabit the living rooms of our homes
You see the African
but refute
the Dutch
the French
the German
the Danish
the English
the Scottish
the Spanish
the Portuguese
the Native American
I grow in the sunlight of my mother's love
grieve the dark mahogany of my father's passing and
learn to set down roots under their tender rainbow

Previously published in *Write This Second*, Prashanti Press, 2015.

Kira Lynne Allen is an Oakland-based author, a four-time VONA/Voices Fellow, Poetry for the People alumna, and a workshop facilitator. Her first book *Write This Second* charts her journey from desecration to divinity, from addict and high school dropout to master's degree recipient, poet, performer, collage artist, activist, and community leader. She hopes to inspire readers to transform their lives by finding and proclaiming their authentic selves. She has a BA in Creative Writing from Mills College and an MA in Transformative Arts from John F. Kennedy University. www.writethissec.com

orienting utopia
Manon Bogerd Wada

they live
inside you & me
through us they feed
with supplanted seeds
wide angle agendas shout to entangle
above & over the camera
not under the common lens
will read may bend
an alternate route to creed
to cruise the perimeter's ends
lead & extend our borders out
to defend & maybe mend
then but when?
remember
they never send notice
we live recorded surveillance
so don't ever quote this
message can't be a passage
it's coded & coated
object of the made ready to go opus
my subject the commodity of whose locus?
however
is there a spectrum to the focus?
orient myopia for a different diagnosis
the coordinates to where utopia lives
perhaps is fictional practice
actively resists pinning down
is wild & boundless
& if ever it can be found
exists inside you & me
between it may be seen

Manon Bogerd Wada was born in New York City and has been based in San Francisco for the past 20 years. She completed her BFA in Community Arts from California College of the Arts. In recent years, Manon has worked as a teaching artist in public elementary schools in the Bay Area as well as in Applied Behavior Analysis therapy working with children with Autism Spectrum Disorder. She has been an active member of Asian American Women Artists Association and A Place of Her Own. Currently, she is an MFA candidate at Rhode Island School of Design in Sculpture.

Manon Bogerd Wada, *Aligning Elevation*, installation, 16 x 3 x 9 ft., 2015. Photo: Reiko Fujii.

Artist statement, right: *Aligning Elevation* explores the symbolism of a chair for a person in this sculptural installation that involved the transformation of personal family furniture. These four chairs are elevated through wooden stilts attached to their legs and have ladders extending from their backs. The parallel backs of these chairs combine to form a lattice of ladders, interlinked to support a roof structure. This installation speaks to notions of home, emotional wellbeing and strength of family as well as community. The installation was partially inspired by traditional Thai houses, which are raised on stilts to protect them from seasonal flooding.

Manon Bogerd Wada
Flux Migration, installation
80 x 24 x 28 in., 2016.

Artist Statement. *Flux Migration* draws upon personal and family history to evoke both isolation and transformation as it occurs with immigration and relocation. The chair in this piece is a family heirloom, cut in half vertically, inverted and reconfigured side by side. As a singular object, it is intended to portray isolation. Upon viewing the objects' reflection in the mirrored sides, the dissected chair halves combine to create two full chairs, and further, a multitude of chairs, expressing transformation. The two doors with mirrors providing two viewing directions reflect a divergence of one's pathway, infinitely and indefinitely.

Manon Bogerd Wada, *Thirsty Ghosts*, installation, 10 x 3 x 4 ft., 2015.

Artist statement: *Thirsty Ghosts* explores the concept of hungry ghosts, found in many Asian cultures, and which are typically characterized as lost or unhappy spirits that haunt the living. Applying this concept to a contemporary context, *Thirsty Ghosts* serves to pair imagery with a feeling of drowning in a substance desired, which continuously runs empty and dry. In this sense, addiction as a metaphor for the insatiable, hungry ghosts that take hold of living beings. The purpose of this piece is not to make a statement about alcoholism, but rather to call out a hungry ghost, which affects a multitude of individuals and their families. In naming it with a visual representation, the intention is to purge and let go of it.

Under construction
Soraiya Domi Lozano

Who knows the sting of a woman
summoned to be small—
The drill next door punctuates first light
until a hum

breaks. Misunderstood, the dead
rat on sidewalk. Under construction
these letters of debt fatten. Apply

clove oil will lighten
dark spots. Our heroes killed.   Toughen
up any loose ends budding, fleeing
when he speaks

Vietnamese men work   hard
next door, Quan Yin on my windowsill,
pinkened clouds park across
the chain link fence, and I feel   freedom

Tai Chi brings as supper cools
the shimmer of our girl
gang, Honey, coffee, first blush, it is
spine and pluck, falling

for one liners & my heart is papel picado
hung   across his eyelids, I want to be
with,   carry this for fertility,   carry
dusk in back pocket

I find his letter   crumpled,
things we cannot swallow:
swords, carbon, jade,   blue
prints for Saturday.

Loop Station
Soraiya Domi Lozano

I'm riding the late bus
crescent backache feet
dreaming, there is a man
                with flowers stolen and showing
off his tattoo, as he runs for the bus,
the ache of a thousand cranes.

      I bite off cuticles tasting metallic
but the sun chases storms, I surrender,

quickly, then brown bodies
climb in and climb out
of their skin.
      To be you skating
on fine lines of race and color, you
must be a theory shouldering
cosmos under thumbnail
bed, me a dark star lit, to be your theory,
if only lotus and chasm, gang stars,

I'm watching the bus stop,
dreaming, there is a man
              with star gazers and taking
off his mask.

You Say Goodbye
Soraiya Domi Lozano

            you say goodbye
i say   goodbye
i   say goodbye
you   say goodbye
then a fissure
a fissure   splits open
here   i stay
            open to you
we've been
strangers in a way   w/o a pen
my bowl   is empty   your
bowl has   no room
as it once had   even the colors
cannot shudder
the graffito scrawl   you and i
once painted   (in our sophomoric dreams)

softens &   fades

        those goodbyes   what made them

                        where are they going

                                    where are they cracking

            where are they unlocking

                                    where are they wandering

Soraiya Domi Lozano is a writer based out of Oakland. She is an MFA graduate of the California College of the Arts Writing program. Her poetry has been published in *Huizache: The Magazine of Latino Literature* and anthologized in *Cantos al Sexto Sol: An Anthology of Aztlanahuac Writing* and *La Lunada* literary anthology. She is a VONA alum, and writes to heal and empower herself and others.

5

mother
father
gifts & ghosts

Shizue Seigel

The Second-Hand Firebird:
A Chinese Man's Journey to America
Li Miao Lovett

My mother has one story about coming to America, and it goes like this. In the winter of 1970 when my father was a poor graduate student at Oklahoma State, we drove across the country to Lake Tahoe, one of the gambling hubs out west, where he found work to get ahead of his debts. Dad had bought a white Pontiac Firebird, a classy convertible with the double headlights, prominent fins and a grill that flared like nostrils. But my dad could only afford a used car, with his family newly arrived from Taiwan and his modest means as a foreign student. The Pontiac had a broken heater, and as my father drove for hours each day, my mother held me in one arm while holding the ripped fabric of the roof with her free hand to shut out the winter's cold.

While my mother worked during the day as a motel maid, my father did menial labor at night to pay the bills, although he was a college graduate. Dad worked hard and didn't complain, but he would literally fall asleep on his feet while washing dishes in the restaurant's kitchen during his second work shift of the day.

I've yet to ask my father, "Why did you come to America?" He doesn't understand why I ask him pesky questions about bygone times. History is written by conquerors, and the obscure do not have their stories revered. We were nobodies, trekking cross country in a beat-up jalopy, like the Joads in John Steinbeck's epic Grapes of Wrath. This fictional family achieved notoriety for fleeing Oklahoma in the Dust Bowl years. Their story was censored and denied existence in the literary canon only to endure as a symbol of American grit persevering against social and economic misfortune. They pushed out West in beat-up trucks because the life had been sucked from their land.

Perhaps my father felt the pull of opportunity in the West. More likely, he was escaping oppression, as was his lot in life. My dad's relationship with his own father throttled him like the Oklahoma dust, and perhaps that was the real impetus to move far away. My father was the unlucky child, and he says to this day he doesn't know why he was the target of his father's wrath. The elder Miao treated my father brutally as a child when their homeland convulsed from the prolonged civil war in China. Landowning families were the nemesis of the emerging Communist party, and Grandfather was repeatedly tortured by inquisitors demanding that he turn over the family wealth. My grandfather must have lashed out at Dad like a wounded animal, one trapped in the steel jaws of a rising regime. Or maybe it was in the Shandong blood of hot-tempered fathers to disdain their more reticent sons.

My father's family escaped to Taiwan in 1946 on one of the boats carrying Nationalist soldiers to the small island, known as Formosa by colonialists. Far from licking their wounds in defeat, Chiang Kai Shek's regime established power in Taiwan and instituted martial law that would last for four decades. Young men had to serve for at least a year in the Taiwanese army. The threat of the People's Republic of China coming to claim its wayward sons who deserted to Taiwan was palpable. My father must have felt the call to defend his adopted land from the countrymen who terrorized his village, upended his childhood, and did untold things to his father whose anger knew no bounds.

Dad did his military service after finishing a bachelor's degree in international commerce. Having been banned from the house and denied supper on many a cold winter's night as a child, my father took the privations of army life in stride. He was often the first to gulp down his evening meal, usually rice with a watery mixture of tofu and vegetables, with meat for special occasions. That put him first in line for the communal bath. Forget about running water. Soldiers had to endure a sweat- and germ-infested tank of bath water after a day of marching with nearly ninety pounds in their backpacks, the weight of several rice sacks with the added discomfort of metal and ammunition protruding into sore backs.

After his service in the army, my dad bided his time teaching school. He must have gotten one stern lecture after another from his father—along with an initial glimpse of independence from this bitter, tyrannical man. As the ancient Chinese adage goes, the sky is high and the emperor is far away. He managed to stay away from his father during his time at the university, then for another year of military service. But once he was back home, he was bound once more to authoritarian rule.

In my mind's eye, it was Grandfather who sent my dad to America by turning to one of his seven brothers, among those who survived or could be located after the Communist takeover. My sixth great uncle was the most prosperous. Grandfather must have told this brother, "Look, I need your help. My no-good son went to a mediocre college after his gluttony cost him entrance to a fine one. My older son, you know, the one who can't spit out two words from those stubborn lips! Give him some seed money to sponsor him as a student abroad. He can go to America. Surely there's more he can do for himself out in the West." The gluttony referred to that giant bowl of seafood my father devoured the night before his college entrance exams, disturbing both bowel and brains enough to alter his academic fortunes irrevocably.

It didn't take long for things to move forward. My father must have endured the lectures that came from his uncle. How to be a man. How to abide by Confucian ideals. The Nationalists never surrendered the ancient beliefs that defined codes of behavior for families and social hierarchies in China for thousands of years. These codes formed immutable lattices of obligations, roles for firstborn sons and fathers, as well as the womenfolk who upheld the patriarchy.

My father suffered through these lectures, as I did on our only family trip back to Taiwan when I was eleven. I remember the ornate, carved wooden furniture, the sparkle of elegant china and silverware, the fine red silk tapestries. Having to sit for hours until it was nearly midnight, while my great uncle droned on with his lectures, I could care less for his wealth or privilege. I aspired to the middle-class suburbs of America (where we later moved), not the gilded life; as a young girl I had to do without the frills of an American upbringing because Mom clung to her familiar tracks in San Francisco's Chinatown. Where I lived, not too different from Taiwan's markets, the grimy streets teemed with stores selling medicines, sweets and produce for the Chinese palate, live fish and whole roasted ducks suspended from the ceiling by hooks. On these crowded streets the elderly men shoved aside unsuspecting children in their path with their walking canes.

There I was, confined to my ornate mahogany chair, too young and bored to ponder why my sixth great uncle would open his gold purse to enable my father's passage to America. Somehow his wealth had survived the political hurricane that swept up the landowning classes who by default were enemies of the great proletariat revolution. Perhaps he had a more even temperament than my grandfather and took pity on my dad. Most likely, he was wed to the same traditions that held the Miao clan together in China for generations, before the Communist takeover ripped apart its fabric. When my dad was a young boy, many of my grandfather's brothers had ventured into provinces to the south to seek business opportunities. Shared wealth had allowed the family to become prosperous, with more than a hundred relatives, close and distant, who lived in a sprawling compound in Shandong province.

Whatever his uncle did to sponsor my dad financially in coming to America to study at Oklahoma State was no small contribution, but in the family lore it was hardly a layer of dust blown off the top of Sixth Great Uncle's coffers.

My father has always thought of himself as the unlucky one. But in the U.S., conditions were ripe for a dramatic shift, an influx of immigrants due to progressive policies that reversed the tide of earlier discrimination. Did my father realize how fortunate he was to have arrived in the U.S. at the cusp of this change?

The Chinese, like Eastern Europeans in the early 20th century, were not welcome in this country once the backbreaking work of building the nation's railroads was done. But going into the 1960s, other countries were moving away from discriminatory policies. The Civil Rights movement pushed the immigration conversations here to the foot of the Statue of Liberty, where President Lyndon Johnson signed this monumental act into law. In 1965, the Hart-Cellar Act opened the gates of immigration for the first time in decades, giving preference for visas to those with professional skills and to relatives of citizens and residents. It was the opening my father needed in his late twenties to escape from the shadows of his past.

In those early photos of our life in America, I see a young man who is my father, but only recently have I caught a glimpse of his youthful ambitions. He bought a Firebird, a sporty convertible. That's not the image I associate with a breadwinner, and someone who has been shy and heavyset his whole life. He came to America at a time of newfound attitudes toward those different in color, language, and traditions. My parents' frugality gave them a leg up into the middle class when the country's prosperity broadened its safety nets and offered them a chance at this bounty. They saved their earnings—his from working in the tech industry, hers from seamstress work when clothes were still made in the USA—toward their first house in San Jose, purchased in 1977 for ninety thousand dollars.

Yet for both my parents, it is never enough. Somehow the frugality of his youth—from emotional deprivation to the ravages of war—has robbed him of the capacity for appreciation. Appreciation that he not only survived a childhood of cold winters without supper in the Shandong countryside, but a revolution that left few unscathed. That he made a new life and found footing in a country that recognized the Chinese only as laundrymen, coolies, cooks, and maids until the mid-20th century. That he moved from menial summer jobs in Lake Tahoe's back alleyways to a budding Silicon Valley, where his company serviced the computers of the U.S. Congress. Indeed, these lawmakers may have been the very men and women who made it possible for immigrants to arrive welcomed, for the first time, not as cheap labor but as skilled men and women with families. My dad was part of that first wave. They came with the weight of their histories, and they came with dreams carried on the flotsam of distant shores.

Li Miao Lovett grew up in San Francisco's Chinatown and the suburbs of San

Jose. She stopped being a good Chinese daughter in her twenties, quitting a corporate job to turn to public service. During her two-decade career in education, she has worked on the struggle to save City College from a corrupt accreditor and to defend union workers. Li does communications for a Stanford-based center focused on learning mindsets and equity in schools. Her novel, *In the Lap of the Gods*, is a tale of love and loss set in China amidst the rising waters of the Three Gorges dam.

Hand-made suits at Ma's Tailoring on Clement Street, 2010. Photos: Shizue Seigel

Jordanian immigrant Zaki Ghishan learned tailoring in Italy in the 1930s. He made suits for the likes of Herb Caen at his thriving Union Square shop. Now he enjoys semi-retirement near his son's Taraval Market, 2017.

My Identity
Keh-Ming Lin

American Dream. In the summer of 1974, having finished medical school and two years of neuropsychiatric training in Taiwan, I arrived at Seattle to start another psychiatric residency, with little idea what I was getting into. Not having been outside of Taiwan until then, I somehow had this idea that I was going to master spoken English in three months and would go on to become a bridge across cultures, uniting things East and West. At the time, I had not heard of the term "Culture Shock" and would not have known what it meant even if I came across it. But shocked I was. Perpetually unsure of what people were saying, and when to say what, I became practically mute. And then, there were challenges that were concrete but even more urgent: for the first time in my life, I needed to buy a car and learn how to drive it, get on and off freeways, find a place to live, negotiate the supermarkets, and search for furniture and clothes at the Goodwill and discount stores. All of these were crucial life skills that I had to learn quickly.

But even more difficult was the question of identity. "Who am I?" and "Where and how do I belong?" had not been questions that crossed my mind until I left Taiwan. In Seattle, my skin color, facial features, accent and mannerisms made it impossible for full assimilation (if indeed that was what I wanted). Compared to many other immigrants and refugees, what I had to go through was not as hard. I had a job, some vague sense of a career path, and I had fall-back positions. I didn't need to worry about food and shelter. But every day there were hundreds of incidents making one feel not "at home." A glance, a frown, a vague gesture, anything could trigger self-doubt and suspicion of ill-will or rejection. Missing half of the conversation was difficult to ignore. Uncertainties with social cues was even harder to deal with.

What made me (more or less) an American? What helped in that initial stage of my "accidental" transformation into an American? For one thing, I didn't feel I had much choice. I could always return to Taiwan, but that would have been regarded as a defeat, and the loss of face would be hard to deal with.

The "kindness of women" helped. My first supervisor was a woman, who from early on decided to take me under her wing, shielding me from criticisms that could be too damaging during my first year there. The nurses and other coworkers were tolerant, and went out of their ways to bridge my communication gaps. It was because of these kind women that I muddled through the most difficult first year, not unscathed, but not irrevocably damaged either.

Nature and scenery helped. Seattle was so green, its air so fresh, and it was surrounded by water everywhere that was so crisp and clean. On rare days when it wasn't cloudy or drizzling, Mt. Rainier would suddenly jump out of nowhere to dazzle us. Within an hour or two, we could get to one of the National Parks and lose ourselves among tall trees that seemed to just keep on marching on, with no end in sight. Going over the Cascades, we could just keep driving through land that was vast, arid, sparsely populated—desolate and majestic. Time and again, by mistake we drove up a mountain, and couldn't turn around. At the top of the mountain, we suddenly entered a meadow with a large expanse of wildflowers. Seeing how big, how diverse, how grand the landscapes were, I started to feel proud of becoming part of this new country of mine. Over the next few decades, such sense of wonder would continue to emerge, making me happy with my decision to stay: Yosemite, Yellowstone, Grand Canyon, Bryce, Banff, Golden Gate Bridge, Death Valley. There was no end to the surprises, compared to smallness of Taiwan.

Unexpectedly, things that had been foreign, puzzling or even repulsive would suddenly become interesting, comforting, and inexplicably moving. Music was a good example. One early evening, as I was driving home from an exhausting day at the VA Hospital, the car radio somehow was tuned on a country music station. On air, someone was wailing about how she missed her hometown down South. Suddenly I started to weep, which caught me by total surprise. That was when I realized that, no matter how far apart we were, how different our upbringings might have been, the country-music singer eloquently expressed what I had had trouble articulating to myself. I was embarrassed by my reaction, thinking how ridiculous I must have looked. But that didn't prevent me from continuing to listen, crying for people I didn't know who were missing their small towns, grandmas, first cars, first loves…

Are they even edible? Adjusting to American food took a long time. Salads were a new concept to me, which puzzled me a great deal, since they looked and tasted like grass, fit only for cows. But, shying away from the salad meant the only choice you had for vegetables were those that were always so overcooked, especially in the hospital cafeteria.

And all the potatoes! How did one even manage to swallow those totally bland, grimy, grubby messes masquerading as food? Gravy might add some indeterminate flavor, but it also made the whole thing even more suspiciously turgid. Yet one night at a restaurant, when the waiter asked me if I wanted chives and sour cream to go with the baked potato, not knowing what he was talking about, and not willing to admit it, I just nodded. It turned out to be such an unexpected treat! From then on, I have always asked for a double serving of chives, although I still go easy on the butter or sour cream.

A taste for steaks and cheese came even later. But I still vividly remember that defining moment, many years later, when, returning from Taiwan, I was suddenly hit by a weird urge for a Black Angus steak. Not only to have a steak, but a bloody one! Why, I did not quite know. This craving lasted for quite some time, but the sense of urgency eventually faded away.

Cheese was another matter. Before I developed lactose intolerance, having cheese wasn't a problem. But other than the soft Laughing Cow chunks that were sweet and creamy, I couldn't tell one kind from another. They were just plain and filling—except brie and blue cheese, which smelled like stinking shoes. Even worse were those with molds that gave you the feeling that you might get killed. Yet there came a day that I surprised myself by finding myself at the supermarket searching for these "disgusting stuffs." A year or two later, the intensity of the craving also subsided, but these experiences assured me that either Americans were not crazy, or I had become crazy like them.

Searching for the Emerald City. Acculturation is a tricky thing. It forces you to change into a different person, which is scary, but it can also be exciting. Often it feels like that no matter how many changes have already taken place, you're still not quite there, and there's still a long way to go. The feeling that it's never going to be complete, that in one way or another you'll always remain an outsider, is deeply unsettling. But hopefully the saying "that which does not kill us makes us stronger" has some truth to it. After forty some years, I haven't yet been killed. So maybe one of these days I'll find myself strong?!

Keh-Ming Lin, MD, MPH, is Professor Emeritus of Psychiatry, UCLA, Distinguished Life-Fellow, American Psychiatric Association. He was the Founding Director of the NIMH/Harbor-UCLA Research Center on the Psychobiology of Ethnicity, Consortium on Asian American Mental Health Training, the Coastal Asian-American Mental Health Center and the Long Beach Asian-American Mental Health Center. His professional publications include four books and more than 200 journal articles and book chapters. Prof. Lin now lives in San Francisco, and joined the Write Now! workshops to work on an in-progress novel and a memoir. He is also enjoying the opportunities to share his work with audiences.

My Sister Went to Tahlequah
For Sandra Mitchell
Gail Mitchell

My sister went to Tahlequah
She wanted to see
where the Trail of Tears ended

My sister went to Tahlequah
She wanted to see for herself
where the Trail of Tears ended
and she took her baby daughter

You see my people come from
Africa, a long time ago but they
also come from Oklahoma

And she had listened
to her grandmother tell
tales of her grandmother
and she knew that blood
could not be divided

She knew that she must integrate
all the people whose blood
ran through her veins

She knew that the heart drum
beat red as well as black
and she knew that you can not
divide blood

My sister went to Tahlequah
to see for herself
where the Trail of Tears ended
She wanted to integrate
all the blood of the nations
that ran through her veins

She knew she could
not integrate the shame
but had lived the pain,
and the tears were there
inside her
hidden away
right behind the eyes,
the silent tears

So she took her baby daughter
to Tahlequah to see where
the Trail of Tears ended
and to teach her that blood
could not be divided and that the
heart drum beat black as well
as red and she rattled
the dance of integration
mixing all the blood
of the nations that ran
through her veins

And the heart drum beat
to tell the story correctly
as she rattled, dancing away
the shame that was not her shame
but integrating the pain so the
tears could fall and she wept
because she knew blood could
not be divided but the truth
could make her whole

"My Sister Went to Tahlequah" was published in *Bone Songs*, Taurean Horn Press, 1999.

Day Work
For Lenora Ross Carrington Rutherford
Gail Mitchell

She said that she made sixty-five cents for ironing a shirt, two dollars for a basket of laundry. There was no hourly wage for day work. If you could get a real job in 1960s San Francisco you made one dollar and sixty-five cents an hour and you earned every cent. There was a battalion of colored women on the streetcar, all of them going to white folks' houses, cooking, cleaning, answering the questions of other peoples' children while their parents worked downtown. Maybe she'd get back before her husband, put the dinner on for her own kids, bring home a bag of hand-me-downs and a check.

Alphabet Blue
For Karen
Gail Mitchell

She will not take her medicine
It is bitter and is just wrong
It will not heal what ails her

Forget-me-nots and blue asters
Turn her vision inward
She would like to dance
but balance can be a peculiar thing

The shawl she is wearing was a gift
Its color suits her
Brings out the warm tones in her skin

Sometimes when she looks out the window
The patterns become something she can almost recall
She tells her son about the net that is holding her together

She says her mother had the most elegant hand
and her missives were kept bound by a blue ribbon
the color of her eyes

Oh! She thinks she was dreaming woke up and the sheets were damp
Her son said that she was incoherent but the syllables fit
and though her tongue felt heavy

She had the oddest sensation she felt each letter that formed
itself in her mouth and skittered across her tongue
and witnessed her despair

Ashes to Ashes
For my father Lawrence Mitchell
Gail Mitchell

Memory is such a strange igniter. One abrupt recall and you are suddenly in the living room of a house you thought would always be home. A place you thought you could always come back to. A place where the bones of old pets are buried in the backyard and where your mother started to die.

In this other world you run your hands along the shelves, you remember the archway around them and how the wood set perfectly in the grooves. How many times did you pick up that old fu and feel the weight of that small blackish-green dog statue brought back from Korea in the 1950s. You remember how it rested in the palms of your hand, small and heavy

There was the sake set embellished with tiny beads of gold paint. It was brown, red and white with the tiniest flowers painted on it. Over and over again those cups were lifted to your eyes and marveled at, for at the bottom of each cup there held a photograph of a woman in traditional dress with her black hair up in a complicated bun.

A child, haunted by memories, where all was lost to fire, to death, to the bluesy flame of strong spirits and even sharper regrets.

In the beginning was the word, and I've drawn on it to map the internal terrain and make sense of the external world, to investigate life and death, traversing a language that leaves me spellbound.

Gail Mitchell is a poet living in San Francisco. The author of *Bone Songs*, she received her MFA from San Francisco State University. I am a native San Franciscan. My parents met here. My mother was from Okmulgee and my father was from New Orleans. My ancestry is Black and Muskogee Nation (Creek Indian) on my mother's side and on my father's side Black, Creole and Italian. There is Indian on my father's side but I could not possibly tell you what tribe. I am undocumented.

Artist Statement: I pick words like gems to make the right necklace to go out into the world. I think of jewelry as amulets to protect and of course as adornment to help one shine. I am a jeweler and a poet. I am a maker. It is a must, a desire that runs as deep as breath.

Día de los Muertos
Linda Gonzáles

Every year as November 1st approaches I do the math to remember how long ago my father passed away on Día de los Muertos. This year I dutifully pulled up my calculator and subtracted 1996 from 2017. Twenty-one years. And then the obvious hits me. I can always know how long it has been since he passed on to his next life by subtracting one year from my twins' age. They are 22 and were just a year old when their abuelo died. I remember carrying Gina down the aisle behind the casket, her and Teo's new life blooming while that same year Tot's had faded.

I set up my altar this week, pulling out the pictures of my dearly departed and adding new ones from this year. The first step is always laying out the cross-stitched mantel with years of stains and a dark mark from when a candle burned too hot. I tape papel picado above the altar, remembering this ritual is not a dirge; it is an opening of the veil to celebrate the lives that touched me and my comunidades. It is a time to think about why I miss them and ponder how to keep them alive in the present moment.

I imagine my dad's disappointed spirit hovering over the Dodgers as they lost in the World Series. I invoke my mom's stove-top magic as I figure out what to do with a bag of zucchini that must be cooked tonight. I remember the mothers who grieve their sons' vibrant spirits every day, and I take a moment send Snapchats to my beloved cuates.

Día de los Muertos is so ingrained in my being that I am startled to see people in costume; my mind wonders for a second, "What's that all about?" This is amazing because I was so involved in Halloween while my children were growing up—making costumes, figuring out the healthiest candy to hand out, trading my children's candy for money so they were not overloaded with sugar (and I could store their loot for the next Halloween).

In years past I have hosted gatherings to decorate sugar skulls, loving this tradition of blending death with creativity. I treasured giving my children and their friends the chance to be playful and imaginative with soemthing that so many people fear. As a writer I live in that crevice of light and shadow, writing drafts only to end their existence for another version and then another and then yet another.

I love the transparency of life and death, the calaveras that dance and meditate and watch TV. Each skeleton could be anyone of us and one day we will know what our antepasados experienced after their last out-breath. One day we will see there is no separation between any of us, alive and dead.

The first and only altar in my parents' home was the one we created on a cake after my dad's funeral, laying out the detallitos of his life that he allowed to be visible. The secrets were still within him, wisps of energy that over the years encircled us with cariño or strangled our voices or tripped us as we ran.

As I set up my altar year after year, I breathe in the musty smell of the newspapers I have carried from home to home. These crinkled papelitos wrap and unwrap memories and give space for those I loved and lost to whisper consejos in the stillness. I unbind my heart wounds and apply the salve gained from another year of living—that little bit more of perspective and wisdom nestled in my corazón that wraps around me like a soft, colorful rebozo.

Linda González is the author of the memoir *The Cost of Our Lives*. She has published essays in literary journals and books, is a storyteller, and received her MFA from Goddard College. She is a four-time VONA/Voices alum. You can read more of her writing at www.lindagonzalez.net and learn about her thriving practice as a life coach, assisting writers and others to discover and reach their precious goals.

Born in Los Angeles, Linda has called the San Francisco Bay Area her home for 30+ years and lives and plays tennis in Marin County. She is still raising and being raised by her beloved millennial twins Teotli and Gina.

Shaking Earth
Joy Ng

In the thick of July summer heat in 1989, Yue Ming was eight months pregnant with her second child, while raising her 6-year old daughter and navigating U.S immigration. By this time, Yue Ming became a naturalized citizen and managed to petition her parents' immigration to the U.S from China with minimal English skills. She arrived in San Francisco in 1981, at 21 with her new husband. At first, she wept every night, missing her siblings and her parents and thinking of home, a farm oceans away in a small village in Toisan. She could not speak a word of English, nor could she read the street signs. She memorized walking routes and bus routes along Geary Boulevard, counting the number of blocks, and memorizing buildings and landmarks. Over the years, she navigated her own learning with a small pocket-sized Chinese-English dictionary that was covered in matte red plastic, and took notes of words that she could not pronounce or understand. She had her first daughter, Yola, in 1983, and by summer of 1989, she was ready to burst with a second daughter on the way.

Yue Ming successfully facilitated her parents' journey from Toisan to Guangzhou to Hong Kong. They finally arrived at SFO on August 9, only ten days before her second daughter was born. Without much of a maternity leave, her parents' arrival meant that her newborn would be in the full-time care of grandparents while she worked as a seamstress during the day. They all lived together in the steep hills of the Outer Mission, where Yue Ming and her husband rented an in-law studio behind the garage of a two-story home.

Two months after the birth, the San Francisco earthquake of 1989 struck in October, decimating the Bay Area to piles of rubble. Yue Ming was working in a basement sweatshop around the corner of the site of the old International Hotel in Manilatown. When the quake struck, the old ceiling of the basement began to crack, crumbling into pieces, crashing down in chunks of old clay and clouds of dust. Sparks flew from electric sockets. Piles of unfinished coats and shirts slid down from tabletops, and chairs skidded along the shaking ground. Hanging lights flickered and swung violently overhead before giving into a complete blackout.

Terrified, Yue Ming took cover under a stairwell as the other seamstresses quickly scrambled out of the basement. When she peeked out from under the stairs, everyone was gone. Crouching in the dark, she came to realize her surroundings and her thoughts immediately jumped to her children. *Is the baby okay? Where is Yola?* She felt her way through the darkness, hands moving over piles of dust and debris for a phone. Yue Ming's mother was watching her two-month old newborn at home and little Yola should be at her mother-in-law's flat in the Tenderloin. Yue Ming picked up the phone and met a dead line. No dial tone. In disbelief, she hung up the receiver and tried again.

With landlines down, she headed out on foot, flying through the chaos that befell the streets of San Francisco. Cars stopped on the road, honking, unable to move. Yue Ming ran from the edges of Chinatown to the Tenderloin. She ran past the Chinese elderly nervously shuffling in and out of the Chinatown parks. She ran through a startled crowd of shoppers that spilled out of Macy's into Union Square. She ran down Geary Boulevard, racing past the Curran Theatre. She ran up the narrow, twisting stairs of the five-story Taylor Street apartment building. Bursting through the front door, she found Yola, safe and sound with her paternal grandparents.

Barely catching her breath, Yue Ming picked up her mother-in-law's cherry red rotary telephone. No dial tone. Forced to wait hours before she could see her mother and newborn, Yue Ming shuffled towards Union Square with Yola and her in-laws, where they were picked up by her husband, quickly heading home in their white 1987 Toyota Camry. When Yue Ming finally returned to their studio behind the garage, she was greeted by her newborn, asleep in the arms of her anxious mother. Her mother recounted the events. Initially, she been unaware of the earthquake. She'd been feeding the baby when the walls began to shake. "Ai-ya! I thought the upstairs people were just vacuuming!" her mother exclaimed. "But then the vases shook and flew off the wall. Absolutely shattered."

*   *

Three generations of women, from infant to elder, shaken by the earth; standing still in a shaking, changing, and chaotic world could topple you like a vase on the shelf. Now in her 50s, Yue Ming tells this earthquake story with enthused animation, dressed in a long powder-blue nightgown, balling her fists and swinging her elbows to pantomime running through San Francisco streets. As she recalls memories from her 20s, I sit across from her, at a gray marbled counter in her new kitchen, in a house in the quiet suburbs of San Diego—far away from the Chinatown basement sweatshop, far away from the Taylor Street apartment, both of us very far away from the studio behind the garage.

Joy Ng is a San Francisco born-and-raised, second-generation Chinese American community worker and writer. Joy currently works at a non-profit agency in downtown San Francisco, providing social services to seniors and adults with disabilities. This piece was posted at joyngsf.wordpress.com on Nov. 9, 2017 part of *High Tides,* a series of non-fiction short stories.

Nyeen Nyeen Has the Last Word
April Yee

As a child I loved being dropped off at at my grandmother Nyeen Nyeen's house on weekday mornings, with the sun shining brightly on the moss green carpets. The smell of toasting bread, butter, and syrup streamed out of the warm kitchen and *Sesame Street* called from the TV. "Sunny day, chasing the clouds away…" For a preschooler, these were all the comforts I needed.

The atmosphere that Nyeen Nyeen and Yeh Yeh, my paternal grandparents, created for my siblings and me was a respite from the rest of the world. At their house, we were carefree and catered to, with our sofa-pillow forts, a backyard filled with insects to investigate and capture, and all the TV and snacks we wanted. I can only remember one time when Nyeen Nyeen got so angry with me that she threatened to hit me with her wood-spined feather duster. I had drawn all over the hallway walls with a pencil and only escaped the feather duster by slipping under her bed and hiding where she couldn't reach me.

But her life was more than childcare. Nyeen Nyeen had endured a harsh childhood, and a tough immigrant's life. She survived—indeed thrived—through strength, strong will, and determination. Everyone in my family inherited her survival skills because she provided such a steadfast example throughout our lives. Nyeen Nyeen became a binding force for our family.

She was born Bowe Kane Gee in 1919 in Toisan, China, in the villages of the Guangdong Province. She obtained a 6th-grade education, which was common for girls at that time. However, she was fond of studying on her own. Throughout the years, she read Chinese classics and memorized Chinese poems that she was still able to recite into her 90s. She lived through the 1920s, '30s and '40s, when war and famine spread across China. Because she experienced lack, uncertainty, and death, she hated to see anything wasted. We had to clean our plates at every meal—eat every grain of rice.

She married Kwok Poy Yee at the age of 16 in 1935, but was separated from him for over ten years during World War II while he was in the U.S. Navy. He was able to bring her to the United States in 1947 as a war bride, and they settled in San Francisco's Chinatown. Nyeen Nyeen had to adjust quickly to both a new city and to motherhood. She gave birth to daughters in consecutive years in 1947, 1948, and 1949, and to a son in 1952.

Lack of money and resources were issues for a new immigrant family that grew so quickly. During her Chinatown years, she mustered her strong will and determination to build survival strategies. She converted to Christianity out of gratitude to earlier arrivals who were slightly more established in

Chinatown. These women saw Nyeen Nyeen's struggle and reached out to help with what little they had. Converting to their new religion was her way of repaying their kindness. Her strong will and determination also sparked an entrepreneurial spirit. She worked as a seamstress and took English classes. Then she encouraged her husband to purchase businesses, which she ran: a laundromat, then a grocery store, and eventually a sewing factory, all within a 20-year period. Her husband, who worked at the Navy Shipyard since 1951, helped with the businesses at the end of his workday. They both put in long hours, and their kids helped out after school when they were old enough. Because of their collective efforts, they never struggled to put food on the table after the early years.

By the time I was born in 1980, Nyeen Nyeen had retired and Yeh Yeh would retire soon after. They cared for me and my siblings while my parents both worked full-time. At that time, Nyeen Nyeen's hair was still almost all black with short curls. She had a robust figure with a solid bone structure, not fragile and small. I was always able to run to her and grab a strong hand, sit on a generous lap, or be folded into a bosomy embrace.

Nyeen Nyeen taught me how to write some Chinese characters, and I can understand a good amount of conversational Cantonese and Toisanese (our village dialect) from hearing her speak. And speak she did, quite often and loudly, telling stories, singing church songs, and talking about God. When she converted, she took on the role of "good Christian" like another job. She wanted everyone to convert and go to church, but her self-righteous tactics only pushed family members further away from organized religion. When I was small, she sang songs about God in her high falsetto. She talked to me about how good He was while I sat on her lap having my hair woven into a fishtail braid. She pulled hard, using a comb that felt sharp on my soft scalp, and applying baby oil to secure any stray strands.

As I got older, I saw that her interactions with my family members could be quite judgmental and critical. She let others know exactly what she thought and felt, often to her own detriment. She pushed her own children until they exploded in anger, yelling back in order to defend themselves or prove her wrong. Why, they asked themselves silently, had they been given a mother who constantly tried their patience, complained, attacked their character, and questioned their decisions?

If Nyeen Nyeen was stressed out or overly worried about something, she imposed the burden onto others, phoning my father or one of her other children and immediately unloading her concerns without pause, for minutes at a time. She only hung up when she was done speaking and her burden felt reduced.

The listener stayed on the line out of respect, feeling bludgeoned and defeated, reluctant to experience it again, yet knowing a recurrence was inevitable.

Once, after Friday night dinner at her house, a shouting match began between Nyeen Nyeen and my father. Though not uncommon, this one reached a level of emotional violence that frightened me. I was nine years old, watching TV and trying to ignore the angry voices. My mother stayed out of it; she never got in the middle of their arguments. Finally my father stormed out of the kitchen and down the stairs. Then I heard Nyeen Nyeen crying. This was different from other times. I peered into the kitchen to see her at the table, her face in her hands as she sobbed. It was the first time I'd seen her vulnerability. Her hurt seeped into me. I went to her and put my arm around her shoulders to comfort her. She sobbed in Toisanese, "You're the only one that cares about me. Everyone else just yells at me." I felt like her protector and her only hope—it was a burden that I was willing to carry. I even felt a little indignant at my father, blaming him for unfairly causing her pain. Thinking back, I'm sure both of them were unfair to each other. Most likely Nyeen Nyeen even started it all, but none of that entered my head at the time.

Everyone who has known and loved Nyeen Nyeen has been greatly irritated, hurt, and frustrated at some point by her demands or criticisms. Yet they returned to her out of respect or obligation—some sense that they owed her a debt. They loved this woman who made it so difficult for them to do so. She battered people with her need to take care of others in the way she felt was correct. She inundated them with her opinions, her values, and her sense of what was right and wrong.

Her family had to stand their ground with her, stand up to her crushing, stubborn, accusing ways. Was nothing good enough for this woman? Interacting with her built personal strength, growth, determination, and in the long-term, patience. Somehow, forgiveness, or a willingness to look past a fight and try to understand her perspective made way for reconciliation—or simple resignation. It wasn't worth it to argue with her. Later in our lives, my relatives began to realize that Nyeen Nyeen's behavior arose from love and good intentions, and that learning to be patient with Nyeen Nyeen taught them patience with life.

As I got older, I too felt conflicting feelings about her. I always looked forward to seeing her and remembered her with adoration and respect. But when I was with her, her critical remarks immediately grated on me. "You're not married yet. I want to see you married before I die. You know I don't have many more years left on Earth." Sometimes she said that I was too fat—while piling my plate with food. The next time, she'd say I was too skinny and piled my plate with food. My annoyance made me distance myself. Seeing this, my father reminded me that Nyeen Nyeen showed her love through food. Making sure we had enough to eat was a remnant of her past experience with famine. I wanted to snap back at Dad, "You should think of that the next time she shows her love for you and you get angry!" But of course, I didn't.

As the matriarch of the family, Nyeen Nyeen could be bitter and biting, but she could be generous as well. She helped sponsor relatives from China to the U.S. several times in her life and provided support while they adjusted to being here. And in her later years when she had enough abundance to do so, she shared her generosity by treating family and friends to meals at restaurants, always over-ordering food so that we could all take home leftovers.

Later in life, she dealt with major health crises, and the losses of her husband, her most supportive daughter, and many friends. I watched her repose at our family gatherings, dressed like many Chinese women of her generation in a polyester patterned blouse, a purple knit vest with gold buttons down the front, and navy-blue crepe pants. She sat silent in an armchair observing everyone around her chattering in English. I couldn't tell if she felt lonely and left out or content and happy. Did she feel defeated by old age, or was she gratified to be surrounded by her little kingdom—family members happy, full, and present. These were the people she helped raise, the ones with her blood running through their veins, along with the ones she invited into her family. Her little kingdom.

Whenever I had the chance to see Nyeen Nyeen in her last years, her face lit up with what seemed to be joy and pride. She greeted me with her signature laugh and a loud "Hi, hon-ney!" I loved feeling like I was five years old again, running into her strong arms for a bosomy embrace.

At her funeral service in December 2013, a priest read her eulogy and praised her strong Christian values. Then he introduced a small surprise in the program, an older Chinese gentleman who was a congregation member from Nyeen Nyeen's church. He read a list of our names, followed by Nyeen Nyeen's last words to us, urging us to convert to Christianity so that our souls could be saved and we could reunite with her in Heaven. I gasped in surprise, feeling incredulous at Nyeen Nyeen's last attempt to push her influence on us, even as she lay still and cold in her shiny, plush coffin. Then pride and recognition flooded me and I laughed out loud—Nyeen Nyeen had the last word after all! How right it was, how like her, to do something like this.

Nyeen Nyeen was part of my life for so long—she was my last living grandparent, living until she was 94 and I was 33. I miss her presence and hearing her voice speak in Toisanese. I miss the matriarch of our family, the one who imprinted herself on us, the one with the long memory of those she loved, the one who had the largest and most trying presence of us all, the one whose hurts and fears and weaknesses died with her, yet whose strength, will, and determination live on in us. And I feel her blood flowing through me when life metes out its harsh lessons and I have no choice but to move forward, as she would have done. Hers was a soul that I needed to know in my life, that I am lucky to have been nurtured by, in order to grow and proceed—to hone my survival skills—through this life in which she helped pave the way. I will never know another woman like her.

April Yee is a San Francisco native, having attended Rooftop Elementary School, Herbert Hoover Middle School, and Lowell High School before graduating from UC Santa Cruz. She lived in New York City for three years in her early 30s. In 2015, she developed endocarditis without knowing until it was almost too late. She underwent emergency cardiothoracic surgery, which saved her life and uprooted her from New York City. Being back in San Francisco, April enjoys reading, writing, spending time with people in her life, and daily practices around healing.

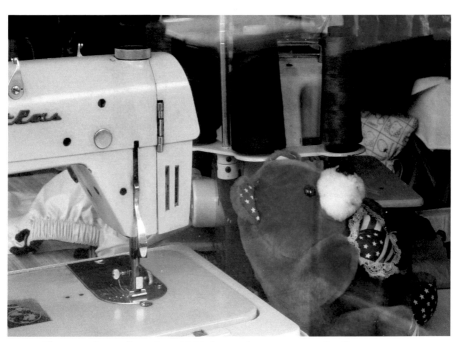

Clement Street laundry, 2008 (proprietors now retired). Shizue Seigel.

I don't know you but I love you
Tina Kashiwagi

My mother's mother was a country girl.
When she found out that she was to be in an arranged marriage,
She ran away to the big city—
Ha Noi.

She had no education, which led her to work a job as a taxi dancer
at a local dance hall.
That's where she met my grandfather.
She had eight children.
She never went outside before 4 pm because that's when
the sun was at its brightest
And she wanted to stay as light as possible.
Her breakfast every morning was a glass of orange juice.

She passed away on February 1, 1971.
She was 44 years old.
I never had the chance to meet her because she died so young.

As I get older, the more I find myself thinking about her.
How difficult her life was, being under the circumstances she was in
How she lived through the harsh economy of VietNam during the time.

I have so much to thank her for—

The least that I can do is to tell her story and let her name be said.

Her name was Tống Thị Hiều.

I never knew her personally
but I love her so much

For she is also my ancestor
She lives through me and guides me every day.

Tina Michiko Kashiwagi is a femme Japanese & Vietnamese interdisciplinary artist residing in Berkeley, California. Kashiwagi's creative process usually involves a lot of experimentation and "play." Her work often tells personal stories such as her cultural heritage and struggles with mental illness. Kashiwagi aims to create dream-like environments that induce viewers to feel a sense of nostalgia. Recently she has been most interested in exploring the realm of performance art. Kashiwagi received her BFA in Art Education at San Francisco State University and contributes to the visual direction of Oakland art collective, Macro Waves. Photo courtesy of Tina Kashiwagi.

All About My Mother
Jennifer Nguyen

My mother was college-aged when she fled Vietnam in 1978. She was never able to get a formal education, but she is the smartest person I know—possessing an infectious wonder when it comes to learning. The list of things she has managed to teach herself is impressive: guitar, English, installing hardwood floors, navigating a new country, making weird handcrafted fruit baskets with watermelons, and raising two American daughters in Houston, Texas. The list is infinite because she is constantly learning. When I returned home during a recent Christmas holiday, my mother had taught herself how to route the basic functions of our house through her smart phone—any of my attempts to turn up the heat was immediately vetoed by my mother with a push of her iPhone.

Along with being the smartest person I know, my mother is also the strongest woman I know. The favorite mother-moment ingrained in my memory was witnessing her negotiate the price of my first car. I remember her intentionally choosing a young, Vietnamese salesperson who exhibited a self-assured swagger. I can hear her asking inane questions about the car ("Oh, the windows roll down automatically?") as a part of her bait-and-switch strategy. I can still recall the walk down that sterile dealership hallway, knowing I was about to witness the equivalent of a spider roping in and feasting on a frantic ant imprisoned in its web.

She sat down in the nondescript office, continued a few pleasantries in Vietnamese, drank a glass of water. When the salesman nudged the conversation towards the car, she named her price in English and then proceeded to sit there like a Buddhist monk, or a rock, or any object exhibiting disinterested inertia. Counter offers were rebuffed, always in English, by threats to walk—this salesman was unaware that my mother and I had spent months creating a full inventory of cars and their features within a 40-mile circumference of our house. After all these years, I vividly remember the color of his shirt—a maroon button down, its hue becoming deeper with each drop of pit sweat until he finally relented at her price. It was his first sale. She was happy for him.

This was the way she approached most things in life—methodically, strategically, never waiting for a call because the most worthwhile things in life would call her.

I give this context so that we can step to 2016, a few days before the presidential election. I'm parked in my San Francisco driveway, on the phone with my mother in Houston. I'm exhausted from the day, but we're engaged in a confusingly tense conversation. She's revealed that she won't be voting for

Hillary Clinton, who she fully supported in 2008. I'm trying to process and decipher the strands of conversation. Is this about healthcare, or the economy, or about a need for change? I'm still the researcher and she's still the negotiator, but we're no longer working together.

"They're both bad candidates, but I've never liked my female bosses," she says to me. "I just don't think women make good leaders or presidents."

I couldn't summon up much to say after that statement, but I wish I could have said, "Mom, do you even know who you are?"

* *

For the better part of two decades, my mother had applied her patient, methodical, and strategic approach to her career. She steadily rose from stripping fiber optics cables on an assembly line to being the line's leader, which led to an opportunity to do clerical work for the line, which morphed into an office manager position. If the rise was slow, the fall was sudden and at the whims of Texas' boom-or-bust economy. In 2016, as the oil prices dipped, she was without a job—her livelihood, her community, and her healthcare—for the first time in nearly 20 years.

After the election, my near daily conversations with my mother took on a monotonous rhythm—my work, her upcoming marathon in Berlin, and insignificant, daily occurrences that helped us avoid speaking about politics.

When we finally broached the topic of politics, I found myself again in my San Francisco driveway, conversing with her from thousands of miles away. This time, I had readied an arsenal of facts ranging from cost effectiveness to the moral argument for universal healthcare. I had esoteric, intellectual bullet points to pit against the substantial, difficult changes she had just experienced in her life.

She listened with her characteristic calm, then replied, "I used to think like you, believe me. I don't like to be anti-anything, but when you have nothing, it's hard. I can't tell you that I know everything, but I just want to tell you how I feel."

At that moment, I couldn't figure out how to out-fact feeling. It wasn't enough to remind her who she was.

Posted at http://jennifervinguyen.com on April 4, 2017.

Jennifer Nguyen. I am a San Francisco based Vietnamese American writer and educator. I was born and raised in Houston, Texas. You can read more of my work at www.jennifervinguyen.com.

About *Hunting Blackbirds*
Shizue Seigel

George and Kazue Yamasaki, my relatives by marriage, were born around 1910 to Japanese immigrants living in Santa Clara County. George was bright and ambitious, but after marrying and starting a family, he quit college for farm work. His wages didn't go far during the Depression, so Kazue foraged for wild mushrooms and mustard greens to supplement the family diet.

After Pearl Harbor, they and their four children were incarcerated in the horse stables of the Santa Anita Racetrack in Los Angeles before being shipped off to the Heart Mountain concentration camp in Wyoming. In the summer of 1944, George and other incarcerees were permitted to leave camp to harvest sugar beets in nearby Cowley, Wyoming. As the workers stooped in the field, George was shot by a .22 caliber bullet that passed through several internal organs and lodged near his spine. The shooter, a local rancher's son, claimed it was an accident. He was "hunting blackbirds," he said; the jury acquitted him.

George never recovered his health. When the family returned to San Jose, they were so destitute that a neighbor offered a corner of his barn to house them. George"s family lovingly cared for him through three decades of poor health. I never met him, but his wife and daughter were quiet beacons of hope who drew upon a deep Buddhist faith to sustain them.

The matriarchs on both sides of my family, my grandmas, aunties, and mom, relied on that same faith—a deeply felt sense of shinjin, or true faith, that helped them cope with frustration and loss. Theirs was no rarified practice of sitting in secluded meditation; they walked the eightfold path every moment of their lives. They forgave human fallibilies with the understanding that no one was perfect, but they cultivated gratitude, not bitterness or fear. Instead of hoarding or lusting for more, they appreciated what little they had and shared it willingly. —That didn't mean they didn't save and re-use every paper or plastic bag that came their way, or crochet cut-up beer cans into hats that only the most dutiful recipients would put on their heads.

But in the most pure-hearted way, their faith was based on the Jodo Shinshu Buddhism developed by Shinran Shonin in 13th-century Japan. Shinran was introduced to the transitory nature of life by losing both his parents at an early age. In the poem he wrote when he entered a monastery at age eight, Shinran mused, "Like the cherry blossom, the heart planning on tomorrow is ephemeral indeed—what sudden storm may not arise in the middle of the night?" My relatives learned to weather storms by letting go of expectations and finding joy in what was in front of them.

6

targeted

Shizue Seigel, *Hunting Blackbirds*, photo collage, 24 x 24 in., 2010.

What Grows in Our Garden
Sandra Bass

Native Bay Area black folks like myself are all too familiar with a form of NIMBYism that lives in progressive places. This strand of parochialism is less about the ills of urban development (although that certainly exists), than the dogged belief that this region has somehow escaped the litany of "isms' that plague the rest of the country. Over the years friends, colleagues, and even random strangers have earnestly assured me that prejudice and discrimination do not exist in _____, fill in the city or the organization or the industry; that my experiences of bias, unequal treatment, or disrespect were isolated events or misunderstandings—on my part; and that we (really, me) were fortunate to live in a place that embraced difference and where moving up in life came to those who had earned it. Racism? Not here. Not in our backyard. And then the 2016 Presidential race with its virulent celebration of rage took us all down the rabbit hole into this country's foundational hatreds and landed squarely in the Bay Area.

Evidence that Bay Area folks are not in fact living in a post-racial paradise came to light during the presidential campaign when Trump made a stop in San Jose. His visit incited a street melee between supporters and opponents the likes of which this native San Josean can't recall seeing in my lifetime. Then, within weeks of 45 ascending to the presidency, student Republicans at UC Berkeley decided to test the University's commitment to free speech by inviting a host of hard-right pundits to speak on campus.

My relationship with the campus reaches back over 20 years. As a graduate student, protest was as much a part of my campus life as foraging for cheap eats and all-night grading sessions. Recently, as part of the administration, I volunteered to observe protest actions planned for the Milo Yiannopolis speaking engagement. Milo, a self-proclaimed troll, had spent much of the past year belittling marginalized people on college campuses across the country before bringing his show to Berkeley. On the evening that Milo was scheduled to speak, a small group of provocateurs thought to be left-wing anarchists and known as the Black Bloc launched an attack against the police and against campus property. Less than 10 minutes after their arrival, the event was cancelled, and we observers were sent home.

Walking to my car, I came across a group of large white men making their way up to Sproul Plaza, the campus's public square. Three men broke away from the current of the crowd and lunged towards me with unexpected speed. A wall of rosy, fleshy faces wearing down vests, blue jeans, and MAGA caps backed me up against the side of a building, chanting "Build the Wall! Build the Wall! Build the Wall!" In that moment, all I could see was their faces, their eyes, their curling, sputtering lips animated with mirthful rage. Within seconds, it was over, and they disappeared back into the roiling mass.

So here is what's true: Despite the extensive media coverage, the motley mix of white supremacists, neo-Nazis, Proud Boys, and Trump supporters in Berkeley, as well as at extremist rallies around the country, were vastly outnumbered by opposing protesters at every turn. And while these events were not always free of violence, the majority of those protesting were animated but peaceful.

What is also true: Many of the right extremists were homegrown Californians. White nationalism is on the rise throughout the state, and hate crimes, just one measure of the growth of this movement, were up nearly 15% in 2016 in California's largest cities. Two Berkeley residents lost their jobs after they were identified as participants at white supremacist rallies on the East Coast. Nathan Damigo, founder of the white nationalist group Identity Evropa, spent his childhood in my hometown of San Jose. And while the line between overt racial hate and supporting Trump is not always straight or consistent, it was sobering to learn that over 20% of San Joseans voted for him—a truth that hit close to home when several of my high-school friends revealed their support for his candidacy on Facebook and then unfriended me with a quickness when I questioned some of their more incendiary posts. Racism wasn't just in my backyard, it was sitting on my front porch smiling and sipping tea, earnestly telling me its existence was a just matter of my misunderstanding.

In this beautiful place with its beautiful people, a strange and bitter crop has found fertile ground and is unfurling its twisted leaves under the welcoming heat emanating from the highest office in the land. Yet despite this surge of extremism, despite my own near miss with empowered white rage, my hope has not waned. What looks like new growth is more likely the last desperate attempts of an old and dying order to take root and find relevancy. And besides, authentic hope is not a belief in a preordained happy ending or an untempered attitude of optimism, but a levelheaded practice that grows in strength as we rise up together to right wrongs and cultivate new realities.

I see this in my work every day with Cal students. Mind you, at times their idealistic admonishments and youthful impatience challenge the best of us. But planted in the hearts of these students are the possibilities for co-creating a society centered on radical inclusiveness, systemic transformation, communal responsibility for our planetary home, and transitioning from a country dominated by self-interested survivalists and fictive corporate persons to one held in the tender care of our collective souls.

And so we are faced with a choice, not just in this moment but for our lifetimes, and for many lives and lifetimes beyond our own. Will we continue to deny or give sustenance to old yet persistent injustices or will we act to ensure that what grows in our garden is what we love? Now is the time to unleash our collective imaginations to till the soil, nourish the seeds of change with our aspirations, and bolster fledgling shoots promising new possibilities with ageless wisdoms, compassion, and courage. Not because we're certain that our labors will bear a harvest, but because we know that it is only through daily acts of loving and serving with and for each other that we live into our boundless, sacred humanity. Constant gardeners we must be, ever preparing the earth for full and abundant life.

Sandra Bass, PhD, promotes transformative social change as assistant dean and director of UC Berkeley's Public Service Center. She served for six years as board chair of the Ella Baker Center for Human Rights and ten years as program officer at David and Lucile Packard Foundation, where she managed an $8 million grants portfolio for education, women's leadership, and reproductive health programs in Sub-Saharan Africa. She holds a BA from San Jose State University and an MA and PhD from UC Berkeley, both in political science. Born and raised in San Jose, she now resides in San Francisco, where she can be still stereotyped as homeless by those who see only her skin color.

Survivor—A Love Poem
Tiny

Once upon a time there was a daughter of a mama with a broken heart
who was a daughter of a mama with a broken heart
who was a daughter of a daughter with only a piece of a heart.

These mamas and daughters held their broken hearts in their hands,
cut in so many places they almost couldn't be held—
slipping thru their broken fingers like sand or water or blood—

They taught each other cracked dreams of how not to be broken—
they walked thru life and mama-hood with nothing but blood drips and
unclear desires for something that didn't hurt.

They fell into men and each other like it would end the break-endings
and the break-ups
ripping new tears into their chest.
Their black and blue eyes would look out from black and blue lives.

Bruises felt like hope.
Slaps and cracked bones soothed the ache of alone.
Violence was an ointment to rub on the bleeding scabs of loss.

They re-wrote horror stores as love stories—writing want into every torn page.

One of the daughters thrown out of the love-car and left to die on the side of
the love-road
burning from the ache
holding onto a shard of maybes with one broken fingernail
erased with the terror of alone
precipice holding
woke up one day
realizing something that she wanted to be love
so bad that she had made it love—
realizing that everything that loved her was already around her and it didn't
taste like blood or pain or loss
realizing that maybe
she wasn't
completely
broken
at all.

The Tenderloin Take

Tiny

The TL—where there used to be
    Brown & Black Faces
In every one of these beautiful places

Now there are barely traces
after the sharp Knife of Displacement
cuts us out of all those Tenderloin
spaces

Gentrification has hit
Where Art isn't any SAFER
Where Snow Storms are born
Removing & Displacing
Poor peoples of ALL races

The Tenderloin
Last Poor People Frontier
But NEVER fear
The kkkolonizers are HERE

Take Long looks
Our Herstories aren't in the
kkkolonizer His-STORY books

Our stories, Our Lives
are Breathing, Screaming, Crying,
Get Me Out Of Here …

This ain't an exhibit
Or Art installation
No Fetishized Grant Dance HERE

Our evictions, Our Addictions
And Then..
Mysterious Fires Appear

A few of us remain
Holding on by a thread
Screaming out our Forgotten Names

Until the thread breaks
and the ScamLords
and Devil-opers
Get out their Rakes

Building condos, hospitals and
    cafes with all the money our
    broken bodies
can make

Tiny (aka Lisa Gray-Garcia) has innovated several revolutionary media, arts and education programs for youth, adults and elders including the first welfare-to-work journalism program in the U.S. for poor mothers transitioning off of welfare, Poor News Network—an online magazine and monthly radio show on KPFA, and several cultural projects such as the Po' Poets Project, Youth in Media, welfareQUEENs, and many more. She is also a prolific writer who has authored over a hundred articles on issues ranging from poor women and families, interdependence, and the cult of individualism to gentrification, homelessness, police brutality, incarceration, art, and global and local poverty.

philanthro-pimps
Tiny

Had a dream—
not to save the world
but to save other unhoused disabled mamaz & little girls

U see i was that baby wit my mama
holding that sign
the one you turned away from
pretending i wasn't alive

Grew up wit mama—
her and me almost made it thru the poverty/racism/houselessness drama
hustled for food—
never had the rent

Until mama sed chase that dream—
write a grant—take a chance
u got skills Tiny
U can do the grant dance

U see—we the philathro-pimps
u a sexy young thing with at least one grant circle we can
exploit
just come and sniff a little of this grant guidelines oil…

You can do whatever you want
(Deep Star Wars voice) BUT ALWAYS DO WHAT WE SAY

SO happy
created a job for my uncle, houseless friends and my mommy

Wow—self-determination
liberation words, and dreams
helping each other

And then—
what? you ain't doing what we say & reporting on each other

Keep those feet up—the philanthro-pimps say
that grant might run out
cuz, well u ain't sexy anymore—anyway

The year that bad became good
Shizue Seigel

1987 turns up like a bad penny,
growing ever more tarnished with every return.

Each noon in the deep dark canyons of finance
the sidewalk people await handouts
from workers scrambling for quiche and latte
and maybe some dry cleaning on their mid-day break.

One woman is there, yet not there.
She folds her legs in a yoga pose
soles upturned toward the sky,
straight back refusing support
from the polished granite behind her,
eyes closed in determined repose
so she doesn't have to see
the gum-spotted pavement
her scant scattering of coins
curious looks of strangers.

Beside her, a talisman of better times,
a briefcase—oiled leather with chipped initials.
Every day she sits like an open sore,
begging us to guess a story she cannot bear to tell.
As days blur into weeks and months
her trenchcoat grows dingy,
the velvet ribbon in her grey hair droops,
her face grows gaunt. And one day she is gone.

But Annie on the next corner hangs in there.
though her husband died of AIDS
and SSI only covers half the month's rent,
Annie's smile moves the cops to nod back
and her landlord stores her bags
when she has to sleep on the street.
Annie's gums are so loose
she pulls out teeth with her fingers,
but Annie knows how to capture sun
and share it with anyone who says hello.

Entering the cage that will shoot me
up to my cubicle on the 24th floor
the elevator darkens when the CEO strides in.
His wrestler's shoulders strain the seams of his Italian suit;
his five-o'clock glower pins us
against the stainless steel paneling.
As we rise noiselessly higher, we hardly know
we're moving 'til we're nearing a stop.

One day, when the CEO is away,
His assistant confides she needs an aspirin.
Her boss made her take his mistress
for an abortion that morning,
then spend her lunch hour at Tiffany's
choosing a diamond bracelet for his wife.

Shizue Seigel

Villanelle on Los Angeles 1992
Jennifer Hasegawa

She was half his size, but her arm was light years long.
He was straight-backed and strode in never-been-wet boat shoes.
How his soft honey hair jerked when Schoolgirl knocked him down.

Dookie braids escaped gravity on her head made strong
by the verdict of twelve strangers. No change of venue
as her fist to his face broadcast the news light years long.

Our heads bobbed against hazy bus windows all along
the route from Slauson to downtown, but as her fist flew
at McClintock, we all knew that Schoolgirl knocked him down.

The driver whistled low and switched his radio on
as the motor moaned to damns signaling corner coups
that would reveal a city, burn down blocks light years long.

Shopping carts rattled, careened unboxed TVs sidelong.
Out store doors flattened shoeboxes bloomed their grey pulp hues
while men on roofs held rifles 'cause Schoolgirl knocked him down.

Hair trigger, DUI, orange juice, and truncheon wrong
into law of brick and fire. Oh pyriscence, you cruise,
burn through resins, put a spit-shine on fear light years long.
Kam sam ni da. How you like us now? Schoolgirl knocked him down.

Jennifer Hasegawa is a poet and information architect. She grew up in Hilo HI and has lived in the San Francisco Bay Area for 25 years. Her poetry and short stories have appeared in Tule Review, Standing Strong! Fillmore & Japantown: An Anthology, and the San Francisco Bay Guardian. Her poetry manuscript, La Chica's Field Guide to Banzai Living, was awarded the San Francisco Foundation's Joseph Henry Jackson literary award in 2014. She is currently engaged in the study of several paranormal phenomena, including alien encounters, Marian apparitions, Sinéad O'Connor, and Bitcoin.

Artist Statement. Historically, my work has steered clear of the political, focusing instead on the personal. In these challenging times, my voice as a poet can no longer have that luxury as humanity continues to inch toward a tipping point into extinction. And I don't even mean physical extinction. I mean the extinction of humane connections, empathy, truth, and history. These are the muscles that help keep the intangible alive. I submit for your consideration a few poems that I hope can help fend off an endangered status for humanity.

O Beautiful, Ain't
After Katharine Lee Bates and Nina Simone
Jennifer Hasegawa

O beautiful, for spacious skies
For amber waves of grain
For purple mountain majesties

Ain't got no home, ain't got no shoes

O beautiful, for pilgrim feet
For chains in migration
For all the nasty women

Ain't got no money, ain't got no class

O beautiful, for heroes proved
For deals and all time highs
For new jobs and stock market buys

Ain't got nowhere, ain't got no job

O beautiful, for patriot dream
For loser terrorists
For internet recruitment ploys

Ain't got no father, ain't got no
mother

O beautiful, for halcyon skies
For hot Friday nights and
For the Great State of Alabama

Ain't got no money, no place to stay

O beautiful, for pilgrims feet
For American hands
For iron aluminum steel

Ain't got no friends, ain't got no
schooling

O beautiful, for glory-tale
For nuclear rogue states
For little success and great threats

Ain't got no children, ain't got no
sisters

O beautiful, for patriot dream
For shadow heroes held
For having no choice but to destroy

Ain't got no earth, ain't got no
faith

O beautiful, for spacious skies
For long gas lines forming
For the Rocket Man and too bad!

Ain't got no touch, ain't got no god

O beautiful, for pilgrim feet
For the walls and fences
For deplorables who returned

Ain't got no love

O beautiful, for heroes proved
For a meeting with Moon
For the privilege of staying tuned

Ain't got no wine, no cigarettes

O beautiful, for patriot dream
For prototyping walls
For consumer confidence

Ain't got no clothes, no country

O beautiful, for halcyon skies
For cutting the red tape
For being caught red handed

Ain't got no god

O beautiful, for pilgrim feet
For moving the capital
For happy birthday CIA

I said I ain't got no clothes

O beautiful, for glory-tale
For the most trusted name
For #journalismisdead

Ain't got long to live

O beautiful, for patriot dream
For ferocious anger
For making American great again

And I ain't got no love

But what have I got?

That nobody's gonna take away.

Got life. Oh beautiful. I got my life.

Kamikazes à Paris
Jennifer Hasegawa

Tunisian sisters
lived in a quaint flat downtown
then, they moved into

a handful of dust. Have you
been to Paris? What was it like?
*

Ghosts sell stale bread in
the market. It will be a
while until even

the Mother of Satan shows
her gleaming face there again.
*

The girl knew it was
time to go, but kept dancing
toward a home always

just another mile away.
Liberty legs took her there.
*

If they were allowed
to carry, it would have been
a much, much different

situation. Carry it
now: baby, book, water, head.
*

They found a finger.
They found the brother and showed
it to him and asked

Did you loosen it, sever
it from the body now too

small and multitudinous
to be placed into a bag?
*

An explosion is
the product of entropy.
Unmasked, confident:

Choose your seeds with intention,
sow 3, 4 times, then reload.

My Cambodian Prince
Queennandi X

Boy, I never would have seen this coming, especially at the time of my life when I needed someone the most. At this difficult time I was trying to figure out how I allowed for a madman to misuse and brutally abuse myself and my young daughter and the burning question was. How was I going to escape this alive?"

On one Friday night when I had a break from the madman (also known as the rolling stone), I put the kid to sleep and put on the movie *What's Love Got to Do with It?* I'd seen the movie before, but this time when the scene came on when Tina Turner finally broke and ran from the hotel after being assaulted by Ike Turner, the powerful, Cameo-like tune of the guitar and the whole melody itself tapped into my being, and tears began to flow down my cheeks. It was like the song was telling me to run like hell, just like how Ms. Tina was running, and that's exactly what I did.

Somehow he got wise to the fact that I was gaining the courage to end this relationship and he barricaded himself and our daughter inside of my apartment armed with a razor blade and began to play this weird, satanic music while laughing in this disturbed fashion acting as if he was trying to invoke satan himself. He always expressed that "he'd rather die than go back to prison" and he was sure to harm himself and our kid if the kops were called.

I was desperate to get my daughter out of his grasp, so I sought the help of some "gangsta homies" that I can't name because I forgot their names as a result of being a "Bob Marley" fan over the years. However, these were the "no women, no children" kind of gangstas, so when I asked for them to help me get my child from this "mack-wannabe, first philli-negro to worship satan in da hood"-ass maniac, they did not hesitate to assist me.

The plan was to get this nut to open the door, so I had the homeboys lean up against the side of walls where he could not see their figures through the peephole. I pleaded with him to let me in and swore I wouldn't leave him. When he opened the door, the homeboy on the left pushed his way in, pistol ready and was like "Man, give homegirl her baby back and get the fuhk outta here!" The madman was taken by surprise because combating men wasn't his bag, only beating and pimping women.

He gave me that "What I do?" look and the homeboy on the right was like "What you want to do?" I said "I want his sick ass away from me and my daughter! I don't want him back into this building and if you see him, don't let him up!"

Real gangstas did not terrorize the community; they protected it. Any young girl could go up to the homeboys and let them know if she had any problems, and sometimes they would escort all the girls home.

Although I had finally broken free from the Maniac (I would not give him the fame to speak his name, it was "something" with champagne). He left us with nothing, so I had to go do what needed doing cuz I had a kid that needed to eat. He found me and began to stalk and harass me, but by this time I was pissed and wasn't running no more!

Then that same night on Lev and Turk Street I saw that young, dark, almond-eyed man that took me decades to find out that he was a true love. "Solo!!! Woah! Where have you been?" After many hugs, I leaned back up against the car and made the expression on my face a serious one. "Hey Sol, could I pay you to post up with me? You know, like an enforcer?" I'd known Solo since he was a young, feisty kid, and the trust from our friendly bond was still intact.

"You know I got your back, fo sho."

He kept his word far as looking out for me. The madman stopped stalking me, so the nightmare was over for now. Shortly afterwards, Solo moved in with myself and Isis, and that made me feel more safe. This was my very first apartment ever, and after leaving that abusive relationship, my domain needed a protector.

My young, Cambodian enforcer eventually became my lover. Solo felt as if the Prince should be with his Queen, not on the couch. And I gave in to his will with very little resistance. He sure nuff spoiled me rotten! I still smile to myself to this day when I flash back to when we would cook Cambodian food in our tiny kitchen, and Solo would chop up the veggies with lightning speed while I watched over what was already in the skillet.

"Baby, why we don't have a rice cooker? You know we need one!" he would lightly scold every time he looked at our small-ass pot that only made 2 cups of rice. "C'mon, Daddy, you know you could pick one out better than me!" I joked to him. He looked back at me with that bad-boy smile. "Fuck you!" and instead of getting offended, I was aroused. "Ooooh baby, you promise??" He was like "Hell yeah!" Then we both laughed.

Why Solo was able to deliver me out of the hell I was going through both physically and mentally but felt that despair was the only destiny he deserved is beyond me. I loved him and I was in love with him, and so he was with me. For us to be as close as we were and still feel that it was a weak thing to say the "L" word … It was that way of thinking that brought our true love crashing to a sad and painful halt.

170

"The Mighty Solo" as I had known him was strong, protective, funny, fierce, and quick-tempered—especially when someone would make the fool-azz mistake of believing that Solo was the "cry me a river and build me a bridge" type. On the flip side, I was the one who truly saw the "soft side" of this man. Solo never struck me nor did he ever make me feel less than a woman, but nonetheless we were young, hustlin, crazy but unified.

Our downfall was dem devil-azz drugs and the fact that we let our guards down around those whom we thought was our "truez," meaning real comrades. To this day, I think about how we had too many people in our circle that didn't care that we all were doing ourselves in, that didn't care about the sacrifice of our son Osiris—Hell, I didn't care! Every beautiful thing that Solo and I created or ever would have created was irredeemably destroyed, and at the end of the day, not too many people had a kind gesture for our downfall at all.

If I am to point fingers, it would be towards myself because that's who I blame. Solo was the King/Enforcer and I was the brains and Psychic/Queen of the crew, so I was in a position to be able to see bullshyt coming. When polluting your temple with the "Devil's Poisons," your eyes are always the first to go. I was very young and very dumb, and despite all Solo's craziness, as one would call it, he was truly the love of my life.

It hurt my heart so much to lose this man who rescued myself and my daughter Isis from brutality AND death when her own father tried to poison her. Solo showed me that us "beasts" are the ones with the most genuine, loving hearts, but yet we both acted as if the "L" word was Kryptonite when the "L" word was one word that would have saved us. Folks judge him for his flaws and dictate a doomed destiny and walk around like they never had a pimple on their azz, but let me tell you some truth about Solo, my Cambodian "Beast." He is one of the most beautiful-souled men I have ever met in my life. He is a fearless, kick-yo-azz-no-matter-who-you-are, radio-toting, sistuh-loving, thuggish-ruggin, hated-to-see-me-bugging—the John Wayne of "chewdogs" (weed laced with cocaine) and I miss him dearly.

Someone had lied and told me years ago that he was dead, so when I found out from his brother that he was still alive, something in my heart resurrected every moment, every touch, every smell, and every sound. My head began to spin as I thought back to all those "weird" dreams I've had. The dreams that someone was shouting that they needed me and where the hell was I. I had to take a drink as I thought back to the dream I had of Solo and woke damn near breathless. Later on, I took a stroll down to the "L's," the Tenderloin, and walked the very blocks we used to dominate. I saw us all, Lace, Mel, RayRay, Joe, Fat Boi, Tears, Madison, Ra, Shell, Woody—and Solo! I closed my eyes and inhaled the cologne, perfume, beer, piss, cracksmoke, shyt and dried blood and allowed myself to embrace the spirits of dem days when us "Fog City Children," we all together.

Solo and a few of those mentioned before were eventually deported and shipped away from us, their families. When Solo was deported so was my security. I felt as if I was left here to be devoured by wild-dog men who never even thought about showing me a pinch of the love that Solo did. I was just a Trophy Queen to these "fraction spineless ones." The deportation of my friends and family made me feel really depressed and alone. I feel angry at the fact that thieves of a land have the authority to say who's illegal and who's not. You would think that the thief of all the lands would be the first illegal, if there is a such thing. "The first barred because of documented destruction." I like that term better.

Criminalize and deport instead of giving the children what they need and have the right to—decent housing, healthcare, education, mental health services, cultural refugee restoration and linguistic recognition. These are the things that children like Solo and myself were denied and that would have assisted in the healing from cultural trauma and displacement from our Motherland(s). More than half of the "ruling and fooling" class would be deported from this beautiful country based upon "criminal activity." The president himself may even get deported back to hell! To be able to label us and deport with impunity is a sickening power. Myself, my Khmerikkkan, Latino, Afrikkkan, Asian and other blessed identities that are my relatives are the "Conscious Amerikkkans"—that's if you wanna waste time with labels!

This past May I started my quest to reconnect with my lost love, Solo. I went to Cambodia where Solo is in the cocoon stage of regrowth, like myself and this writing. His angel's wings are tireless; so long as he is still alive he has that blessed word and blessed hugs coming. To put it another way, the story is still being written! Peace.

Queennandi X. Born 'n' raised in the Fillmore. Daughter of Carolyn X, granddaughter of Our Lady Saint Lillie Mae Brantley, grandniece of Our Lady Saint Beverly and niece of Queens Janet Brantley and Nikki Swan, for without them, there would be no "me." Raised by the "Black Sheep" Queen in the concrete jungle of SF's OCP housing complex, Queennandi is a survivor of poverty, betrayal, brutality and death. At a very young age, she chose the pen as her weapon to defend her community, her existence and all who are suffering from oppression on Mother Earth. She is a strong voice for the voiceless—a motivational speaker, poet, author, actress and revolutionary thinker.

Thank You Note to the Dirty Old Man
Rose Berryessa

Dear Dirty Old Man,

It's been a half century since we last met. You've had a lasting effect on my life—a positive impact, I can now report. I didn't always feel this way, but I've done my "hone" work, transmuted your base metal inward, making gold bullion for me to employ again, and again, and share, yes!

On that historic day of our unfortunate yet enriching encounter, I uncovered a creative use of girl power, naive/native discernment, and an unmatched strength to safeguard a friend … such a harsh gift ….

You first approached our bevy of girls and asked us if we wanted all-day suckers. Who wouldn't want those lollypops? They really did last the day, even with frequent pulls and sucks on them. And they cost more than a Welch's sucker, which we seldom—or in secret—bought, since they were owned by the John Birch Society.

So you handed my sister a dollar and directed her to the corner store on Clement and 22nd. I wanted to accompany my big sis. I didn't want to remain with you; I sulked while straddling my tricycle. Sister said, "You stay here, I'll check this out at Stanley's." (That was our favorite nearby mom-and-pop store because it housed a better selection of penny and nickel candy.) Our neighbor Ann and I remained on the street with a couple of other kids, talking to you, hoping you'd give us money for one of those tasty suckers, too. Something in my gut whispered otherwise ….

Sister returned empty-handed. You said, "Try the store in the other direction—try Appel and Dietrich." So sister took off. Now I was frustrated with being left behind, so I started crying. "Shhhh, hush, shhh," you said, looking vaguely uncomfortable. Sis arrived back unsuccessful. You disbelieved her foraging skills, so you sent her again to the first store.

The other kids dispersed. Somehow you steered Ann and me toward the side hallway of our building, to the left of the garage, where the trash cans live. You shut the trash door behind us. I could almost taste the brown, fog-dampened redwood walls of this spot that was used to let go of what was not needed: vegetable parings mixed with decaying meat, sharp tin-can lids, and sour dairy refuse. I gulped in all these olfactory messages, and felt creepy and claustrophobic. Why were we hiding here with this old man?

I stood with my back against the door in full view of you and my friend. Ann was distressed when you grabbed hold of her and pressed your decaying manhood against her strong yet timid twelve-year-old body. She tried to pull away and you covered her mouth with one hand, as your other roving hand molded itself around her budding chest. Squirming Ann, squirmy me in my own discomfort with this nonconsensual nonsensical scene. You looked at me and mouthed "SHHHHH." I watched as your hand moved toward the top of her capri pants, now fingering the elastic.

That's when I screamed and furiously began kicking the trash-can door. Something was really askew here and it had to stop NOW! *Kick, scream, kick, scream!* I got the door unlocked, threw it open and ran out with Ann unfrozen and racing behind me. We careened upstairs where her father lived, out of breath, our lungs and hearts pounding, but with our freedom intact. Ann's dad went rushing down, waving his big revolver. I'd only seen that on *Rawhide* or in cartoons. But this was real. He wanted to protect us against YOU!! But you were gone. I dealt with you and I protected my friend more meaningfully and successfully than any gun!

I was a superheroine at age five. Heroic tendencies thrive inside me and I've expanded my repertoire to include ALL people who say NO to injustice and boundary crossing.

Peace!

Rose Berryessa grew up in San Francisco and lived there until being displaced to Berkeley. She writes, "Have kept a diary since age seven, sifting through the past, which graces my present. Historical roots spanning six generations in Califa. Former elementary health educator and current community gardener. Long time believer in applying painterly 'chiaroscuro' (light/dark) in writing. Am in Chiapas and heading to Belize for a Permaculture Design Course."

Victor Navarette
Unititled Artworks

Cuban artist Victor Navarette grew up near Santiago, Cuba. He began studying art at 15 and moved to Havana a few years later to to study sculpture and graphic arts at the prestigious Academia Nacional de Bellas Artes San Alejandro. He left school before graduation to design book covers and propaganda posters for the Castro government.

But he didn't feel free to make the art he wanted to. One of his friends received a hefty prison sentence for pasting Fidel Castro's face on a ballerina's body. Navarrete was barred from traveling to Italy for an art exhibit, and later sent to a work camp for a year on charges of "ideological diversion." In 1980, he and two fellow artists left Cuba in a small boat, landing at Key West, Florida.

He has been in the United States for more than 30 years. He worked as a photographer for Spanish-language newspapers in the Mission, and bought Radio Habana Social Club from a compatriot fifteen years ago. The cafe is crammed with quirky, surrealist sculptures that he fashions from castoffs and thrift-store finds at his studio at the Hunters Point Shipyard.

Above: Radio Habana Social Club, 2010. Shizue Seigel.

Leila Mansur, *Homage to Archile Gorky* and *Homage, Cachao,* pastel. Leila Mansur, Victor Navarette's wife, draws upon from a mixed ancestry—Iraqi and Armenian, with European American roots reaching to Susan B. Anthony and the Revolutionary War.

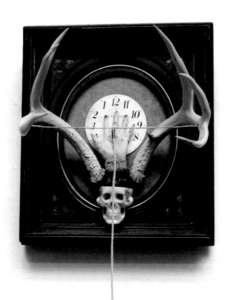

Victor
Navarette,
untitled
artworks.
All photos
of Navarette
and Mansur's
artwork
by Martin
Revolo.

Knock, Knock
Grace Morizawa

Aunty Junko said they came
6 PM December 7, 1941.
[Knock, knock,]
Two tall men in long overcoats and hats
Stood in the doorway

[Knock, knock]
Mr. Ikeya, Mr. Kaiji Ikeya?

No time to say good-by to his
Beloved wife who was taking a bath.
No time to get his toothbrush.

[Knock, knock]
[Knock, knock]
1,173 Issei picked up that day.

[Knock, knock]
[Knock, knock]

17,000 in all

[Knock, knock]

One third of the first generation men
Priests, teachers, community leaders
Imprisoned, Disappeared.

Kaiji Ikeya found to be intelligent
Well-liked, a leader, a member of the Methodist church,

Interned without family,
Interned, denied rehearings,
Interned,

never seen again by Aunty Junko.

They didn't know there were informants
Decades before, surveillance records
Secret lists. Potentially dangerous.

[Knock, knock]
Into the middle of the night

They didn't know their success meant
They were "enemy aliens."

Jerked from camp to camp,
Tuna Canyon, Missoula, Santa Fe,
Honouliuli, Ellis Island

[Knock knock knock]

Can you hear it?

[Knock, knock, knock, knock]

Can you hear it now?

[Knock, knock, knock, knock
[Knock, knock, knock, knock.]

Grace Morizawa is a Sansei, a third-generation Japanese American. Her parents met in the Heart Mountain concentration camp in Wyoming. She grew up in a Japanese American community in eastern Oregon where West Coast Japanese fled to escape incarceration. Japanese Americans from Minidoka, Heart Mountain, Tule Lake, and other American concentration camps voluntarily resettled there during the war and afterwards. Grace taught elementary school in Oakland, worked on a national school reform project, and was a principal of an elementary school in San Pablo, California. Currently she is the Education Coordinator for the National Japanese American Historical Society. She has a BA in English from Pacific University, an MA in Creative Writing from San Francisco State, and an EdD from the Leadership in Education and Equity Program at UC Berkeley.

Quietly This Time (I Don't Think So)
Yukiya Jerry Waki

Quietly
That's how they said we would go
Quietly
That's what they said they don't know
Quietly this time
I don't think so
I don't think so

Ask a Japanese American about picking sides
Ask the Issei and the Nisei about loyalty
Ask what it's like to take only what you can carry
Ask what it's like to be interned
Ask what it's like to be enclosed with barb wire
like animals
Ask what it's like to be 100th or 442nd
Ask what it meant to defend freedom, liberty, and the pursuit of happiness
abroad
And at home,
Seeing signs that read "Japs Keep Moving: This is a White Man's
Neighborhood"

Ask them again
Ask them again
Ask
them
again

Ask a Japanese American about picking sides
Ask what happened when they didn't
Ask them when they did
Ask what happened after
Ask a Japanese American about picking sides
Ask why uncle, auntie and your cousin
don't throw away a damn thing in their house
Find out what happens when you ask them
to see if you can throw something away
Ask why you don't throw anything away
You don't throw anything away
Throw
Nothing
away
Ask them again

Ask them again
Ask
them
again
Ask a Japanese American about picking sides

(Wait, wait, wait…Don't think I'd forget)

Ask other Americans what they did
Ask them how their food tasted
Eating off the china that you low balled to get
Ask them about reaping the benefits from all the fruits of their labor
From fruits that they labored
Vegetables that they labored
Land that they labored
Ask them about what it was like staying on the side
Ask them how deafening their silence was
Ask them if they did something
Ask them if they did nothing

Ask them again
Ask them again
Ask
them
again

Quietly
That's how they said we would go
Quietly
That's what they said they don't know
Quietly
This time
I don't think so
I don't think so

Yukiya Jerry Waki is the creator and host of *The Buffet Show,* a live podcast that showcases artists, community organizers, and educator, highlighting sacrifice and process in their work. Born in Coalinga, California, and raised in Santa Maria, Mr. Waki's experience as a shin-Nisei offers a different perspective of the American experience post incarceration, and post redress and reparations. He currently resides in San Francisco with his wife Johanna and son Sebastian.

18 Minutes

Jennifer Hasegawa

What woke the birds that morning,
woke all.

Shook too soon,
down sparked
as they dropped
into flight.

Visibility
was good that day.

It came in low;
tips see-sawed.

Then,
it inverted
and everything went in.

A vast gray corpse
bloomed from a building.

It was the end
of the long division
between planes
and buildings.

EngineDeskWingChairRudderPaper
    NailSkinHair
No, it was not
a normal flight pattern.

My father said,
"Come, look."
The dull blue TV light
coated his face.

It took 18 minutes
for the words tumbling out
to turn from terror
to the -ism.
That clean
set of seconds
when unimaginable precision
looked like a mistake.

Watching so closely,
we could not see the second
coming.

What dare fly
in this air?

The boom
flipped the room
and bones
dropped from our pockets.

My father sucked his teeth
and my mother demanded
that we turn it off.

She was ready
to take on the day,
not watch this naked,
ragged body struggle
to right itself.
"Don't watch,
it's disrespectful."

We didn't look away
and now, somehow,
all they want us to do
is
watch.

Choppy Oshiro., *Green Spring in Iran,* paper and inkjet, 2011.

Shizue Seigel

The Hijab
Shizue Seigel

On Oct 7, 2001, less than a month after 9/11, United States began dropping bombs on Afghanistan. Outside my window, leaves glistened in the clear autumn sun, but inside my head, dark clouds churned. How many Muslim Americans had been arrested, like my Japanese immigrant grandfathers after Pearl Harbor? How many Afghanis would die from explosions, starvation, exposure, betrayal or terror like the Vietnamese and Central Americans before them because of an American thirst for vengeance?

My emails were choked with announcements of peace vigils, memorials, and meetings. A forward from Hapagrrrl began: "Solidarity Action this Monday! On October 8th, women across the United States, regardless of their faith, will wear a scarf or hat covering their hair. They will wear the hijab to support Muslim women who have been afraid to leave their houses because of ignorant hatred."

I worked at home, and didn't have time to take the bus downtown to join a demonstration, but I wanted to participate somehow, so I decided to put on a head covering when I went to my corner grocery. I'd been going there almost daily since 9/11, to make sure that the Palestinian Arab owner, Bob, was safe.

Bob was a treasure, the kind of neighborhood mainstay that was disappearing even in 2001. He ran tabs of $100 to 200 a month for his regulars, made deliveries to homebound seniors, and signed for our FedEx packages. He carried mini-cans of Vienna sausages for the folks who didn't cook and orzo and olive oil for those who did. More important, he remembered our names and our children's names. When he asked how you were, he really wanted to know.

Bob was a Palestinian Christian whose parents had left their ancestral town of Ramallah after the partition and migrated to Lebanon, then Michigan, and finally San Francisco. I learned that there were so many Arab grocers in San Francisco that they even had their own trade association.

Bob had never seen his ancestral home in the West Bank, but neighborliness was part of his DNA; his father's barbershop had been a social center in his old Ramallah neighborhood. Bob's freezer case was the urban equivalent of a cracker barrel, a place to hang out and hash over the day's events. On 9/11, once I'd registered the meaning of planes flying into buildings and the vengeful talk on TV, I rushed over to Bob's to make sure he was all right. I told him I'd come daily to check in with him.

The next day, we chatted worriedly about the news when a tall, lanky Irishman burst into the store. In a barely perceptible brogue he said, "What kind of demons would kill so many innocent people! The dirty bastards should burn in hell!" Bob and I froze as he paced rapidly, long ginger hair bouncing, arms and legs jutting dangerously in all directions. He towered a good foot-and-a-half above either of us.

"This is a black day for America. A black day!! Say, do you have any newspapers left with that headline across the top: 'BASTARDS!!'? That's going to be a real collector's item. Got to buy a bunch."

Bob shook his head. The Irishman ducked out of the store, and then roared back in. "Listen, I've got an idea! Let's start our own organization, you and me." He jabbed his finger forcefully at Bob. Bob threw his hands up, and backed away, shaking his head. "Leave me out of it. I don't like to get involved," he said.

"No, no, listen to me! We'll start an organization, you and me. We'll call it the United Front for World Sanity—UFWS." He swept his arm toward the produce case. "We'll load up your truck with fruits and vegetables, get all our friends and drive to Washington. We'll line up front of the White House and the Capitol Building and throw fruit at them. Don't you see? It's just crazy. They're all crazy!"

Bob and I looked at each other in disbelief, and the three of us began to laugh. Three San Franciscans with roots reaching to Japan, Palestine and Northern Ireland came together on that terrible Tuesday in the realization that the world's ills had irrevocably breached our shores.

Since that day, the Bush administration had begun a steady march toward war. And I was going to put on a hijab in solidarity with Muslim women all over the world.

I was ambivalent. As much as I respected people's rights to practice their religion as they wished, the sexism of expecting women to cover themselves rather than asking men to control themselves didn't sit well with me.

I sighed as I laid the scarf across my forehead, folded it down over my ears and under my chin. With my heavy jaw and no forehead, I look like an ape. But I could not cheat and expose my bangs like Audrey Hepburn in the 1960s. To Muslims, a woman's hair can symbolize a private spiritual connection with Allah, so every strand had be completely hidden.

The soft cotton fabric refused to hold crisp folds along my temples. I needed bobby pins, but I didn't own any. When I was a kid, Mom imposed despicable torture instruments on my body. But now I had wash-and-wear-hair. And girdles, garter belts, and hard pink hair rollers had been banished from my universe long ago. I had the freedom to choose what I wore and how I looked. And dammit every Muslim woman deserved the same!

I finished fiddling with the scarf and headed out the door. I noticed my steps were dragging. My stomach fluttered, my head thickened, and I had a sudden urge to go back to bed and pull the covers over my head.

Suddenly, an old memory surfaced. It was 1952, and I was six, walking home from school in Baltimore, head down, enjoying the lacy weeds growing up through the cracked sidewalk. Suddenly, I heard, "Ack-ack-ackkkkkkk! Brrrrt-brrrrt- brrrrrrrr- rrrt! It's a Jap plane! Going in at 12 o'clock."

Two big eight-year-old boys barreled down on me, arms outstretched like wings. I froze, sure they were going to knock me over. Instead they veed their arms ahead of them like torpedoes and whizzed narrowly past on either side of me, screaming, "Gotcha, you yellow bastard! Booooom!!" They imitated the screaming whistle of a smoking plane spiraling into the sea, and then erupted into mocking laughter. My ears burned in shame and rage as I walked home in the springtime sun.

"Get a grip!" I told myself. "That was almost fifty years ago." My parents had said at the time. "Let it go. They're just kids. Maybe they lost a relative in Korea or in World War II. Maybe they've just seen too many movies."

I forced myself out the door. Bob's store was only two blocks away. I skulked down the street, eyes locked forward, amazed by how easy it was to slip into old feelings. I had spent my childhood avoiding people's eyes, dreading the flat stare of hatred and the dismissive glance of contempt. That feeling didn't leave me until the 1970s, thirty years after my parents and grandparents had been locked up for being Japanese American.

I straightened my spine and lifted my chin against the thought of another generation of immigrants growing up under hatred and suspicion. As I turned the corner, I marveled that the sun was shining, and my bland stucco-fronted neighborhood looked as safe as always. I even managed to smile at a couple of passersby before I reached Bob's store.

When Bob saw the hijab, he lit up with pleased surprise. He was a Palestinian Christian, but he appreciated my intent. "You're wearing a ..." His hands fluttered around his head.

"A hijab." I told him about the email, and he smiled broadly and then sighed. "Yeah, Muslim women, in some countries, they have it pretty hard."

"Well, not here. Not if I can help it." Bob's eyebrows rose in amusement as I went to pick up a quart of milk and some cheese.

Family-owned Middle Eastern businesses are common in San Francisco. Some are clearly ethnic, and many more are corner groceries, liquor stores, delis and coffee shops. Photos: Shizue Seigel.

Right and below:
Goood Frikin' Chicken

Below: Cafe La Boheme has been run byAwad Faddoul for 25 years.

"There's only one sky above us. In America, Russia, Israel, Palestine, only one sky, one sun, one moon. Why can we not learn to live together in peace?"
—Old Jerusalem Restaurant proprietor
Ahmed Nasser

Samiramis on Mission has carried Middle Eastern groceries since the 1920s.

At Gyro King, across the street from the San Francisco Main Library, Welat Yuksel, a Kurd from Turkey, and his smiling chefs from Central America serve a variety of shish kebab and homemade savory and sweet pastries

188

Fernweh: the need, not desire, to travel
Dena Rod

I'm walking to the bookstore, Bird and Beckett. There's a literary magazine launch party being held there, and one of my poems has been selected for publication. At last, I am a contributing writer. Published and stepping over pigeons sipping gutter water like cocktails, I am arriving, stepping over the threshold of something wondrous and new. I have a spring in my step. There's a man waiting at a bus stop, an unlit cigarette between his fingers. His hand reaches out for me as I pass by. He asks me if I'm American. I immediately tense up, my defenses engage, and I want nothing to do with him.

My mind leaps to the worst possible conclusions, my body remembering strangers stopping me on the walks home from school, asking me if I spoke English. Asking me where I was "from" as the answer "up the street" wasn't good enough for their curiosity. Armoring my body against this man, who is quite possibly a tourist, perhaps just asking for directions or maybe even a lighter for his cigarette? But my tolerance for microaggressions has reached less than 10% in 2017. My steps quicken, my breath shortens as he reaches for me and I yell, "Leave me alone!" I rush past, as he exclaims, "Wait, wait!" I can hear his footsteps behind and my pulse races. Who do I trust in this landscape? What were once seemingly innocuous questions of "Where are you from?" now send signals of fight or flight to my nervous system, alerting my subconscious of someone who desires to categorize me, to other me.

I used to do the same. For the longest time, I compartmentalized parts of myself into corners of my mind, when it was just too uncomfortable to admit the truths in me. There was a time when those words would not have bothered me. I would smile (don't you know you look so much prettier when you smile?) and say, "My parents are from Iran." I would acquiesce, accommodate, and educate all in the name of being seen as a good representation of my culture. I would describe myself as "Persian," the outdated name conjuring images of the ancient, exotic Orient, rather than the modern Islamic Republic. I was one of those "Persians," like a breed of cat or a decorative carpet, a novelty from a far-flung place, except for the fact I was born on U.S. soil. As a Persian ambassador, I wanted to show that we weren't all scary terrorists yelling "Death to America." My parents taught me the importance of tarouf, the Persian custom of hospitality, and I always wanted to show the best face of our culture to Americans who had been inundated with state propaganda.

However I want the world to acknowledge complexity within those of us with migration, exile, and intergenerational trauma in our histories. See us as human. See just how painful it is to be split amongst borders and the brutal mistress of geography. Just as dozens of think pieces sluiced through the headlines in the wake of the 2016 election, pleading with the left wing to understand the plight of the blue-collar Americans struggling with opioid addiction and the pitfalls of global capitalism, and why they would vote for Trump; there is an equal and yet achingly bruised hand reaching out with an olive branch for understanding, held out by those of us whose lives are at stake. There is complexity in my life as a queer Iranian American person. There is love there that deserves to be protected. See me! lest we forget what our humanity and compassion engenders us to feel for others.

I struggle with the paradox of being too much and not enough simultaneously. Am I Iranian enough? Am I queer enough? Do I laugh and speak too loudly? Do I draw too much attention to myself? Am I too angry? Too militant? Too sad? Not angry enough? Am I calling enough representatives? Is it even worth it in a blue state like California? January 27, 2017, was an exercise in feeling my intersections acutely as the world came crashing down upon our communities, and the fire continues to burn. The Muslim Travel Ban executive order was something I tried to block out before the texts of concern came pouring in from my friends and the weight of understanding crashed onto me. I think of my familial history; the toil of immigrants and refugees fleeing a theocratic regime to find what? Freedom? Is that what this was? Or was it liberty? What did they find instead? Assimilation, denigration, and fear; each one heavier than the last. I am tired and exhausted and I'm not even out in these streets every day like my comrades.

For strength I look back to those in my motherland who wrote amidst spilled blood and revolutions, persevering even though their liberties were violated. Forough Farrokhzad resisted poetic conventions and gender expectations at a time of great sexist discrimination in Iran. Simin Behbahani was often called "the lioness of Iran." Her passport was seized by the Iranian government on her way to a reading of her work in Paris. These are my literary foremothers, who resisted the societal roles created for their gender. I often think, who am I to follow in their footsteps? I imagine my ancestors watching my life as I apply my lipstick and shave the sides of my head. What would they think of me? Would I make them proud? Do they clutch their foreheads when I'm abysmally steaming rice in my rice cooker, laughing into their chadors when I pronounce my "gh" sounds like a Turk (so my parents say)?

I only have memories of my mother's parents, snapshot images of what was once comforting as a child. My grandmother's brown knuckles were calloused and scrubbing painfully into my tender flesh in the shower. The water was harder in Iran and so was her touch, toughened after years of labor, sewing clothes, chopping herbs, scrubbing her own children clean from the daily dust. Since my parents are close-lipped about their lives back in Iran, I must imagine what the women in my family must have endured; plagues, famine, drought, invading soldiers from rival empires? They must have because their bloodlines have led me here.

However, I had to fully compartmentalize the complex parts of myself when I came out as queer to my parents. My maman and baba told me to not make a big deal of it, not to tell the rest of the family. My life split into two parts; Iranian for the first half and queer for the next, and the two couldn't meet. I kept Iranian culture and community at arm's length as I immersed myself in the queer fabric of the Bay Area. As a result, I'm not Iranian enough because I can't translate protest or informational signs into Farsi or translate for lawyers hunkered over a laptop in the airport. I gave up on the Farsi alphabet more times than I can count, the serifs and swirls washing over me, never sinking into the curves of my brain.

Assimilation. Denigration. Fear. I'm not Iranian enough because I can't stop crying as I read our stories of denial at the border of a country we called home for decades, who took us in and said, you're safe here (if you behave). I am not Iranian enough because it says, "born in California" on my passport. Therefore, a full week before 45 passed the travel ban on seven Muslim majority countries, I was allowed back in the country by my wife's side returning from our trip to Thailand. I shudder to think how this one geographical act of birth has such ripples through one's life. The weight of U.S. citizenship isn't a heavy burden to bear in comparison to my diasporic family's patchwork of green cards, visas, and web of marriages. But for those of us who would want to bring the rest of our families over, we now can't.

"You're U.S. citizen, you're fine," my mom says. "It's okay, I'm citizen too. I have my papers if anyone asks." The thought of my mother retrieving her naturalization certificate amongst her Iranian marriage license and passport, whorls of Islamic motifs decorating the borders, breaks my heart. The documents of her life's journey, mementos of the land and sea she's traversed to settle, and now she asks if you'd like to open up a Target card to save 5% off?

Immigrant success doesn't always look like doctors researching how to treat rheumatoid arthritis, winning the Fields Medal, or lawyers sitting in airports to free detainees. It can also look like owning a corner store and providing your community with flavors of "back home," driving a cab through traffic that pales in comparison to what you grew up driving in, owning your own business that goes bankrupt twice. Immigrant success looks like your children propelling themselves through the stratospheres you couldn't pierce, the first in your family to go to college, because not all Iranians choose to become doctors, lawyers, or engineers.

I've never been to Iran and now who knows if I ever will? I am not Iranian enough because my parents actively discourage me from visiting the homeland; I'm not "missing much," my dad says. "I talked to the State department."

"You did?"

"Yeah you can go to Iran no problem," he says, voice echoing through the phone receiver.

"That doesn't make sense; the Iranian Ministry came out with a statement…"

"You're free to go and get executed."

I lose my breath over the cruelty of the joke. I try to not let the shock show in my voice. The phone passes to my mother.

"Is this true?" my mom inquires. "You want to go to Iran?"

I sigh, exasperated. It's no secret that it's been a lifelong dream to see the mountain I'm named after, to see the blue tiles in Isfahan, the ruins of Persepolis, Hafez's tomb in Shiraz, and the oil fields of Abadan where my mom grew up. It's something that is always conveniently forgotten by my parents until the next time I mention it. They always feign surprise and shock as to the depth of my desire and longing to see where I come from.

"You're not missing much," my dad repeats with the bitterness of a long abandoned ex-wife. "Go to India, go to Saudi Arabia. Anywhere but Iran."

Anywhere but Iran. If only I could so simply abandon the notion. Yet the amount of tears I have shed watching Iranian travel documentaries hosted by Western travel writing men should say otherwise. I have buckets to cry before I ever set foot on a plane headed in the general direction of the Middle East. There's this pull in my blood, this drive within me to step foot in the land my ancestors hail from, to see the Iran that my parents come from. I would get a better understanding of them by walking in their footsteps. As a substitute, I gobble up images of lakes, cities, and mountains in Iran on Google.

When I was in Bangkok, Thailand, I realized that geographically I was the closest to Iran than I had ever been in my life. It weighed heavier than I expected, and I searched for echoes of Iran everywhere I went. There were Thai pomegranates juiced everywhere, but their thick yellow husk and strawberry red seed differed from the tough-skinned wine hued anar I look forward to every fall. I hunted for the Iranian flag any time we passed street stalls showcasing their collection of international flag patches. "Am I Iranian enough to wear this in the States?" I remember thinking, finally procuring one. "In Trump's America," I concluded, "yes."

Yet I am not Iranian enough because I'm a U.S. citizen. Now I'm banned from traveling to Iran, because the Islamic Republic of Iran might as well have invented pettiness in government policy. The Islamic Republic is no longer issuing visas to U.S. nationals. I am not Iranian enough because I speak Farsi with a heavy Northern Californian accent and am constantly told how "interesting" my grammar is. I'm not Iranian enough because the homeland of my ancestors betrayed my father and he said, "You know what? Fuck you!" as he left, middle fingers in the air as he boarded a plane, never to look behind him again. I am not Iranian enough because I followed in his footsteps and had America betray me over and over as I looked at my student loans, planned an emergency gay wedding in ten days, and protested in airports. We now have that in common.

I have relative privilege in this situation. Not being Iranian enough has shielded me from the front lines of this battle—in the arrival terminals of airports across the nation. Watching videos of head-scarved grandmothers released in wheelchairs finally made clear the full extent of what's at stake here—families' connections to their people. After years of going to protests in San Francisco, folded invisibly into the Latinx contingent, I see Iranians at rallies and protests for the first time. For all I know, they have always been there, but for the first time my eyes are honing in on Iranians. The solidarity that I am witnessing in this community is outstanding, yet it touches a raw emotional place that I am just beginning to articulate. Throughout this ordeal, I've come to accept my United States assimilation as a mode of survival and yet I resent it at the same time.

I'm so fortunate to be in this country, despite it all, with my wife at my side. In Iran, homosexuality is punishable by death. If LGBT Iranians could escape to Turkey and jump through all the hoops their refugee asylum applications entail, the hope was to be resettled in the U.S. The travel ban has put a stop to that. They are stuck in purgatory in Turkey, as Canada is focusing on Syrian refugees and Europe doesn't accept LGBT Iranian refugees. How do we support those who are the most vulnerable in our diasporic community when my own family encouraged me to stay in the closet to the rest of our extended family in the U.S.?

And yet I resist, despite everything. I'm opening windows into the past for a look into the future, reconnecting with loved ones from my childhood, and restoring my self. I think, maybe, finally I might be on the right path. I sustain myself daily on the altar of Audre Lorde's words: "Caring for myself is not self-indulgence, it is self-preservation, and that is an act of political warfare." When the Supreme Court upheld the latest iteration of the travel ban, I truly understood how it was my job to love more fiercely, in deeper kindness and compassion for myself.

On March 20th, first day of spring, the start of the Persian New Year, I FaceTimed with my cousin, whom I hadn't seen in over ten years. She's been a guiding hand ever since I was born; sitting by my infant bassinet, changing my diapers, and much later, teaching me how to apply foundation with a sponge. She was visiting Iran. As we caught up, she flipped the phone over and I saw the sun shining on mountains in Shiraz. The phone wasn't blurry because the Internet connection was shit; I was seeing through my tears as I longed for the soil of my ancestors. How can you be nostalgic for a place you've never been? It forever vexes me. Tonight, I came back from her 35th birthday party in the East Bay, still warm from the hugs of still more long-lost cousins. I feel nourished as we restore these roots of our family tree, stronger against the tide of isolation to come. I am Iranian and American and queer and all these identities can exist together in the matrix of myself. Somehow I'll keep weaving my way through the world and maybe someday I'll see the mountain I'm named after with my American wife by my side.

healing
& community

Charles Dixon, *Bohemian Knuckle Boogie - Mike,* photo collage, 2017.
Collage of several photos taken from 2008 to 2017 inside or near
Sheba Piano Lounge in the Fillmore.

Soul Music
Jesus Francisco Sierra

At around 11 pm on a Friday, I descend the stairs into the Cigar Bar, a bar where you can order a quick drink or pick up a cigar. You can't smoke inside but you can do so in the open-air courtyard that separates the bar from the dance floor on the opposite side, where a live salsa band is playing. I weave my way across the courtyard through the thick smoke and crowded tables until I push open the doors into the other room.

The sound of drums, bass and the familiar clave beat echoes in the courtyard. The singer is belting out "La Banda," a song made popular by Puerto Rican icon Hector Lavoe back in the early seventies when New York salsa rained (as in "poured," not reigned as in "ruled")the groove and the swing of Afro-Cuban music all over the planet and all over San Francisco's Mission District.

I remember those times, being swept by the magic of it, dancing to songs like Pedro Navaja. I would slide my hand around the girl's waist. She would place one hand on my shoulder. I'd hold her other hand in mine and we would move to the beat, always to the beat. We sang the lyrics to each other because those words and that sound reached us.

* *

I drop two dollars in the clear jar that sits on the narrow coat-check counter and hand my sport coat to the young Filipino woman on the other side. She smiles and hands me a numbered ticket. I stroll to the edge of the floor mouthing the words to the song because this is Afro-Cuban music, and it's my soul music. My body feels lighter when I hear it, as if lifted elsewhere, to the sounds that brought me life, to the Havana that I remember.

I see couples dancing half drunk, falling into each other, taking up more space than they should. I see an Asian couple. They are both staring down at their feet counting their steps, trying to remember what they learned during the early evening salsa lesson. Over on the far side of the floor I see this white guy and woman moving as if they were jumping rope to the music. They're not counting anything but they seem to be having a good time.

Then there is the middle-aged black dude too cool for his own good, looking like he's working a hula hoop in slow motion. He's dancing with a Filipino woman wearing a tight sequin dress and tall heels. She gyrates her hips slightly and doesn't seem to want to mess up her hair. Finally, an Indian guy holds his drink in one hand and spins his partner with the other like a top, almost launching her right off the dance floor. The thought that there is a beat to follow seems to elude some of them.

I suppose I should feel proud when I see them dancing. Proud that my music has reached so far and has become such a phenomenon. It has leapt across cultural and geographical boundaries. But they have no idea what the words to the song mean. Pride is not what I feel. Instead there is a heaviness to my legs that anchors me to the floor. My face feels flush and my chest tightens as the music is drowned by memories of a different time, of a different San Francisco.

In the seventies, neighborhood garage parties with red or black lights were also crowded, smoky and yes, we all drank then too. But like the subtitle to Fania All Stars' breakthrough 1971 album *Our Latin Thing*, it was indeed nuestra cosa, our thing. Couples swayed as if riding the same wave, mirroring each other's steps. The bass, the drums and the tat-tat-tat, tat-tat of the clave steadied the rhythms while the horns burst out the melody, and the vocals kept us in the groove, not just with the music but also with each other. There was ease to it all, the ease that came with the familiar. Our moves felt inevitable, like breathing.

* *

But here at Cigar Bar, the music seems to be background noise to the dancers. It seems as if only alcohol or maybe wanting to appropriate our culture as their own spurs them to the dance floor. It's the type of cultural appropriation that's not that different from what I see these days in the Mission, my old neighborhood. What used to be a predominantly Latino neighborhood is seeing a proliferation of new residential condo buildings unaffordable to the working class. The new buildings are named with words like Vida (Life). As if baptizing them with Spanish words will somehow preserve the heritage of the neighborhood. The past is being re-written by these modern day Columbuses: developers and the rich settlers that inhabit their new buildings. I'm reminded of that when I see a bar called "Amnesia" or the "Alamo" Draft House, which now occupies the old New Mission Theater. They kept the marquee sign from the original theater because it was deemed to be historic as it held some level of architectural significance. The Crown Theater across the street used to alternate Mexican movies with American films. It housed innumerable memories for many of us, but it held no such historical significance to them. It, too, is now gone.

The new structures replace old stores like Newberry's at 23rd and Mission. I used to buy shoes there as a kid. There were two large bins on the sidewalk in front of the store: one filled with left-footed shoes, the other with right-footed shoes. If you found one you liked that fit, you needed to rifle through the other bin to find the match. It was always fun to barter if you were to find someone else holding the matching shoe. Although those memories remain, the landscape and the people that evoke them are largely gone.

I don't have to pair my left and my right shoes any more. These days I can afford to buy them together at places like Nordstrom's and they're actually made of leather. But I can't forget because there are those who still have to sort through sidewalk bins, those, who like me, came here imagining a future for the first time, albeit uncertain. Today it'd be places like Newberry's that ICE would come calling to complete their quota of immigrant detainees—like they did not long ago when they raided a Family Center in the Mission or like they have done at countless other places throughout the country. We didn't worry about that as much back then when we still came to this country chasing the illusion of a dream, and felt safe doing it.

* *

Maybe tonight, in this place, what we're really witnessing is a case of acculturation. We, armed with our music and our ways, are bringing together a community. We have things in common after all. We all understand progress. Immigrants by definition seek to improve their lives. We seek progress but understand that progress is not without sacrifice. The question is where do we draw the line? Decimating entire communities in the name of profit is not progress. It erodes the foundation that binds us as a society. A bigger question is, who draws that line? If not us, then who?

I don't mind if the white couple jumps or that the Asians mark their steps or that the black dude thinks he looks cool or if the Indian guy throws the girl off the dance floor. They can dance the music however they choose. I'm okay with it, not that they need my permission. It's hypocritical of me to talk about community if that community only allows a certain kind. They'd do well to consider that before tearing down the next building. In the end, I know who I am and where I come from. I wonder if they do. I've already drawn my line. This is my Vida and no one is going to build any condos where I'm standing.

The song ends and everyone applauds. The crowd disperses. I tap the jump-rope woman on the shoulder as she walks past me, "Would you like to dance?" I ask.

"Sure," she says.

I take hold of her hand and lead her to the dance floor. I slide my right hand around her waist. She smiles as I guide her left hand onto my shoulder. The music starts. I mouth the words to the song. And we dance.

4/4
Sandra García Rivera

Signature of time
creased in my brow
no rest for wrinkles.
Marrow retards,
tempo decreases,
no repeat
at the end of the measure.
From minor to major,
quarter to half to whole,
grace notes diminish,
heartbeats crescendo
pitch and lunge,
tremble mid sea.
The Conductor
keeps score,
measures intervals
between sharp and flat.
I strike a dissonant chord
walk the line
balance the scale,
compose harmony,
in the swing of life.

Friscopino is never forgetting where you came from.
—Tony Robles

From San Francisco, by San Francisco, for San Francisco:
Friscopinos & the *Native Immigrant*
Joy Ng

Seated across from Ro3lay in a humid conference room at the Bayanihan Community Center, I quickly cut to the chase, pressing my old friend for an answer from the heart. "But WHY did you make *Native Immigrant*? What makes this different from your last projects?" Ro3lay spent the last five years making this album, and would spend the next few months showing me the answer.

Native Immigrant is a collaborative Hip Hop album between San Francisco born-and-bred MC Richard "Ro3lay" (pronounced roe-lay) Olayvar and seasoned producer Rey "MISTER REY" Novicio. Five years in the making, *Native Immigrant* reflects a Filipino American San Francisco story, touching on memories and experiences around gentrification, police violence, and even mom's cooking and the Filipino diet.

* *

Against the backdrop of San Francisco, *Native Immigran*t frames a commentary of the quickly changing landscape of the city. Between growing up, and the city growing distant from its roots, its residents continuously fight back as working families are constantly swept from their homes by skyrocketing costs of housing; as beautiful ethnic murals are painted over in the Mission by transplant entrepreneurs; and as local art spaces become luxury condos to accommodate incoming populations of young professionals. These symptoms of gentrification and whitewashing have been wringing out the vibrant soul of San Francisco over the past decade. Additionally, characterized by a trend of profitable evictions, booming tech industry, and police brutality, the city quickly became unrecognizable, and us loyal San Franciscans, near and far, hold fast to our ethnic food, our ethnic art, our ethnic languages, and our collective memories of home.

*   *

Clinging onto every scene of *Piece by Piece* (2005) and *Wild Style* (1983), Ro3lay found a freedom in black books, paint pens and bottomless stacks of postal stickers—otherwise material tools for the intention of leaving a genuine mark on this world through art. By the time Ro3lay and I became friends as teenagers, he was already inseparable from his Sony Discman, rapping along to every word of Nas's *Illmatic*, carrying a thick booklet of CDs in his backpack. At this time in the early 2000s, the rise of mp3s and burned CDs meant that people could start customizing their own playlists, and Ro3lay was hungry for all kinds of music. Because Ro3lay had an unconventional experience as a youth, his knowledge and connection to the fabric of San Francisco stems from his time spent in different neighborhoods—SoMA, Chinatown, and the Sunset. His album, *Native Immigrant,* is a testament to the development of Ro3lay's journey as a growing San Franciscan Filipino American MC and artist.

Throughout the span of Ro3lay's music career thus far, none of his works have been this invested in exploring identity and community as a Filipino American artist. *Native Immigrant* stands out as a body of work that situates itself in the larger context of diaspora, taking a personal step towards adopting a critical outlook of the rapid changes in his hometown of San Francisco and the impacts on his identity as he continued to learn of his own roots in Filipino American history and culture. *Native Immigrant,* as a concept, and oxymoron, digs into complexities of immigration and transnational definitions of home, as well as the now-rare claim of being a born-and-raised San Franciscan experiencing gentrification. The album frequently dives into Ro3lay's memories connected to his own Filipino American identity, citing his mother's journey to the U.S. and acknowledging an ongoing eradication of culture and assimilation in America. With accompanying sounds of the Kulintang, Ro3lay sums up his personal relationship to the Philippines, building a bridge between home and homeland, belonging and return:

> *Native tongue got erased in a classroom*
> *whole country could disappear in a typhoon …*
> *Balikbayan boxes sealed tight with love*
> *I know my hand-me-downs can only do so much*

But still go a long way
From the islands to the Yay
I know I'll be back one day
　　　　　　　　　　　　—Ro3lay, "Native Immigrant /Friscopino II"

Although packaged as an album, *Native Immigrant* as a body of work is an unpacking of Ro3lay, with a personal viewpoint that takes into account the generations that came before him, as well as growing up tough in a Filipino American working-class family in San Francisco. What separates *Native Immigrant* from other Filipino American Hip Hop albums is the direct take on the city of San Francisco as equal parts social commentary, personal documentary, and conceptual ideas of home. This ongoing dialogue between the trajectory of San Francisco and its impacts on Filipino Americans through the personal lens of Ro3lay's viewpoints fits perfectly into the word, "Friscopino."

*   *

With a firm belief in Nina Simone's infamous words, "An artist's duty… is to reflect the times," Ro3lay presents tracks such as "Quick Hands" and "Healing," featuring BWAN of Beatrock Music. Ro3lay takes on gentrification and police violence, paying homage to the modern activism of the Frisco 5 Hunger Strike. With sound clips from rallies and demonstrations, we can hear Equipto's mother Cristina and Davey D denouncing the injustices of deadly police shootings of unarmed Black and Brown young men, including Alex Nieto. As the Black Lives Matter movement for justice and equity arose in response to the unjust murders of Trayvon Martin, Freddie Gray, Mike Brown, and so many more, the deadly killings by police in San Francisco become part of the growing national trend of calling for an end to the militarization of police and the murders of Black and Brown lives across the U.S. *Native Immigrant* takes a protective stance that underlines the entire album, defending youth, working-class, and Black and Brown people struggling to survive in San Francisco.

The making of *Native Immigrant* reflected the community of artists who had a hand in contributing to the ideas of home and resistance, pulling in local educators, activists and organizers. The album was produced in its entirety by Mister Rey, who is also a community worker in the heart of downtown San Francisco. He has worked with artists along the West Coast as well as the Philippines. The album also boasts features from artists such as Nomi of Power Struggle, the Mighty DJ Delrokz, and Dregs One. With these MCs and DJs who are also on the ground working with vulnerable communities—immigrants, youth, seniors, and working class—the album hits a sensitive nerve and paints the contrasting gritty shadow of San Francisco, opposite to the appealing images of San Francisco as a hub for trendy places to live and work.

While the album includes fighting words of resistance, found in tracks like "Freedom Writers," tackling evictions, capitalism, and even Filipino cuisine and eating habits in "Kawali," there are also tracks like "Kiss the Sky" that steer the listener towards taking deep breaths, and taking in the city for its sights, sounds, and heights through its music video.

Following the digital release in August 2016, *Native Immigrant* as an album and as an experience moves to fulfill the notions of Hip Hop as a vehicle for storytelling and social change. The promotion of the album also sought to engage the audience directly within Filipino communities in San Francisco. With frequent visits to Bindlestiff Studio, building connections to community organizers and earning access to communal spaces for team meetings, the way that *Native Immigrant* was shared and disseminated deepened Ro3lay's roots in local Filipino American community spaces.

The I-Hotel remains an enduring symbol of home, gentrification and resistance, not only for people who identified with the struggle, but for those who are willing to tell their stories and stand up for the City. On August 26, 2017, artists including BWAN, Fego Navarro, Rocky G, Ruby Ibarra, SoMA youth organizers YOHANA, and DJ Fonzilla took to the stage to help usher in the *Native Immigrant* album. The I-Hotel saw a rising generation of artists who articulated stories of their survival in San Francisco, touching on immigration, calling out racism, police brutality, and mass evictions. The album's second track, "Native Immigrant/Friscopino II," features a poem by Tony Robles:

Friscopino is the shame we have in the parts of us that are the most beautiful
Friscopino is the Black in us that can't be denied
—Tony Robles, "Native Immigrant/Friscopino II"

Nephew of celebrated poet/activist Al Robles, Tony is celebrated in his own right, as a poet, current President of Manilatown Heritage Foundation, and a seasoned community organizer and anti-eviction advocate.

The release party was held just after the 40th Eviction Commemoration of the I-Hotel. The love and resistance embodied in the performances were a perfect homage to the Manongs who once fought to the bitter end for Manilatown and for their right to exist, live, and thrive in San Francisco.

Through the process of making *Native Immigrant*, Ro3lay comes full circle, from dreaming and craving music as a young teen to creating albums and public experiences that engage the communities that raised him.

This piece was posted at https://joyngsf.wordpress.com, Jan 11, 2018. The album *Native Immigrant* is available on iTunes, Google Play, Bandcamp, and Spotify: https://open.spotify.com/album/3zaAxbBbOuVvKJQdE9n2a0.

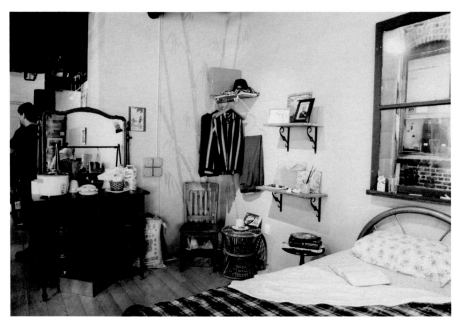

Cris Matos and Cynthia Tom, *Domingo's SRO,* life-size installation,
11 x 17 ft., 2016.

Domingo's SRO was a site-specific installation created at the International Hotel Manilatown Center to mark the 40th anniversary of the 1977 International Hotel Eviction. Sized to the exact footprint of a typical room at the original International Hotel, the piece was created at the request of Caroline Cabading, board vice president at Manilatown Heritage Foundation, to honor the memory of the Manilatown Manongs. To give life to the installation, artists Cris Matos and Cynthia Tom imagined a possible resident:

"Domingo loves to dance, he is a visual artist
and has a little shelf for his paints and canvases.
His dress shirt hangs cleaned and pressed ready for a night out.
He sleeps with his head under his window, so he can look out and dream.
The world is his room."

Cris Matos is a photographer, painter, mixed media artist, and singer/songwriter with Manicato, a Puerto Rican Latin funk, rock and reggae band. His themes include social justice, world unity and love of his home country of Puerto Rico, where his family was badly impacted by Hurricane Maria. www.manicato. com. www.facebook.com//CrisMatos. Cynthia Tom, a Chinese American San Franciscan, is a visual artist, cultural community curator and founder of A Place of Her Own, which helps women define their voice through the arts. She is concerned with social justice, feminism, spirituality. www.cynthiatom.com.

Building Community

The International Hotel Manilatown Center's tradition of activism is based on hard work and collaboration, and also fellowship, music, dancing and food. Caroline Cabading with the I-Hotel Jazz Ensemble and dance instructor Benito Santiago perform at a Club Mandalay get-together in 2016.

An Endangered Heritage
Sandra Yamakishi

Growing older and reflecting on my life, I find my cultural heritage and community have become an endangered species. Although San Francisco's Japantown is not the old community of the past, it still reminds me of my life in the Denver Japantown in the 1950s.

Denver's Japanese community began with immigrants who mostly worked as farmers nearby and in the outlying countryside of Colorado. It wasn't until the forced removal of Japanese Americans from the West Coast in 1942 that Colorado had an enormous influx of families mainly from two sources: the incarceration of West Coast Japanese to the Amache concentration camp located in Colorado, and the declaration from Colorado's Governor Ralph Carr that any Japanese living in Colorado could remain outside of the internment camp. To avoid incarceration, Mom and Dad and their extended families quietly left Los Angeles and drove to Colorado before the "voluntary evacuation" ended on March 29, 1942.

Many stayed after the war to start a new life. In the 1950s when I was growing up, our Japantown filled social and economic needs, with a Japanese-language school for kids, a Japanese-language newspaper, and the Buddhist temple as a center of social and community activities.

My Dad owned a photography studio in the middle of mostly Japanese businesses close to downtown Denver. On one side of the studio, there was a pool hall and hardware store. Next door on the other side was the law office of Min Yasui. I learned decades later that Mr. Yasui challenged the constitutionality of the incarceration in a historic court case in 1942. On the same block was the

Pacific Mercantile market where we shopped for fish, tofu, Japanese vegetables and canned goods. Across the street were a jewelry store, café, drug store, and barbershop.

Because I was the oldest girl in the family, I spent most summers and after school helping Dad at the studio. My time at the studio was lonely, yet I also remember special times with Dad and the Japanese community.

I often stood next to him in the blackness of the darkroom while he developed film and made photo prints; sometimes I slowly waved my fingers through the cold-water bath where he rinsed the photographs after printing and developing. My chores were to clean the freestanding ashtrays of old cigarette butts and ashes, sweep the floors, clean the display cases, and decorate the front window with framed photographs of weddings and portraits placed strategically on black velvet cloth. For fun, I hand colored the customers' black-and-white portraits with special oil-based paints, which was the way to have color prints. I was so bored, sometimes I sat at Dad's work desk looking up at a large poster of portraits of all the U.S. presidents, which I tried to memorize. Lunchtime, I heated Campbell's tomato soup or chicken noodle soup on a hot plate and made baloney sandwiches. My only contact with people was with Japanese customers, an occasional Mexican customer, Japanese shopkeepers, and Dad's Japanese friends who came to the studio to play goh (a strategy game played on a wooden board with black and white round stones). In the back half of our building was a dance studio where a traditionally trained dance instructor taught kabuki-style dance (odori). She produced dance performances and plays held at the Buddhist Temple. I was part of the core of young dancers. Every day, I entered through the back door of the photo studio, into the back stage of the dance studio. I quietly walked to the front of the studio and bowed respectfully to the o-sho-san (respected teacher), with the Japanese greeting "Ko-ni-chi-wa" (good afternoon). I then changed into my practice kimono and proceeded to the stage to practice the dance. My fellow dancers and I had fun in our free time playing jacks on the wooden floor of the dressing room.

Life felt like a cocoon. I was harbored among the Japanese community, with family and friends that looked like me. Home life kept me protected, comforted, and without any tribulations, although we lived frugally and barely sustained a living. My favorite time was celebrating New Year's with the gathering of family to pound rice into a paste to make mochi (molded into dome-shaped mounds), to place in front of the home Buddhist alter and then to eat the traditional ozoni (mochi soup). For New Year's Day, Mom made all the traditional dishes that represented wishes for a prosperous year such as kamaboko (fish cake), gobo (burdock root), kobumaki (kelp rolls), kazunoko (herring roe), kuromame (black soy beans), then she would add more Japanese American fare such as teriyaki chicken, chow mein, tempura shrimp, and baked ham. For the highlight of the food feast, Dad created a large platter-sized fish baked with the head and tail curled up in an elegant presentation.

Then one day, Dad closed his studio. In the early 1960s, Denver's Japantown was disappearing as the Urban Renewal Authority demolished blocks of decaying downtown buildings. The declared intent was to help the Japanese American community sustain the culture by improving the neighborhood, but many small business people like Dad were not able to make a living during the reconstruction. My father took up gardening and mowing lawns, and Mom worked outside of the home for the first time as an assembly-line worker at the Russell Stover Candy Company. She worked the night shift in order to be home for the kids. I'll never forget the times she came home reeking with the smell of chocolate and quickly bathed to get rid of the scent.

With two regular incomes now, Mom and Dad bought a newly built tri-level house in the suburbs, moving away from the downtown area like many other Japanese American families. We lost the neighborhood community of relatives and friends who had lived so close, and were now so far away.

Fast forward to the nineties, through college, careers, marriage, and children. My children were biracial, and growing up in the suburbs without the Japanese American neighborhood, customs or traditions that I'd been raised with. I tried to impart my heritage by taking my kids to Sunday school at the Denver Buddhist Temple. It was the only place left after urban renewal that exposed them to the Japanese American community culture. After the kids graduated high school and entered college, the time came for me to make changes. I yearned for a cultural community and moved to San Francisco.

What I found here in San Francisco was the same situation that had happened in Denver. Urban renewal changed San Francisco's Japantown. Across the U.S., Japantowns swiftly vanished—lost to assimilation, gentrification and commercialization. California, which once had more than 40, now has three major Japantowns left—in Los Angeles, San Francisco, and San Jose. In an attempt to create a new Japantown, San Francisco developers tore down the local business shops and created malls. Most local Japanese businesses couldn't afford the increased rent. They either closed up shop like my Dad or moved to outlying neighborhoods or towns. A truly Japantown community was lost, but that wasn't the only cultural heritage affected by urban renewal.

Urban renewal also impacted African Americans in the Fillmore District next to Japantown. Historically, African Americans had occupied the Fillmore District since the 1906 San Francisco earthquake, but the population boomed during World War II. A large migration of African Americans arrived from the southern states to work in shipbuilding and other defense industries. They moved into the Fillmore because the 1942 incarceration of Japanese Americans had left a large number of vacant homes and businesses in the area.

The Fillmore became a hub for the growing jazz culture, which created a new energy and vitality to the district. The newcomers brought their southern dishes, Cajun flavors, and smoked bar-b-q-ribs. African American migration to the city and district continued at a staggering pace until it reached a peak in the 1970s.

Then in the 1970s the Fillmore District was enveloped in the urban redevelopment effort to help the community rise from poverty. There was a desperate need of rejuvenation, but promises fell short to help the residents return to better housing and to keep the African American culture intact. Instead, the project was a disaster for the overall culture and detrimental to the jazz scene. African American food offerings disappeared. Mini-malls or plazas tried to create the ambiance of the community, but the return of the vitality of the African Americans did not happen.

It was amazing how the landscape for the Japanese Americans and the African Americans in San Francisco was transformed into a pseudo Cultural Center built with concrete malls, superficial enhancements, invasive food fare not necessarily rooted from the two communities. The subsequent generations

Photos courtesy of Sandra Yamakishi

fled into outlying areas that provided better housing and living standards but in exchange they abandoned the roots of their heritage.

Living in San Francisco, without the old Japantown or any relatives living close by, there is no return to reminisce about my childhood, or family, intimacy, and heritage. As any typical American, I can easily buy take-out, eat fast food, shop at box stores such as Costco and Target, and celebrate family events at restaurants instead of home gatherings.

The lack of community traditions, customs, and heritage results in selfishness where every person strives for self-identity and material success. People forget about other people because there is nothing to bind them together: none of the memories, music, greetings, or customs that make people into a community. This is what happens when the endangered species of cultural communities die.

However, there are hidden jewels of refuge to be found. I have come full circle, back home to the Buddhist Temple where I have reconnected spiritually and found friends who continue to instill the heritage. A heritage that blends old Japan with the American customs that we've inherited from our first and second generations of Japanese Americans. Maybe endangered but still surviving.

Sandra Yamakishi. I was born just after World War II in Denver, Colorado. My father was from Japan and Mom was a second-generation Nisei from Sacramento, California. After graduating from University of Colorado, I moved to San Francisco, New York City, then back to Denver. Retiring from University of California San Francisco, I spent over two years in Belize as a Peace Corps volunteer before returning to San Francisco.

Black Girl Origin Story
Kelechi Ubozoh

The black woman is god,
but they have forgotten.
Their strength was forged from the fire of the sun.
Black girl, you were a moon goddess before they told you those lies.
You are creation, they came spilling from your thighs.
Your wet caves adorned with diamonds.
Ebony sunset.
They have forgotten.
Black girl
maybe, someone told you.
But could you hear it?
Was it just a whisper?
Or did it come from your mama?
Did you believe it?
That you're made of fallen stars plucked from the night, that light your eyes.
That black girl magic is real.
Are you starting to remember?
To unlearn those lies?
They want to be you so badly,
did you ever wonder why?
From you lips to hips,
fluid motion
your swag to your sway.
The strength is but a cover to eclipse the soft, gentle warmth inside.
The black girl forgot her origin story.
Magical ethos
ebony sunset
galaxies
lights in her eyes
sways in her hips
free spirit
That's how she was made.
The secret of her softness is hidden in her strength.

How the Bay Taught Me That The Black Woman Is God (and She Can Breathe Too)
Rochelle Spencer

"Is the Black woman god?" I asked my friend Stacia years ago.

"Yes," she answered. There was no hesitation.

Stacia is a member of the Five-Percent Nation and grew up with a lot of cultural pride. She carries herself like royalty, tells me about "knowledge of self," laughs at my kumbaya notions of the world—"No, Ro, racism wouldn't disappear even if the government did hand out free, weed-infused chocolate."

I'm not as militant as Stacia, but I'm not one of the Black people who's entered "the sunken place," Jordan Peele's term for Black people who've swallowed the white supremacist Kool-Aid and have literally Sammy Sosa'd/ Michael Jackson'd their souls. But after several years of graduate school, of reading theory written almost entirely by Whites (even when I was writing about Black fiction), I'd lost my confidence—and damn near lost my mind. Moving to the Bay deepened this confusion at first, but it's also helped me to understand people better—to recognize folks as complex.

What's confusing about the Bay is it's the type of place where a White person can explain Critical Race Theory and quote the Black Panthers' 10-Point Platform, but still won't hire you for a job. It's the kind of place where White people protest in the streets but when you go to their house, your Black ass is the only PoC at the party.

My mind started to clear last July at the *The Black Woman is God*, an exhibition at SOMArts Cultural Center curated by Karen Seneferu and Melorra Green and featuring 60 intergenerational artists.

I almost didn't go to the opening. I was broke, as usual, and feeling too lazy to travel from the East Bay to SF. I don't know. I was feeling terrible. My father-in-law had passed away. The U.S. had elected a new president—a scary, pig-faced man who snorted racist and sexist remarks. I fought often with my husband (I was irritable, and he was understandably upset); I was freelancing but couldn't sell a story even if I wrapped it in a homemade sweet potato pie. My dissertation advisors said my chapters lacked focus (how can a discussion of the AfroSurreal qualities of five postmodern novels exploring time travel, the Diaspora's historical trauma, and futuristic ways of generating social change possibly lack … well, maybe they had a point). I was in one of those moods when I could have stayed in bed.

But here's the thing: some kind of weird, psychic energy invades the Bay. I think all the collective goodwill from helping each other create art whips people into a frenzy and forces them outside of themselves. You're drawn, if you're in the region—if you're in Oakland or San Francisco or Hayward or Emeryville—to find out what the people around you are doing and creating.

At the exhibition, there was music, drums, art, love. I saw writers I knew—Black women who were creators. We hugged, smiled. After weeks of feeling inadequate, I felt powerful. I was reminded of what could be accomplished with vision and hard work; I walked out of the exhibition feeling as though some of that collective creativity and intelligence belonged to me, too.

In October, I saw *Black Women Over Breathing,* curated by Adrian Octavius Walker and Danielle McCoy, at Oakland's Betti Ono Gallery. It erased some of the feeling of "What can we do?" that had floated through me for several months. At the panel discussion, Black women addressed real social issues, including the Black women and girls like Aiyana Stanley-Jones and Sandra Bland, who had died as a result of police violence.

In December, Kelechi Ubozoh's Moon Drop Productions had a tribute to *The Black Woman Is God* that featured writers Nazelah Jamison, Joyce Lee, Thea Matthews, Vanessa Rochelle Lewis, Jenee Darden and musician Melissa Jones. And in one sentence, Nazelah's lightening-hot poem, "Ode to Oakland," summed up everything I've been feeling about the Bay's magic: "Oakland is a Black girl and I love her."

Rochelle Spencer is the author of *AfroSurrealism: The African Diaspora's Surrealist Fiction* (Routledge 2018), and co-editor with Jina Ortiz of *All About Skin: Short Fiction* by Women of Color (University of Wisconsin Press 2014).

Photo: Shizue Seigel

Photos: Shizue Seigel

Homes for the Homies
Cynthia De Losa

I'm a third-generation native San Francisco "Homegirl." I grew up in Noe Valley and the Mission; my mother is from North Beach and my father and grandfather from the Fillmore District (now known as the "Western Addition"). I was born at Mary's Help Hospital at 145 Guerrero Street on the corner of Clinton Park Street. I grew up in Noe Valley and the Mission. I went to school at Marshal, Leconte, and Bayview Elementary Schools; James Lick Junior High; and Mission High. I still live and work in the beautiful Mission District.

I love my hometown dearly, but over six decades I've seen lots of change. I personally experienced gentrification and displacement when I was "downsized" out of my job with United Airlines and later became a victim of an "Ellis Act" eviction after living in my Day Street home for nearly 40 years.

In my "Homes for the Homies" diorama series, I tried to capture the soul and essence of the old Mission before it all disappears. These intimately scaled dioramas are nostalgic representations of the Mission, North Beach, and other special memories and moments in San Francisco.

Elaine Chu and Marina Perez-Wong
Twin Walls Mural Company

"The smaller the world expects us to be, the larger the surfaces we'll paint!"

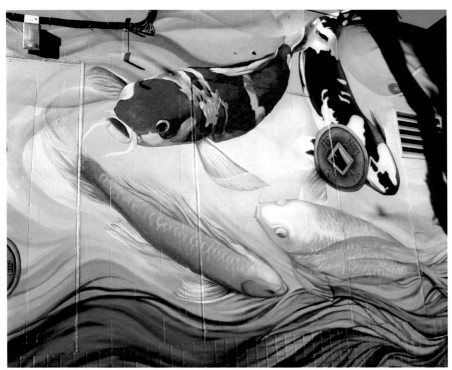

Above: *Koi, La Mission*, 2700-24th Street, San Francisco. Below: *La Flor de la Vida*, 3473-25th Street, San Francisco. Photos: Twin Walls Mural Company.

HOPE. ACT. The Fight For Freedom. Hemlock Alley, San Francisco.

We are both San Francisco natives who met in high school while attending the School of the Arts. Instantly connecting both in styles and interests, we collaborated on many murals in the city and learned mural painting by working with Precita Eyes Muralists in the Mission. Marina Perez-Wong graduated from California College of the Arts with a BFA in painting, and Elaine Chu graduated from the Maryland Institute College of Arts with a BFA in painting.

With a strong community art focus, we strive to create murals that reflect the community we are painting in. History and stories preserved through street art educates and inspires people that live in the neighborhood and pass by it everyday. Our style is influenced by the Mujeres Muralistas and strong local women muralists like Susan Cervantes, Juana Alicia, and Miranda Bergman. We also realize the importance of setting an example for future generations of strong, independent women in the art world, especially as women of color. We noticed how young women responded and reacted to our work but we especially noticed our importance as lady painters because the most common phrase we tend to hear is: "Oh YOU'RE painting that? I thought it was guys. I didn't realize girls were doing that." Another one of our favorites that we get daily when working on scaffolding is "Be careful up there!" (always from men of various ages). Most of those remarks are entertaining and frustrating simultaneously.

One of the best parts of being muralists in the Bay Area is how much we continue to learn about the city through research and also through storytelling through visuals. We work collaboratively through listening and thoughtful research to tell a story through street art that is not just a beautiful image but reflects the beauty, culture, and diversity of San Francisco.

Shizue Seigel

A community art project by Mission-Bernal Merchants Association and Galleria de la Raza features three generations of women who ran Playa Azul retaurant, one of 9 businesses and 58 residents displaced by the 3300 Mission fire. The building, bought in 2004 for $1.5 million, is now for sale for $3.5 M.

218

8

artivists
activate

Rene Yañez, *Attack on the Future*, mixed media, 2018.

Rene Yañez

René Yañez is a Mexican American artist, curator, and producer who lives and works in San Francisco. He has a quietly self-effacing yet powerful presence. Since the early 1970s, he has collaborated with and promoted the work of so many talented visual and performing artists that his own ever-evolving artwork can be overshadowed. Yañez co-founded Galería de la Raza in 1970, and served as its first artistic director for fifteen years. In 1972, he was one of the first curators to introduce Mexico's Day of the Dead to the U.S. in a contemporary context. The visually stunning *Día de los Muertos* exhibitions he has curated at SOMArts Cultural Center since 2001 are seen by thousands every year. He has acted as visual and performing arts curator for exhibitions at SF MOMA, the Yerba Buena Center of the Arts, the de Young Museum, the Mexican Museum and elsewhere. The *Chicano Visions: American Painters on the Verge* exhibition her curated traveled to 15 venues around the U.S. Yañez remains a powerful role model and a vital cultural force in the San Francisco arts community.

Artist Statement. As an artist in San Francisco, I've learned to be very versatile when it comes to making a living. In working as a curator and organizing over 300 exhibits, it's vital to acquaint yourself with artist and subject and delve into projects with passion and understanding. By working with and directing the comedy group Culture Clash and performance artist Guillermo Gomez-Peña, and bringing the group ASCO from Los Angeles to perform at Galería de la Raza, I learned the great satisfaction of connecting with the audience. As a curator I appreciate the opportunity to work with great artists, architects, and lighting and sound technicians to bring about successful exhibitions.

In my own work, I have always experimented with different media as they become available to artists. In the 1970s, I worked with color Xerox machines with slide attachments, Gestetner and mimeo, and silkscreen printing processes. Today I am working with giclée prints that I scan from original artworks in my sketchbooks, and then layer with paint, colored pencil, and collage. I also create street expression and interventions by posting artwork on Mission walls. The alleys are teeming with art, with stencil-spray art on the sidewalks and with stickers everywhere. This art is just meant for the streets.

In my career as an artist-curator, the thing I love most is being able to work and collaborate with my son Rio, curating *Day of the Dead* at SOMArts and flipping art tortillas with Jos Sances and Art Hazelwood in our Great Tortilla Conspiracy. Being an artist, all I can say is that commitment and passion are part of the life.

Rene Yañez, *Frida Apparition*, mixed media, 2018.

Frida Kahlo figures iconically in many of Yañez's works. He fills pages and pages of his black sketchbooks with ideas that he develops and explores in many iterations, adding textural richness with paint, bleach, pastels, cut paper, and found objects. He then creates more variations on giclée prints.

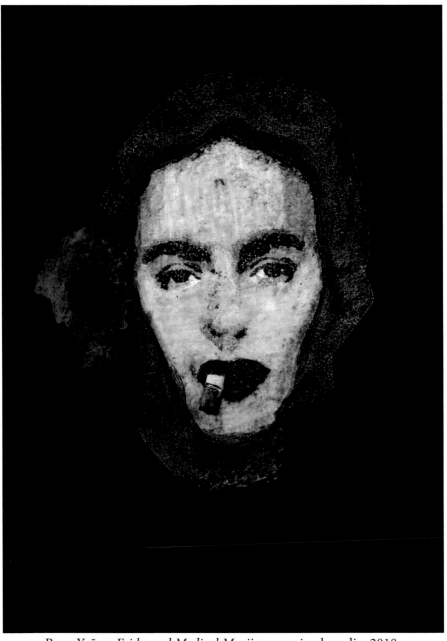

Rene Yañez, *Frida and Medical Marijuana*, mixed media, 2018.

Yañez has begun a new series of works exploring the medical and creative components and effects of marijuana. He celebrates the legalization of marijuana, especially now, as he undergoes medical treatments that necessitate the use of medical mariajuna.

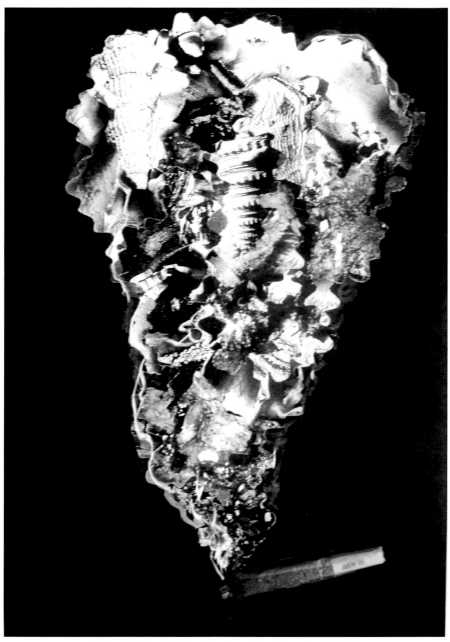

Rene Yañez, *Up in Smoke*, mixed media, 2018.

Hallucinations are one of the side effects of the drug. Yañez uses the smoke to analyze feelings and visions that he tries to capture on paper. They become a series of reflections on medical marijuana and a long, rich life. He affixes actual joints to some of his work.

Mark Harris, *Untitled - Flag*, mixed media on found wood, 18 x 24 in., 2014.

The Activist Art of Mark Harris

Mark Harris is a San Francisco-based artist whose work has appeared at numerous galleries, including the USF Thacher Gallery, San Francisco; Rock, Paper, Scissors Collective, Oakland; 111 Minna Gallery, San Francisco; Marin Museum of Contemporary Art, Novato; and The Whitney Young Cultural Center, San Francisco, among others. Harris has combined his passions for social justice, activism, and art making to create a unique visual vocabulary that he uses to engage his audience on some of the most critical issues facing society today. He is equally passionate about working with youth, and has taught in both public and private schools in San Francisco and the surrounding Bay Area. www.markharrisstudiosf.com

From his newsletter: "This spring I had the privilege of speaking at four different schools in the East Side Union High School District in San Jose, CA. I presented work from my "State of Denial" series and talked about using political art to make a statement and inspire critical thinking. I encouraged the students to use their voices to speak out about issues concerning their future.

"Earlier this year my art was censored and removed from an exhibit by the Superintendent of the East Side Union High School District. As a result, the story received a lot of media coverage. This has given me more of a platform to use my art in helping create change by giving a voice to what is right and just."

Mark Harris, *Original Gangsters*, mixed media collage on paper,
24 x 18 in., 2014.

After reading about the removal of Harris' artwork from the lobby of the administrative offices of the East Side Union High School District in San Jose, San Francisco Museum of Modern Art invited him to make a video about his role as an artist working in public spaces, and about about the role of the artist as public intellectual in society today. The video can be seen here: https://openspace.sfmoma.org/2017/05/state-of-denial/

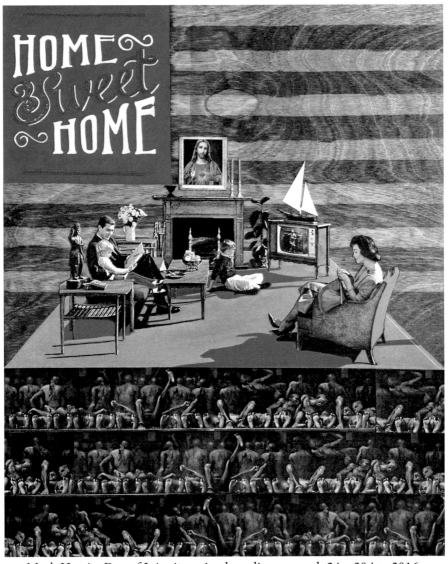

Mark Harris, *Den of Iniquity*, mixed media on panel, 24 x 20 in., 2016.

Mark Harris, *Freedom Isn't Free*, mixed media collage on panel,
20 x 16 in., 2016.

Ode to the Enduring Woman
Venus Zuhura Noble

Is there a befitting sonnet that can capture all her strength?
Doubtful for this heroine thrives
Her patience and compassion will stretch to any length
Her beauty transcends definitions from all lexicons; or picture of any model
She is sustained by an obscured superior powerful love
Often unrecognized.
She withstands continual battles
Her name is Wanda…the one who emerged as an activist
When the cop couldn't tell the difference between a taser and a gun
His self-righteous indignation unbelievable, after he shot Oscar her son!
Her Name is Lucy. Her name is Samaria…
When young Jordan and young Tamir were snatched away by rogue racists
She stood stern and resolute staring at their faces
Don't forget Sandra Bland.
Who they called depressed; found hanging in her cell.
Her blood cries out defiantly … asking … Who me? Suicide? What the hell?
Alan's Momma Jeralyn …. We all know her, right?
She had to accept his diploma after he was killed. It ignited her vigilant fight!
Her is name is Sybrina
Trayvon was a real danger you see …
For wearing a hoody and carrying Skittles; his killer they set free!
A lapse of logic prevailed when Valerie contested
Citing a system that hunts Black men
Philando died on camera with no justice
Eric and Erica should not have died
Gwen and Gloria lamented
As their murderers tried to hide
The cowardly deeds so vicious and contrived
These women came from obscurity
Forming a justice league
Starting a movement for all to see. Demanding lasting peace.

Live from Planet Woke
Kwan Booth

On a morning that was remarkable in no other way, the famous sports star stared into the bathroom mirror, into his own face, and the huge problem hovering above it.

A kinky revolution had sprouted atop his head as he'd slept. A tiny 2-inch afro now stood triumphantly after toppling his close-cropped Caesar like a corrupt regime.

After breaking two sets of clippers and chipping his favorite sheers trying to rid himself of the stubborn scruff, he headed down to breakfast, where he lamented to his wife while devouring an egg-white omelette.

The news was on. A young woman had been shot by police the night before and there were protests happening all over the country. The famous sports star ignored the journalist's voice like he always did, but had to call his wife's name loudly to draw her attention away from the big screen.

He complained about the new edition to his profile and worried that it would be taken the wrong way. Like some kind of political statement or act of defiance.

Indeed this new face, with it's black power coils, did resemble the pictures of the old activists and rabble rousers he'd seen in the books his wife was always reading. Books with titles that promised of uprisings and critical examinations of things that the famous sports star had either taken for granted or never fully understood.

His wife listened to his concerns, clutching a large mug of tea in front of her chest and nodding with the rhythms of a compassionate lover.

She told him that he was overreacting. That it was probably just temporary. And besides, if some people were rattled by a little something like this, then those people needed to have their coat tails pulled to the ways of the world that they were living in.

The famous sports star trusted his wife and knew that she had a much better grasp on these things. So he sighed with heavy breath, pulled his jersey over his head with a bit more difficulty than usual, and headed out to practice, where he avoided questions about his new hairstyle and led the team through their morning routine.

By the end of the month his mini fro had blown out into a perfect 12-inch sphere and a short beard and goatee had sprouted up to match. He'd begun to resemble some of the men on his father's side, with their oak skin and drawls that stretched clear back to Mississippi. The ones that the god-fearing Catholics on his mother's side didn't like very much.

And despite his early fears, and the fact that he'd made a point to stay away from the bruising debates on race and sex and oppression that had been igniting all over the country, his new 'do was taking a political stance for him.

He noticed the new attention whenever he wore a hoodie, stood in elevators with white women or made late night grocery store runs. Not famous sports star attention. But something else entirely.

Once his fro reached two feet in length, certain friends said that they were shocked and slightly dismayed that he'd decided to play the race card. They'd never seen that side of him before.

"We didn't think you were one of those people."

At three feet, photos of the star and his new hairstyle were leaked to the media. Sports commentators and pundits denounced his actions and questioned his allegiances. They fumed. Sport was no place to insert one's personal political opinions.

By the time his afro topped four feet in circumference, the town where he'd grown up, which happened to have more churches per capita than any city in the United States, was torn in two.

At the local pizza parlor where he used to work—someone painted a Hitler moustache on his portrait, right before someone else covered it in kisses.

Another restaurant named a hot dog in his honor, while someone else hung a mannequin with an afro from the Oak tree in front of the house he'd grown up in.

By the time the season rolled around the sport star's afro was the size of the state of Virginia and there was no way that he could play in his current condition.

Which suited him just fine. At his wife's encouragement he'd began reading the stacks of books that she had placed strategically around the house. And the more he read, the more that the protests erupting across the country started to resonate.

He'd taken to spending the majority of his time with his books and his thoughts and his wife and the growing movement of people who'd begun to gather around him—drawn by the news reports and social media feeds and the buzz of change. It was like his hair had its own gravitational pull as people from all over the world were drawn to the man with the planet sized afro. Together, under the shade of his curly hair, they'd discuss politics and philosophy and revolution, while mapping out a new world that the famous former sports star now knew that he played a part in creating.

Before long, the afro eclipsed all of the West Coast and some of the more adventurous had began to climb to its peak, scaling the sides to hike across its wide expanse in order to see the world from a new vantage.

Over time they discovered that the kinky curls were excellent for growing crops. A little digging revealed a network of underground freshwater streams. Carpenters sheared off long planks of the dense curls to build libraries and schools and more and more like-minded people began to join.

The famous former sports star's wife was elected to oversee the development. Villages began popping up on the hairy surface, with small houses and customs and names that reflected the values this group of idealists were working towards.

At a press conference, when he was asked about the developing community and what he was hoping to accomplish, the famous now-former sports star said that he was just doing his part to create the world that we all wanted to see.

"We're just trying to be our best selves," he said, staring right into the cameras and the flashing bulbs.

"We believe that it's time to build a world where that can happen."

And high above them the sound of hammers and working drifted down to the press conference. The sounds of children and singing soon followed, as the promise of something better floated just above them all—between the ground and the sky—huge, living, and clearly visible to anyone with the courage to just look up.

Previously published online at Chicago Literati.com, Afrofuturism issue, May 7, 2017.

Kwan Booth is an award-winning writer and strategist focused on the intersection of media, technology and social justice. He is the editor of the anthology *Black Futurists Speak* and has been published in *The Guardian, Fusion, CHORUS: a literary mixtape,* and *Beyond the Frontier: African American Poets for the 21st Century*. He has developed media and technology projects for Facebook, the Knight Center for Digital Media, the Kapor Center for Social Impact, and the National Conference on Media Reform. He has been twice nominated for the Pushcart Prize. www.Boothism.org.

Colin Choy Kimzey, *Here Signifies*, silkscreen, 25 x 19 in., 2016.

Colin Choy Kimzey is a mixed-race, Chinese American culture worker born, raised, and based in San Francisco. With a degree in Art Practice from Stanford University, he studies Asian Pacific American activist art as an archivist for Kearny Street Workshop, the oldest Asian Pacific interdisciplinary arts organization in the country. He is interested in how histories of social movements, labor, and migration construct urban space, particularly as battlegrounds between communities of color and larger systems of capitalism and colonialism.

THE MOST RADICAL THING I EVER DID WAS TO STAY PUT

GRACE LEE BOGGS

Colin Choy Kimzey, *Radical Thing*, silkscreen, 25 x19 in., 2016.

San Francisco is a unique site of political experimentation, multiracial organizing, cultural production, and systemic inequity. Gentrification threatens the ability of communities of color to stay in their neighborhoods and tell their alternative stories of the city. These conflicts over space and narrative are major themes in my work. I primarily use silkscreen for its history as a tool of social protest, instigating intergenerational conversation with the Bay Area's contested spaces and communities.

Choppy Oshiro

Choppy Oshiro, a graphic designer/illustrator, loves creating things by hand. She grew up in Hawaii and moved to San Francisco, earning a BFA from the Academy of Art. Experienced in graphic design and print production, she specializes in design, publishing, and arts-based projects. She complements her passion for creating art around community and social justice issues by providing design and photojournalism services for Oakland-based California Nurses Association/National Nurses United and has served on the board of directors for Kearny Street Workshop. Her work is created with cut-paper techniques based on katagami (Japanese textile stenciling).

Statement: For me, the drive to create a piece of art has always been the message. My art is me shouting from atop my soapbox, and my soapbox is built on the shoulders of all the community activists striving to create equity.

Choppy Oshiro, *Historias*, mixed media installation, 2012. An homage to labor history exhibited at SOMArts' Día de los Muertos. Photo: Bob Hsiang.

Above: *Presente*, installation honoring Silvia Parra, Cynthia "Kiki" Wallis, and Martha Rodriguez, paper with *Dear Orlando*, paper and fabric, 2016. Below left: *Skyscraped*, 24 x 18 in., blacklight poster board. Below right: *For Yuri*, 2014. For samples of her work, see www.creativehotlist. com/coshiro2.

Water is Life: Recollections from Standing Rock
Leon Sun

September-October 2016. Riding along the highway from Bismarck to Standing Rock over the easy rolling hills of North Dakota, I couldn't help but note how the natural beauty of the land contrasted with the violence that was being perpetrated upon the peoples of this land.

We knew we were approaching Oceti Sakowin Camp when we saw lots of banners strung on the wire fencing alongside the highway. The banners were placed there by peoples who had come from all over the continent in a historic show of Native unity. There were also flags from different parts of the world. I saw a Palestinian flag among them. Later on in the visit, I met indigenous

peoples from as far away as Norway and Tibet. The call of freedom and justice was heard all over the world, and no power could keep apart the oneness of the human spirit.

Entering Oceti Sakowin camp, I felt like I was walking into history being made. One of the first things I noticed was the self-sufficiency of the place. For instance, off to the side of the flag-lined driveway was a solar-powered generator donated by a 100% Diné-owned engineering company. In another corner, food was being prepared, cooked and served to anyone who needed it. Later on our visit we were treated to a performance by school children. Because many had settled in for the long haul, a school had been set up for the children so as not to miss any classes. Tribes from all over sent or came with donations of food, water, firewood and other necessities. An art tent was set up where Native and ally artists like myself came to paint signs and banners. There was a media center set up with Digital Smoke Signals sending out communications to the world from the ground and from the air with drones.

In the middle of the camp was a fire circle, where the fire never went out. Across from the circle was a stage with a sound system where elders gave continuous talks, along with announcements as they came up. It was where our delegation declared our solidarity and exchanged gifts with the elders in a welcoming ceremony. It soon occurred to me that, more than being a base of operations for the water protectors, Standing Rock was a living example of Native self-determination.

At Standing Rock I learned about the meaning and power of prayer. Throughout my stay I heard, from all the tribes that came, a common refrain:

"We came to pray" and "We are still here." Spiritually I felt a great connection with the people I met, as many Native beliefs and practices resonated with my Chinese culture: in particular, the respect and reverence for ancestors who remain in the present as teachers and protectors. Perhaps all the rivers running though our collective memory came from the same source. Water is Life.

239

Standing Rock, North Dakota
Kimi Sugioka

The evidence is clear,
There are only false leaders here
Who use their power to stuff their pockets

The true leaders
Carry signs and pray
Tell the pipeline pushers
To own their disgrace,
Make their money
In an honest way

Shame their persecutors into calling off their dogs
Tell the hired thugs to go home
And ask their mothers and grandmothers
If they should strike down
Unarmed mothers and grandmothers
Who brazenly pray to save
The born and unborn
Of all our relations

Water and land protectors
Stand with their faces to the wind
In the middle of open prairies
No cities, no witnesses, no media

They do not live in Herod's court
They do not feast on the bones of the beloved
But walk and pray with songs and drums and eagle feathers

The protectors have come to heal
The wounds of the earth
I can see them from here
Their faces shine with ceremony
The singing rock people
Are not alone
And neither
Are we.

Sweet Nothings
Kimi Sugioka

I have decided to whisper sweet nothings into your ear tonight
Cause it's all I really know how to do
I learned early from the maid who took care of me
When my mother could not
A black woman who knew
The weight and size and shape of color
In Moncore, North Carolina

I didn't know what color I was
My birth certificate said "white"
But I was an almond-eyed anomaly
Born into the whiskey laced womb of the south
To a white mother and a Japanese father
Whose animosity for one another
Clawed well past color and culture

Not that I could see color
Til I moved to Berkeley, California
Onto Telegraph Avenue
In 1965
I mean I saw it in the picture shows: Gunsmoke and Wagon Train
Where I mistook myself, not for the Indian princess,
But for the blue-eyed blonde
It must have been the humidity

But that's a long time ago
I have been identified as native:
Navajo, Cherokee, Hawaiian, Eskimo
To the eye of my beholders
For so long, I finally gave up and invisibly claimed that heritage
Proud to wear the hair and eyes of the disenfranchised
And the wiser for walking those irrefutably ambiguous borderlines

Here I am
Knowing nothing
So well
I can practically
Taste it.

Descant on the faces of love
Kimi Sugioka

In the mirror of night
my true nature
sings and arcs
above infraction & censure

The text of despair
erased and retooled
with wit
with artifice
refracting into
disrepair
in the name of
Silence
to atone for the cacophony
raging between the pages
of my sins

descant
descent

into a skinwalker's greed
I of lust and determination
am the shadow
in his path

where berated souls
bloom false-petaled,
vagabond intimacy

and shatter the mirror
or the illusion
of the mirror

Having slung the moon
in the left side pocket
I have come
with crystal plate
and crusted spoon
Namesake
Keepsake

Slaker of thirst & longing
For wounded gods
with broken tongues
My heart is a penny
in your boot
to remind you
of the price
one pays
for love

Kimi Sugioka is a poet, songwriter and eduator who earned an MFA from Naropa University's Jack Kerouac School of Disembodied Poetics. A San Francisco Poetry Slam winner, and a founding member of the spoken word group, Bloodtest, she has a book published by Manic D Press, *The Language of Birds*, and a recording of her songs. She takes measure of the world through the lens of a utopian educator in a dystopian system, a bi-cultural woman of color, and a single mother.

Making Art That's Uncomfortable
Nancy Wang, MSW

Eight standing ovations!! In Tennessee, Utah, Washington, California! And then after the last performance … a letter came.

Now, I knew my piece, *Red Altar,* contained many truths and facts that could be very uncomfortable for some European Americans. Even as I wrote this story of my ancestors, I had to overcome my "be nice" Asian way of not wanting to offend anyone. But how could I write an historical play without some very uncomfortable facts?

The history of the early Chinese who came over in the time of the Gold Rush is not pretty. Not many know about it either. It is not in the history books. It is not part of our American knowledge base. And so, as an artist, I felt I needed to be as specific and revelatory as possible about what was happening on the West Coast to the Chinese.

And, I needed to make sure to include white people who were allies for balance, though there was not much balance back then!

Writing *Red Altar*: So, in my most non-offensive way, I wrote *Red Altar,* a multimedia, storytelling, and interdisciplinary performance theater piece. It follows three generations of one Chinese family that started the fishing industry in the Monterey Bay area. I spent years doing research, interviewing family members, did readings for feedback, and it is still evolving. When is an art piece ever really done? Art is not dead. It lives, it breathes, it grows.

Red Altar tells the personalized story of how, in 1850, six teens sailed their junk boat from the Pearl River Delta region of Southern China to California, heading for San Francisco. But, caught in a torrential storm, they were blown south of San Francisco and crashed into Carmel Bay, California. Rescued by the Esselen-Rumsen, they began to build their lives. And, they were successful, very successful, and they pretty much lived in harmony with the Mexicans in what had been Mexico's territory up until 1848. However, when more Europeans began to move into Monterey, things began to change.

Suddenly, there was name-calling, small violent infractions against the Chinese while just walking down the street. The European Americans began to pass laws specifically against Chinese fishermen in order to get rid of them. However, the Chinese proved to be resilient and determined. Their courage and ability to reinvent themselves over and over again became evident, and the Chinese remained.

For example, a law was passed forbidding the Chinese from fishing during the day. So the Chinese fishermen fished at night for squid. They then built a very successful industry.

Then a law was passed saying that the Chinese could no longer dry their squid. If they couldn't dry their squid, how could they preserve it to ship to China or sell to the Chinese communities throughout the West Coast? So they gathered the rotten fish innards dumped on a public beach outside a certain Italian immigrant-owned cannery and turned it into fish emulsion and fish fertilizer, selling it to the farmers in the valley. Again, they were very successful.

But it was not just in the Monterey area. Throughout the West Coast, violence and discrimination were rampant against the Chinese. In my piece, we project newspaper illustrations that portray the Chinese as bats, rats, monkeys, pigs; and headlines about special taxes charging Chinese only, about lynchings, mob rule, the marching out of entire Chinese communities, and the burning of Chinese villages. *Red Altar* is based on and inspired by historical true events.

In our multimedia storytelling theater play, we mention Europeans who supported the Chinese or who befriended the Chinese and did what they could to help. But, the tide against the Chinese was too big and too strong for fair play. Still, we survived, even after the fishing village was burned down and the fish emulsion factory was destroyed by fire. And, coincidentally, a new fish emulsion factory was soon built next to the Italian cannery.

But, we not only survived, we thrived. And, we're still here. But …

"But it's not over." This phrase marks the end of *Red Altar*, followed by images of Black Lives Matter, photos of people murdered because of the color of their skin, and pictures of people marching against racism. Finally, one more phrase—"Lift the lamp higher"—asks all of us to shine the light higher and stronger into the darkness.

We end the performance uplifting, inclusive, non-judgmental, with standing ovations at every performance.

And then that letter came.

The Letter: The first words of the letter are: "I was deeply hurt and offended by the *Red Altar* performance on Saturday night …. Can't you ever show kindness and appreciation for all we've done for you …" And "How could your businesses thrive without the patronage of white people?" And she suggests that we end our play with "a loving word to lo fon," a Chinese name for Caucasians, and "… perhaps asking the entire audience to sing a song together."

Finally, she asks me to write into my play all the wonderful things white people have done, and asks how I would like it if I had to sit through over-an-hour play of how all the Chinese did bad things to white people. That would be

244

a play for her to write, not me; she missed the point that this was a historical rendition of my own family history!

Many thoughts and feelings thread throughout her two-page letter in defense of her whiteness. Truly, I read the letter with my mouth agape, closing and opening it many times! I am sure that the things she wrote are typical of what many others think and feel out there. And so I found it very interesting.

Basically, this woman was asking me to "white wash" my piece so that she could feel better. She was asking me to take care of her feelings by writing a piece that tells how wonderful European Americans are in the face of this particular set of historical truths and facts. She thought I should add that things are so much better now, and that the Chinese are "better off in America than in China."

She goes on to accuse me of being racist and hateful because of this storytelling play. She asks why I can't just say nice things about white people.

All of this is the epitome of "white privilege."

White Privilege: So here's the thing: "white privilege" is not personal. People with white skin are born into white privilege. The choice was not theirs. Nonetheless, white privilege provides them unearned privileges that the rest of us don't get automatically. America has been Euro-centric from the beginning, and their culture demands everyone else measure up to them as the standard— in the way we express ourselves, in the way we dress, in how we speak, in what we eat, in how we pray, in the way we look. European Americans, consciously or unconsciously, are saying to us that we are more desirable as human beings if we are like them. They feel more comfortable if we are. At its worst, if you are not like them, you are considered and treated as less worthy. This attitude is institutionalized. It is pervasive. It has been the "norm" for so long that most of us are unaware of it, including people of color. It's just the way it is. It's like being the fish in that saying: "Does a fish know it's in water?"

This letter writer, as a European American, found it difficult to hear a different point of view other than her own European American point of view. And most probably, there were others in our audiences like that. *Red Altar* was difficult to hear because it required her to step out of her position of white privilege and to experience life from someone else's perspective and position. I know that this woman loves plays like *South Pacific, Flower Drum Song, The World of Suzy Wong*, and the like—all written about Asians by Caucasiansfrom a European American point of view. If *Red Altar* were like those stories, portraying Asian Americans as cute, exotic, harmless, song-and-dance making, keeping our issues light and funny, we probably would not have gotten that letter.

My use of the words European American (or EuroAmerican) instead of "white" is very much based on how white privilege operates. It is important and even necessary that white Americans know they come from somewhere else, too. If we are Asian American because our ancestors are from Asia, then they need to be identified as European American so that they and others understand their ancestors are from Europe. They are not the only and "real" Americans, maintaining that the rest of us are the "other"—the marginalized Americans, the "ethnics," not "true" Americans like they are.

Recently I was turned down for a grant because of my "languaging." When I asked for examples, one of them was "Well, what's a EuroAmerican?" When I explained it, he simply said "We use the term white." I asked who was on the panel, and he said it was a multicultural panel. So, we can all be that fish in that water. It is not just European Americans.

I am not saying that all European Americans are like this. Absolutely not.

In Need of Allies: European Americans were the majority of our *Red Altar* audiences—anywhere from 75% to 99%. These audiences gave us standing ovations and expressed appreciation, shock, gratitude, and a heartfelt compassion for our history, even apologies for what happened. They want to learn because they are dedicated to eradicating racism and prejudice, both systemic and personal. We need all the partners we can get; we need each other.

Including the woman who wrote the letter.

After all, she came to the performance. She took the time to write the letter. This is good. This is an opening. This is someone who is willing to dialogue. Perhaps nothing will change, but it is an opportunity. If nothing else, we have learned so much about the kind of thinking that is out there.

So, my co-director Robert Kikuchi-Yngojo and I decided to respond to her letter. Here was an opportunity to figure out how to express our point of view in a way that this self-described liberal yet racist woman could understand without getting further offended. There are many like her in our country and this was a chance to hear it, think about it, and look into our own set of beliefs so we could write about them without creating a greater distance between us. (Yes, as usual, victims of a perpetration need to be the educators. Learning, changing, healing would not get done if we did not speak up.)

In her own way, she, like us, is fully committed to being part of the solution. But, no problem can be solved if the problem is not thoroughly understood. She didn't like hearing about the racism and violence, so she wanted us to "leave it behind" and "get over it and move on." Oh, if it were that simple.

There are too many parts of her letter—and our responses—to write here. However, my co-director summed it all up beautifully:

1) Can we agree that this chapter of our immigration story was hurtful and painful for the Chinese immigrants?

2) Can we agree that the important stories of people who have had a direct experience of historic events need to be told and heard, honored and respected?

3) Can we agree that the many stories, uncomfortable and painful, must not be ignored because that would be tantamount to suppression? We must listen to truthful stories and not sweep our pain and suffering or history under the rug. Knowing the past is precedent to moving the present into a better future.

4) Can we agree that all Allies—progressives for social change—need to be a multicultural Euro-Afro-Asian-Latino-Native coalition? If so, we need to respect each other's history.

5) Can we agree that positiveness and happy feelings must not mask over important stories and experiences? In healing society, just as in healing victims of trauma, rape and other atrocities, victims must be allowed to express themselves, unfettered, unchanged, and un-censored by the perpetrators or by those who just do not want to hear about it. It is irresponsible to democracy.

6) Ultimately we CAN agree that we all aim for a better world of peace, love and understanding.

We can DISAGREE on our methods and approaches. We have our ways as artists. You have different approaches. Use them. Good luck with them. Let's all hope our combined efforts work. As we said in the play "It is NOT over..."

Art That is Uncomfortable: So yes! I made art that made people uncomfortable, because I also know many yearn for meaning and depth in the artistic events they attend. If we are to create a knowledgeable community of allies, I have an inner mandate, as an artist and an activist, to provide for that! There are many Americans who are willing to be allies, and they need what we have to offer.

Make uncomfortable art with respect and honor. Make uncomfortable art that speaks truth to power. Make uncomfortable art if it's from your heart. You will learn, and others will learn a great deal from it.

Red Altar is not offensive, but this woman was offended. These are two very different things. I know I did not make offensive art—uncomfortable for some, yes, but being offended is a choice made by the receiver.

In the end, my integrity remained intact. I did not make little of a very horrible era in America's history or pretend all is fine now. No, it is not over.

Make that art that speaks truth to power and have it make a difference in how we all come to live our lives together in peace and harmony. We need more of this. Enough of frivolity, though it has its place. We all need to help create balance in a world that is terribly out of balance right now.

I am so glad that in this lifetime, at this particular time, I am an artist!

Nancy Wang, MSW. Growing up in New Orleans and Chicago resulted in different perspectives for Nancy as a Chinese American. Coming west, San Francisco's Chinatown was as alien to her as it would be to someone from Iowa. Eventually finding her roots in the city, Nancy's performances and workshops are a celebration of diversity and of her Asian identity. With co-director Robert Kikuchi-Yngojo, she performs around the world reaching millions as Eth-Noh-Tec, kinetic story theater. With a background in modern and ethnic dance, theater and playwriting, she co-scripts and sculpts Eth-Noh-Tec's synchronistic and seamless tandem movements to create lyrical, rhythmic and evocative visuals in their storytelling and theater pieces. www.ethnohtec.org

Artist Statement: Eth-Noh-Tec's mission is to create art that heals the divides within us and between us.

Our mission statement is inseparable from our personal vision and purpose. This is how we intend to live the moments in our lives.

I did not choose to be an artist. It was just there. It is a way of thinking, being and seeing the world that is different than, for example, a scientist or a real-estate person. We are all creative as human beings, but creativity in the arts is an all-encompassing way of living.

Luckily, I am both right-brained and left-brained. I am also a psychotherapist and love being able to connect to my clients. In my private practice, which I closed last year, I was able to apply my mission. There is nothing more sublime than being in the presence of someone's vulnerability and courage as they dig deep to discover the root of a problem and find resolution. Lucky me.

Then, there's my right creative-art brain. Dancing, writing, performing, singing, even arts and crafts make my day! It is joyful. It is what gives me energy, calm, purpose, and aliveness I just don't get from balancing my checkbook or cleaning the house or even throwing a party!

I hope to be able to continue until I'm not in this world anymore, doing what I do. I just need to get someone else to balance the books and clean the house.

9

spirit
sustains

Shizue Seigel. *I Am a Link*, photo collage, 17 x 11 in., 2009.

The Fly
Shizue Seigel

When I was nine, Mom and I went to live with Baachan and Jiichan, my Japanese immigrant Grandma and Grandpa. Ten years after their release from incarceration, they'd finally earned enough from sharecropping strawberries to buy land of their own. It was nothing compared to the 140-acre seaside ranch from before the war. This was ten, hot dusty acres south of San Jose, off the old Hwy. 101—"Blood Alley," they called it, because cars could get hit by fast-moving traffic as they tried to pull onto the highway.

Every week, Mom dragged me to the Buddhist Sunday School on a nearby farm. Boring! We sat on hard folding chairs, in a bare, whitewashed room with a piano and a small Buddhist shrine. We listened to the traveling minister sing corny Christian-sounding hymns and read boring sutras out loud. If I started swinging my legs to pass the time, Mom gave my thigh a sharp, quick squeeze, so I chewed the inside of my cheek instead and twirled the tassel of my ojuzu prayer beads. But I did believe in the Buddha. Every time we said the prayer called the Golden Chain, it etched deeper into my heart and brain.

"I am a link in Amida's golden chain of love that stretches around the world. I must keep my link bright and strong. I will try to be kind to all living things and protect all who are weaker than myself. I will try to think pure and beautiful thoughts, to say pure and beautiful words, and to do pure and beautiful deeds, knowing that on what I do now depends not only my happiness or unhappiness, but also that of others. May every link in Amida's golden chain of love become bright and strong, and may we all attain perfect peace."

How can I protect all those weaker than myself? I worried. I'm just a kid! I couldn't stop thinking about it. I visualized my parents, grandparents, and all my aunties and uncles lined up in a row, expecting me to take care of my link. They weren't angry, just disappointed, which made it worse.

Baachan, Jiichan and Mom had all become devout Buddhists in camp. They'd had a lot of time on their hands, baking in the heat in their bare tar-paper barracks wondering why, why, why had this happened to them. To find peace from fear and anger, they went to church and to informal prayer groups called zadan-kai to listen to those who had found shinjin, faith. They learned from the teachings of Shinran Shonin that if they were in hell, it was a self-created one. Each of us created our present through our past actions. Karma was inevitable. We reaped what we sowed; we could not change the past, only accept its consequences with grace. Life was what it was, and all the anger and blame and wishing could not change it until it was ready to change. As surely as night followed day, loss followed gain. There was a time for ganbatte, determination and hard work, and there was a time for shikata ga nai, letting go. As long we saw the world as duality—good-bad, like-dislike—instead of as a unified field of gratitude, suffering was inevitable.

It was all too deep for me. To keep me from doing things that would create bad karma, Baachan simply told me that Amida was all-powerful and all-seeing. He lived in the sky and kept track of everything. He sounded a little like the Christians' God, but without the beard and the vengeance. Anyway, Baachan said if we did good things, good things would happen. If we did bad things, bad things would happen. That was karma, and you couldn't escape it.

Of course that didn't keep Baachan from covering her bets. She prayed to Amida Buddha in the black-and-gold shrine in the dining room, and she prayed to Kamisama in the kitchen, perched in a simple pine shrine on a high shelf above the fridge. She prayed to the natural spirits around her. Before the war, when the plow turned up arrowheads, she brought in a Shinto priest to offer a prayer to the old ones, and ask their permission to farm their land.

But it was hard to be good all the time. One day, I was sitting on the front porch steps, feeling bored in the lazy heat of summer. An enormous housefly buzzed around my head. I flicked it away, but it kept coming back. Bzzzz. Bzzzz. Bzzt. Bzzt. It landed on the steps and rubbed its feelers together. Its huge red eyes bulged from the sides of its head. I wondered if it saw hundreds of little girls bending down to look at it.

What would the fly look like dead? I pushed the thought away. I will try to be kind to all living things. But the thought came back. I wonder what will happen if I killed it.

There was no one around: Mom was at work, Baachan and Jiichan were out in the fields. I glanced up at the sky. It was a sharp clean blue without a cloud in it. "It's only a fly. Maybe Amida won't see," I thought. I mentally manufactured a dense grey cloud and pulled it across the sky. Then I took off my shoe and swatted the fly. When I lifted the shoe, the fly didn't look much different, except for thick yellow guts oozing out, and a red smear of blood. Its blood was the same color as mine!

From then on, whenever Jiichan bounced the pickup over the railroad tracks and waited for a gap in traffic to turn onto Blood Alley, I could almost feel a giant flyswatter hovering in the sky above us.

Published online as part of a longer piece, "Of Christmas and Karma," at *Persimmon Tree*, Winter 2015, http://www.persimmontree.org/v2/winter-2016/of-christmas-and-karma/

Aurora Borealis
Edna Cabcabin Moran

As a child, I lived in Iceland where it was a treat to bundle up in a heavy coat with itchy wool collars and a thick-knitted face mask pulled down over my head and wait under dark skies for the aurora borealis. After what felt like an eternity, it showed up. The aurora borealis started in the corner of the horizon, a cluster of shimmering lights. And it grew, expanding as a green glow of shapes that danced on a syrupy sky. On rare occasions, we witnessed a light show of purples and reds radiating like a heavenly crown floating against the black of night.

When I turned six, we moved from Keflavik to California and the aurora borealis came with me. It showed up in the pictures that my first-grade teacher, Miss Henderson, encouraged me to paint. Each day, I planted myself in front of the classroom easel where I pushed pigment onto paper half my size. Streams of colors emerged from beneath my hand. I brushed on red melding into yellow and thought of dad who was en route to Vietnam on the USS *Delta*. I painted in blues and violets, and thought of the dark tunnel of the quonset hut where we lived. Mom wasn't the same since we left Iceland. Her sadness sat in the pit of my stomach. But whenever I painted, I floated and flew. And all of the colors were there.

Edna Cabcabin Moran: I grew up in a military family, the first American-born child of Filipino immigrants. I'm drawn to the arts, nature, multicultural stories, and environmental and social justice. I love to paint, dance hula, and read and write poetry, children's literature and memoir pieces. My forthcoming book, HONU AND MOA, (BeachHouse Publishing) will release in 2018. www.KidLitEdna.com

Edna Cabcabin Moran, *Aurora Borealis*, mixed media, 2018.

The Missing Lamp
Rishad Qahar

I am not sure how I am still alive
After drinking that cup of love
I am not sure how I am still sane
After drinking that cup of poison
That cup which upon sipping will enslave you for lifetime, yet
That cup which upon sipping will grant you the happiness of lifetime
Oh if I had been wise and listened
       to those who had drunk before me from that cup
I wouldn't have been here
I wouldn't have lost that joyous playful lad that once lived in thy heart
How I'd give the world for that joyous playful lad
Because that lad and only that lad can bring light into my dark cold world
The world which there is no day only endless nights
Oh how I search throughout the busy world filled with little dim lights
For my bright lamp
Yet the only light I see is emanating brighter than the sun
from the castle of the evil witch who had once fed me from that cup
What does one do who has come to the crossroads of life
Live in the dark lonely world as a free man
Or
Live in the bright glamorous castle as a prisoner
What does one do, what does one do
Or
Does one learn to become a robber to rob others' lights,
to become a sucker to suck others' energy,
to become a feeder to feed others from thy cup,
to become a lover and to love others
but how can one be a lover when one can't love thyself

Oh how I pray and I pray and I only pray to you
the one and only the creator of the ups and downs, heavens and hells,
light and dark, righteousness and wretchedness,
yesterday and today, today and tomorrow, life and death, love and hate,
to free my light from that witch or free my body from this earth
for I'm just an empty vessel with no soul, roaming the endless road of life
I don't know where it's taking me

but I pray to you, I pray to you and only you
to give me the light so I can see again
What will you lose? Nothing
It's as if a drop of water is given from the ocean
or a grain of sand is given from the desert
so I ask you again what will you lose
oh divine one

Rishad Qahar. I am a Persian from the Korasaan region of Afghanistan. When Taliban took over, my family moved to Pakistan and then fled to America so that my seven siblings and I could get a chance in life. I was 8 when I started 2nd grade in America. I became Americanized pretty quickly, but my mom was a Farsi teacher who helped keep me in touch with my roots. I grew up with Persian music, arts, and literature.

Upon graduating college, I moved to Fremont, California, to get a sense of independence and then moved to Orange County before rejoining my family in conservative Pennsylvania and finally multicultural Virginia. For a time I was writing a historical novel but for some reason I lost my ways of writing. As a young adult all I wanted to do was live the party life, thinking this is what I needed. I did it for a bit, but I still wasn't happy. Once I rejoined my family, I started to read the Quran and all of sudden I was able to write again—this time in a poetic way. With any piece that I write I can honestly say that my fingers are moving the pen but the words that come to me are a gift of the almighty's. I'm very blessed because he has given me the noor (light) again.

Ben Pease.

Tuyet Cong-Ton-Nu, *Om, Peace, Love*, watercolor, pen & ink, 6 x 6 in., 2015.

Tuyet Cong-Ton-Nu

I was born in Saigon, Viet Nam and by divine grace and incredible courage and sacrifice, my mother made the decision early on during the war to emigrate us to Germany, France, and then finally to the United States. I moved to San Francisco in my early twenties and it was a transformative time, a rebirth, a rejuvenation of my spirit that still continues. My multicultural background, along with my experiences in computer programming, yoga, nutrition, art, and spirituality have given me much joy in exploring the infinite possibilities and potentials that arise in each moment of this precious life.

Tuyet Cong-Ton-Nu, *Squash Blossom*, digital photograph, 2017.

Artist Statement
Tuyet Cong-Ton-Nu

I am interested in my soul's journey in this lifetime and beyond. Exploring through writing, photography, painting and drawing, I let the soul reveal the preciousness of whatever is arising. Simplicity and grace underlie my intention to express the honesty of what is happening in each moment.

I love using watercolor and pen and ink because the flowing, spontaneous quality produces unexpected, magical results. Accidents are beautiful.

Photographing fruits, vegetables, and flowers from my garden nourishes my soul. I appreciate the generosity and beauty of Mother Earth. My love of cooking is inspired by the produce that is so fresh, alive, and delicious.

Art for me is a sacred place where there are no rules, just the freedom to create with abandonment, passion, and authenticity.

All the challenges and learnings from my childhood have shaped my soul in a unique way, and my spiritual practice and my art let me access an inner life that is full of richness and mystery. I am discovering that my true nature is pure, loving, and indestructible.

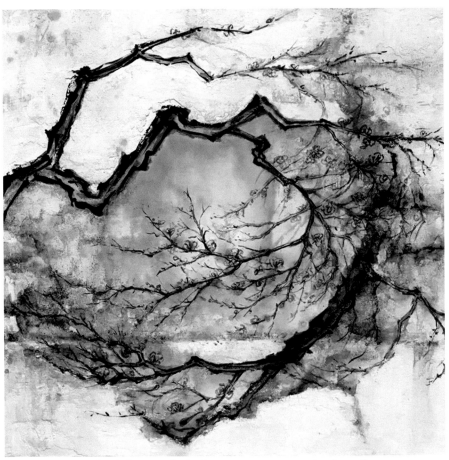

Cindy Shih, *Spiral of Silence,* 18 x 18 in., mixed media.

Scarification
Cindy Shih

Where do we stand, in today's race to black or white?

Growing up, spiraling downward
We've been cast as blooms promised but seeds never manifested—
Because the sun will always shift its golden light.

Because everything, everyone—casts a shadow.

Cindy Shih, *Friend of Winter*, 18 x 18 in., mixed media.

So we keep twisting, cracking, and breaking through each painful growth;
Because our day will someday come.
Because the only difference between the crimson red of wounds and the rose
of gold is where you stand in another's light.

Remember, a period of dormancy is required to bear fruit ...
    Just after each petal withers, and every flower falls off

---

Cindy Shih is a Taiwanese-American visual artist living and working in San
Francisco. Her work explores nature as metaphor. She combines Western-
inspired fresco painting techniques and abstraction with the visual vocabulary
of traditional Chinese landscape painting.

El aroma de un corazón

Adrián

Había una vez un hombre
que después de tanto buscar el amor y no encontrarlo
se sacó el corazón del pecho y lo quemó en su balcón.
Los vientos llevaron el aroma del corazón
más allá de valles y montañas
hasta donde una muchacha descansaba.
Ella despertó y siguió ese aroma fascinante
por desiertos y ciudades
cruzando fronteras y océanos
escondiéndose de los uniformes
y traspasando el miedo hasta llegar a una casa y tocó la puerta.
El hombre sin corazón abrió y sus ojos
no pudieron resistir las lágrimas
El corazón de la muchacha palpitó doblemente
entonces ella sopló sobre el pecho de él
y un nuevo corazón le empezó a crecer
pequeño y poderoso
como el primer día de primavera.

The aroma of a heart

There was once a man
that after so much looking for love and not finding it
he took his heart out of his chest and burned it on his balcony.
The winds carried the aroma of the heart
beyond valleys and mountains
where a girl rested.
She woke up and followed that fascinating scent
through deserts and cities
crossing borders and oceans
hiding from the uniforms
and going beyond fear until she reached a house and knocked on the door.
The man without a heart opened and his eyes
they could not resist the tears
The girl's heart throbbed doubly
then she blew on his chest
and a new heart began to grow
small and powerful
like the first day of spring.

Adrián, *Angel of the New Revolution*, pencil, charcoal, red wine, rainwater on Arches 300, 20 x 28 in., 2017.

Adrían, *Angel with pencil arrow*, pencil, charcoal, rainwater on Arches 300.
20 x 20 in., 2017.

Ofrenda del tiempo
Adrián

Nuestras infinitas manos
delicadas y fuertes
tocando algo ahora, olvidándolo después
la memoria es una cosa extraña
que dice su verdad y se esfuma.

El calor de la belleza nos mantiene vivos
acariciamos su luz como una delicada pluma
con su aroma hacemos poesía
con su textura podemos transformarnos en lo que sea,
memoria sin miedo.

La vida está más allá de la memoria
la vida es un baile
¿bailas conmigo?

Offering of time

Our infinite hands
delicate and strong
touching something now, forgetting it later
memory is a strange thing
that says its truth and vanishes.

The heat of beauty keeps us alive
we caress its light like a delicate feather
with its aroma we make poetry
with its texture we can transform into whatever it is,
memory without fear.

Life is beyond memory
life is a dance
dance with me?

Adrián, *Angel Protector of Future Life*, pencil, charcoal, tea, rainwater on Arches 300, 20 x28 in., 2017.

Tejer
Adrián

Tejer un camino
hilvanando olvidos con recuerdos
es como medir la distancia
entre lo que se fue
y lo que nunca has tenido.

To Knit

Weave a path
weaving forgetting with memories
it is like measuring the distance
between what went
and what you've never had.

Adrián Arias is a multidisciplinary poet and visual artist, born in Peru in 1961 and resident in the San Francisco Bay Area since 2000. His poetry, visual art, video-installations, photography, and performances have been seen at the De Young Museum, Mission Cultural Center for Latino Arts, Gallería de la Raza, SOMArts *Día de los Muertos,* and the San Francisco International Arts Festival.

Adrián believes that poetry is in constant motion that feeds on each discipline to continue among us. Sometimes it is a photograph of a feather lying on the shore, sometimes a book-object talking about the future, sometimes a naked body moving slowly between blue lights, dancing with paper, honoring roots and drawing hope.

The absurd, the light, the sensual, the shadow, and dreams are often elements in the daily life of Adrián, who in addition to declaring himself a poet in motion, is an art teacher, a cultural organizer of events, and a contemplator. "You have to look at the wall and cross it, be on the other side, and stay here at the same time. There is no magic in art, because art is magic, the only one in which I believe. To feel life as a gift, a little gift to change the world, the only thing you need to do is produce beauty." www.adrianarias.com.

The Sun Carriers: for June Jordan
Sriram Shamasunder

Your hardwood floors match the color of my skin
I wait for you to enter the sky lit kitchen
sunlight settles on the countertop
specks of air are made visible and touchable
Until i try to bring them into my palm

When you finally enter the room
Treading lightly as ever on the ground
You come to stand
statue solid when and where you choose
sun tints your short hair

we wait
in your house
together
for a doctor's phone call
determine if cancer has spread
to your brain

you light a cigarette or
move towards the hot printer
to find
an essay
revised and reddened
any movement to keep pace with the cancer
something as to not stand still

I want to say then:
The story goes
The Sun at dusk doesn't just disappear
chosen folks wait behind the hill
cradle the sun as it falls
Store shiny slices

and
morning only comes when
the chosen gather and pack
fire tight like snow balls
hurl the sun back into sky
my auntie always said
Sun carriers come closest to saints
Can be told apart

266

during the day
cuz
traces of sun left in spines
pour beautiful through eyes
Or even a belly button

Are you one of those people?
Is that why they call you June?
Is that why you stand up so straight?
To respect the sun you must carry?

I want to ask all this and
Simultaneously say:

do not worry about legacy
when lying crows all around crowing
to tell the truth is much
to carry the sun for so long is enough.

But I say nothing
and
After so much silence
Your sister says
"Could I please be alone with June
I hope you understand"

What can I say or do now
Except spread my arms
always to embrace the exact
size of your
diminished frame
And try to carry along some of the sun

You: 65 and dying
I: 23
You stay and
I leave

Shizue Seigel

epitaph # 1
Sriram Shamasunder

tell them
i stood
side by side
the doctors and the dreamers
a poem in my left hand
a scalpel in the right
tried and tried to funnel
lilies and light
from poems
into the tip of my scalpel
cut a slice of bread
for the hungry

Index by Author

Acknowledgements

I'm grateful to the following for contributing in large and small ways to this project: proofreaders Rosalie Cavallero and Linda Gonzáles, publisher Pease Press, printer Edition One, publicist Sally Douglas Arce; editorial consultant Corinne Westphal, and administrative assistance from Landa Williams, Kathleen Wallace, and Tamiko Wong.

The project was made possible with the support of a San Francisco Arts Commission Individual Artist Commission. Thank you to SFAC staff members Barbara Mumby, the late Ebony McKinney, and Robynn Takayama for their support of cultural equity. Thank you to Joan Jasper and Michael Hinton of the San Francisco Main Library for meeting space, and to At the Inkwell reading series at Alley Cat Books, Bay Area Generations, Eastwind Books of Berkeley, Eth-Noh-Tec, the Gears Turning poetry series at Adobe Books, James Tracy and the Howard Zinn Book Fair, Bay Area Generations, La Lunada Literary Salon at Galería de la Raza, LitQuake, the Manilatown Heritage Foundation, the Nihonmachi Street Fair and the National Japanese American Historical Society, the San Francisco African American Historical and Cultural Center, and the Soul-Making Keats Literary Competition for reading opportunities.

Additional thanks for outreach opportunities and inspiration to the African American Arts & Culture Complex, the Asian American Women's Artists Association, Rene and Rio Yañez's *Día de los Muertos* art exhibitions at SOMArts Cultural Center, the Fillmore Jazz Festival, Kearny Street Workshop, San Francisco Juneteenth celebrations, SOMArts Cultural Center, The Black Woman Is God project, the Writers Grotto, the Writing Salon, and VONA/ Voices of Our Nations Arts Foundation and to Elmaz Abinader, Faith Adiele, Tomo Arai, Michelle Antone, Dennis J. Bernstein, Nikos Diaman, Lyndsey Ellis, Susan Ito, Lewis Kawahara, Kathleen McClung, Eileen Malone, Ahmed Nasser, Margo Perin, the Reverie Writers, Sandra García Rivera, Tony Robles, Deborah Santana, Bob Shatara, San Francisco Poet Laureate Kim Shuck, Denise Sullivan, Truong Tran, and Midori Yenari.

About the Editor

Shizue Seigel is a third-generation Japanese American writer, visual artist, and community activist. She has actively explored complex intersections of history, culture, and spirituality through prose, poetry, and visual art for over twenty years. She was born in 1946 shortly after her family's release from incarceration. She grew up as an Army brat in segregated Baltimore, Occupied Japan, California farm labor camps, and skid-row Stockton. After her family moved to San Francisco in 1958, she experienced many of the city's changes, such as Western Addition redevelopment and the Haight-Ashbury counterculture in the 1960s, feminism and the alternative schools movement in the 1970s, Financial District corporate life in the 1980s, and HIV prevention efforts in the 1990s. For the past twenty years, she has been a writer, designer, and cartographer active in San Francisco's nonprofit activist arts community.

Endangered Species, Enduring Values is her fifth book. She also edited *Standing Strong! Fillmore & Japantown* (Pease Press, 2016) and *Distillations: Meditations on the Japanese American Experience from Four Sansei Artists* (Pease Press, 2010). She authored *In Good Conscience: Supporting Japanese Americans During the Internment* (AACP, Inc., 2006), and co-authored *A Century of Change: The Memoirs of Nellie Nakamura* (2002). She was co-cartographer of Rebecca Solnit's *Infinite City: A San Francisco Atlas* (UC Press, 2010), chief cartographer of *Unfathomable City: A New Orleans Atlas* (UC Press, 2012), and editor of *Nikkei Heritage*, the National Japanese American Historical Society's quarterly magazine from 1999 to 2001.

Her prose and poetry have been published in numerous anthologies and journals. She has twice been awarded a San Francisco Arts Commission Individual Arts Commission. She's a two-time VONA/Voices alum and a two-time Associate Artist at the Atlantic Center for the Arts. She has also been awarded grants and residencies by the API Cultural Center (APICC), Jentel, Newnan Art Rez, and Hypatia-in-the-Woods. Her papers are archived at UC Santa Barbara's California Ethnic and Multicultural Archives (CEMA).

For more about her writing and artwork, see www. shizueseigel.com.

For information about her ongoing community writing projects, see www. WriteNowSF.com.